Policing Pop

Sound Matters

a series edited by Michael Jarrett

Policing Pop

EDITED BY

Martin Cloonan and Reebee Garofalo

TEMPLE UNIVERSITY PRESS

PHILADELPHIA

Temple University Press, Philadelphia 19122
Copyright © 2003 by Martin Cloonan and Reebee Garofalo
All rights reserved
Published 2003
Printed in the United States of America

⊖ The paper used in this publication meets the requirements of the American National Standard for Information Sciences—Permanence of Paper for Printed Library Materials, ANSI Z39.48-1984.

Library of Congress Cataloging-in-Publication Data

Policing pop / edited by Martin Cloonan and Reebee Garofalo.
      p.   cm. — (Sound matters)
   Includes bibliographical references.
   ISBN 1-56639-989-0 (cloth : alk. paper) — ISBN 1-56639-990-4 (pbk. : alk. paper)
     1. Popular music—Censorship.   2. Popular music—Social aspects.   3. Popular music—Political aspects. I. Cloonan, Martin. II. Garofalo, Reebee. III. Series.
ML3918.P67 P65 2003
306.4'84–dc21
                                                       2002020419

Lyrics from "Carcass" (pp. 98–99 herein) are reprinted by permission of Dan Tobin, Earache Records.

Lyrics from "Bitchcraft" (p. 144 herein) are reprinted by permission of Vasja Ocvirk, Strelnikoff.

This book is dedicated to all musicians
who have fought for freedom of musical expression

Contents

Part III. Up Against the State

Acknowledgments

This book would not have been possible without the International Association for the Study of Popular Music (IASPM), which has offered a space to study, debate, analyze, and just listen to popular music for over twenty years. We acknowledge with gratitude the debt which we owe to IASPM and give out thanks to its members for being who and how they are. For more on IASPM please go to <www.iaspm.net>. And join.

Our very special thanks go to Johan Fornäs for inspiring this book and being its instigator. Johan and Hillevi Ganetz first raised issues of freedom of musical expression within IASPM and thus provided a focus for our work. We remain in Johan's debt and would like to thank him for all his work and inspiration.

We would also like to say thanks to all the contributors for putting up with our endless requests for clarifications and modifications and for all the hard work that each of them put into his or her chapter.

We are both grateful to Janet Francendese at Temple University Press for all her help, and to series editor Michael Jarrett for his detailed comments on the manuscript.

Very special thanks to Marianne Rowan for proofreading.

Martin would like to thank Lucy for her ongoing support and encouragement with this book and endless other matters. Colleagues in the Department of Adult and Continuing Education at the University of Glasgow have offered friendship and all sorts of help.

Reebee acknowledges Debby for her love and support in all things. As a two-term board member of the American Civil Liberties Union of Massachusetts, he had occasion to work closely with a number of free speech activists whose dedication and integrity are noteworthy. They include John Roberts, Nancy Ryan, Bob Chatelle, Jim D'Entremont, Susan Flannery, Seth Finkelstein, and Nina Crowley, who runs

the Mass Music Industry Coalition (MassMIC), a superb anticensorship organization that can be found on the web at <www.massmic.com>.

Finally, as this book was being written, FREEMUSE, an organization dedicated
to monitoring and fighting music censorship across the globe, came into being. We
hope that its work will inspire future activists, musicians, and researchers and urge
readers to visit its website at <www.freemuse.org>.

Policing Pop

Introduction

In the aftermath of the destruction of the twin towers of the World Trade Center and a section of the Pentagon on 11 September 2001, Clear Channel, the largest radio chain in the United States, circulated a list of some 150 songs that executives considered "insensitive." The list included Metallica's "Seek and Destroy" and AC/DC's "Shot Down in Flames," Carole King's "I Feel the Earth Move" and the Bangles' "Walk Like an Egyptian," as well as "all Rage Against the Machine songs." Defended as a simple act of sensitivity toward the victims' families, and denounced as the latest move in a continuing and needless attempt to regulate popular music, the Clear Channel list quickly took its place in a running debate pitting civil liberties and freedom of expression against the perceived need for unity and stronger national security. The fact that the list also included John Lennon's "Imagine" made it all the more interesting that Neil Young chose to perform that song on the *America: Tribute to Heroes* telecast that was promoted by every major network and cable outlet in the country to raise funds for the victims' families. As usual, popular music was at the center of the battle for dominant values, where every act of repression is accompanied by an act of resistance. This is the stuff of *Policing Pop.*

As the new millennium takes shape, the tension between freedom of expression and the regulation of various cultural forms remains as fraught as ever. In an era of globalization and apparently expanding avenues of communication, the prospect of censorship remains the pea under the princess's mattress—irritating, annoying, almost bewildering. The question of where to draw the line, far from being solved, has become the moving target of shifting cultural and political values the world over. Nowhere is this more the case than with that most globalized of artistic forms—popular music. As multinational media corporations lobby governments and pursue their agendas at international trade meetings, the strategic deployment of popular music and control of the mass media have become ever more powerful tools in the state's arsenal. While most governments willingly assist transnational corporations in the eradication of trade barriers, those same governments often seek to blunt the edge of popular culture by imposing restrictions on websites, consumer videos, sound recordings, live music performances, and a range of other cultural practices.

If one response to globalization at a governmental level has been the attempt to close borders and reinforce national identity, another involves efforts by non-governmental organizations to mold the nation's morality by restricting its popular culture. In Britain, for example, a long-standing pressure group, the National Viewers and Listeners Association, renamed itself Media Watch UK in 2001 and vowed to continue the fight for "cleaner" popular culture. Its activities were mirrored in the United States by campaigns to restrict the breadth and appeal of popular music launched by the Parents Music and Resource Center (PMRC) in the 1980s and carried on through the efforts of Christian fundamentalist organizations such as Focus on the Family and the Christian Coalition, and political activists and elected officials such as William Bennett, Joseph Lieberman, and Dr. C. Delores Tucker.

Religious zealotry has long played a role in silencing aspects of popular culture. While the actions of Christian fundamentalists have perhaps been the most familiar to observers in the west, the rise of Islamic fundamentalism in Afghanistan, Algeria, Pakistan, Saudi Arabia, and other parts of the world has been accompanied by less tolerance of cultural diversity and many forms of cultural expression. The attempt by the former Taliban regime in Afghanistan to outlaw most musical forms is but the most extreme example of attacks against popular music taking place across the globe.

In places that have a strong tradition of and commitment to freedom of expression, acts of overt repression are usually greeted with an automatic negative response. The discussion becomes measurably more complicated, however, when the topic turns to, say, the cultural boycott of South Africa during the apartheid regime, a misogynistic Death Metal scene, or Nazi rock in contemporary Germany. For many, the maxim of the American Civil Liberties Union—that the antidote to hate speech is more speech—remains in force even in these instances. Others are willing to consider certain forms of censorship as a progressive strategy, which offers a very different perspective on the notion of "policing."

Meanwhile, at the industry level, the global music business has become embroiled in attempts to fortify its bottom line by harnessing new technologies for the production and distribution of music. Its first goal has been to prevent peer-to-peer internet services such as Napster and Gnutella from providing users with free access to thousands of recordings as it prepares to enter the internet music business on its own terms. This enterprise has led the industry down the path of restrictive copyright legislation and punitive litigation—yet another form of policing—rather than providing useful services.

Policing Pop takes up these struggles at the point where regulation and repression meet resistance and revolt. Its contributors provide a wealth of examples of both attempts to stifle the creativity of popular musicians and the strategies used to resist such pressures. To this end, we have consciously chosen the metaphor of "policing," rather than the narrower concept of censorship, to describe the activities in question—not simply for its alliterative value, but also to convey the variety of ways in which popular music can be regulated, restricted, and repressed. These 13 chapters include instances of direct and indirect acts of censorship by government functionaries, social pressure brought to bear by conservative religious and cultural groups, organized boycotts spearheaded by liberal and progressive causes, proposed legislation that threatens to restrict everything from live performances and T-shirts to portable playback devices and digital downloads, market forces that limit the range and styles of music available, and, finally, prior capitulation to any of the above, which leads to that most pernicious of all forms of censorship—self-censorship. Our focus goes beyond the suppression of content to include issues of access, ownership, and the use of popular music and other forms of popular culture. Many of the incidents described in *Policing Pop* are fully covered here for the first time. Our goal is to explore the range of practices which limit popular music, determine the agents and the mechanisms of these practices, and illustrate strategies for resistance and positive change.

Policing Pop falls into three parts. The first, "Defining Issues and Themes," contextualizes the regulation and censorship of popular music within the broader notion of policing. It introduces some of the major themes which recur throughout the book, including problems associated with definitions and boundaries, the importance of changing technologies and attendant legislation, and the diversity of censorial and regulatory practices. These opening chapters explore the basic parameters and historical underpinnings of policing. What is it? How does it affect pop? How widespread is it? Does it occur in routine operations of the music industry? Can it be countered? Must it always occur?

Martin Cloonan deals with the problem of definition in the opening chapter. Examining the concept of censorship as it applies to popular music, Cloonan argues that many commentators have been quick to use the word in the case of popular music without considering its meaning. He illustrates the need for more precision by considering various definitions and levels of censorship and the ways in which pop music has been censored. Cloonan suggests that acts of censorship are related to the artistic form in question and that censorship does not have to involve deliberate imposition of moral or political codes, since the routine machinations of the market can have censorial implications. Having thus moved the notion of censorship beyond the relatively narrow confines of governmental acts into broader social actions, he explores the implications of such an approach through some illustrative cases. His conclusion that the PMRC's stickering campaign was not a form of censorship provides a provocative opening for the book.

While Cloonan is concerned with perennial issues, Reebee Garofalo's chapter is firmly located in the age of hyperspace. Highlighting the censorial implications of changing technology, it examines perhaps the most contentious area of policing pop today—the regulation of the internet. Garofalo situates his work in the history of U.S. copyright law and music industry practice, detailing a pronounced shift in emphasis away from users' rights toward corporate self-interest. He shows how by using terms such as "theft" and "piracy"—while at the same time influencing copyright legislation to narrow the terrain of fair use and the public domain, the music industry has been able to defend its ability to profit while simultaneously masquerading as a defender of artistic freedom. The result is an enforcement mentality hopelessly mired in an impossible search for secure file formats rather than a focus on providing consumers with affordable, user-friendly services. Thus, in common with Cloonan, Garofalo discusses the ways in which daily business practices seek to curtail artistic expression, but takes the issue further by adding the important dimensions of audience access to and use of that expression.

The varied ways in which pop is policed are illustrated further in Chapter 3, where Vanessa Bastian and Dave Laing review *Index on Censorship*'s coverage of musical censorship around the world over a 20-year period. Drawing on more than two hundred examples, they identify the most censorious countries and chart the range of issues which have resulted in pop's being censored. While *Index* generally concentrates on government censorship, Bastian and Laing show that censorship is practiced by a variety of agents, including state regulators, broadcasters, pressure groups, and guerrilla groups. Thus, their chapter illustrates a key theme of *Policing Pop*—that it is not only governments who police the popular music terrain.

This idea is taken further in Chapter 4, where Steve Greenfield and Guy Osborn review the policing of pop within the music industry. They show that the notion of policing goes beyond outright censorship to include the control and regulation of artistic output. Focusing on the experience of the United Kingdom and drawing on a range of legal documents, they show how copyright—in many ways the very foundation of the popular music industry—can serve to stifle artistic freedom. Their examples include artists such as Abba, the Rolling Stones, and Bruce Springsteen. Picking up on themes explored by Cloonan and Garofalo, the chapter also examines the potentially censorial impact of standard music industry contracts. Changing technology again emerges as a key issue as Greenfield and Osborn show how the law struggles to keep pace with technological developments such as samplers and the internet. The result is that the policing of pop continues to be undermined by new technologies. Battle lines are continually redrawn, but the war never ends.

Many of the themes included in Part I of *Policing Pop*—issues of definition, changing technology, the roles of various agents, and the key role played by the music industry—return in the second part, "Controlling the Artistic Process." Moving from the general to the specific, the four chapters here deal with the ways in which individual artists experience the prospect of censorship and what happens to their music as it becomes subject to broader social forces. Contributors explore the censorial implications of moving from small subcultures and relatively isolated "scenes" to mainstream scrutiny, the attendant pressures toward self-censorship, ways of countering attempts to prosecute, and the roles which popular musicians can play in fighting censorship.

Keith Kahn-Harris's chapter on the limits of musical expression within the death metal scene demonstrates that a book on censorship is almost guaranteed to take the reader to places that are most uncomfortable. Analyzing the horrific musical text "Fucked with a Knife" by the band Cannibal Corpse, Kahn-Harris's work is important in that it addresses freedom of expression in a situation that puts it to the test. His exploration was motivated by his concern about the text and the band's larger body of work, which is almost wholly devoted to explorations of the abject. While the content of the song is fully discussed in the chapter, the complete lyric text does not appear. The reader is directed to a Cannibal Corpse website, where the lyrics can be accessed in the context of the band's complete body of work. This decision to omit the lyrics, of course, forced all of us to grapple with the prospect of our own self-censorship—certainly an irony in a book on censorship. Ultimately, we all agreed that the decision was a sound one. In deploying the concept of a "scene," which provides a cultural and aesthetic frame for the music, Kahn-Harris finds a disjuncture between "text" and "practice" in the death metal scene. He suggests that while death metal produces texts that are "transgressive," the scene itself is not—partly because it is self-consciously anti-political—a fact that prompts the author to look for signs of social utility in the notion of transgression. One of the defining characteristics of the death metal scene is its near complete insularity. Until the political enters, Kahn-Harris suggests, the scene—and the internal acceptance of its own misogynist and exclusionary practices—will remain intact. Kahn-Harris's contentious view is that intellectuals have a role in exposing the scene to greater scrutiny and thus making it engage more overtly with the political and especially with its unreconstructed sexual politics. Kahn-Harris warns against the "critical paralysis" which can result from over-analyzing any given phenomenon; he opts, instead, for a form of "policing" based on intellectual monitoring, analysis, and evaluation, which holds a given text up to the light of day and moves towards a more egalitarian scene via self-criticism and confronting regressive practices.

Mike Jones's chapter is based on self-reflection concerning the fate of Latin Quarter, the band of which he was a member. Best known for the hit "Radio Africa," Latin

Quarter were an overtly political band from Sheffield, England. Their history revisits some of the issues raised in Part I as Jones again shows how the daily workings of the popular music industry acted to stifle both the band's politics and its creativity. In an industry based more on entertainment and escape than on art and engagement, it is predictable that a band with serious material will have difficulty surviving. Although the industry will accept *some* overtly political texts from artists who can fulfill its other requirements (Bruce Springsteen, U2, and Billy Bragg come to mind), Jones suggests that it has trouble coping with artists who place politics in *all* their work (Rage Against the Machine stands out as one notable exception). Jones locates the difficulties that Latin Quarter faced not in overt acts of censorship, but rather in the very process of pop commodification, as he reflects on how he censored his own work in order to produce a product that suited the politics he was anxious to convey. His conclusion that the political instincts of Latin Quarter were entirely inappropriate for success in the pop world—too pop for the politically committed and too political for pop fans—acts as a somber warning to those who would follow in the band's wake.

In Chapter 7 Rob Bowman relates the story of an attempt to censor the Canadian band the Dayglo Abortions. Bowman charts the band's career and then explores the minutiae of a censorship battle, basing his work on a wealth of newly uncovered material. Importantly, he shows how fighting censorship can have repercussions for artists. In this instance it helped to exacerbate existing tensions between the band and its record company, Fringe Product. The defense's case was further undermined by a dispute between the company owner, Ben Hoffman, and his lawyer, Marlys Edwardh. Drawing upon correspondence between the two, Bowman reveals the complexity of an attempt to defend popular music from censorship. Eventually, thanks to the support of a number of experts and astute defense tactics, the Abortions' case was won and their records were acquitted. However, Bowman also shows that some potentially key allies were reluctant to help. Moreover, in the fallout from the case Fringe scaled down its activities, and other record companies became more cautious about what they released. This case thus shows the need not only to defend pop—and to do so loudly and clearly—but also to do so in ways which offer victims support in the longer term.

Chapter 8 moves from North America to Eastern Europe and again shows the need for allies, albeit in a rather different climate where rights to free expression are less well established. The subject is the Slovenian band Strelnikoff, whose members have been engaged in a long-running censorship battle with the Slovenian Catholic Church and its political allies in the Christian Democratic Party. The dispute centers on the band's "Bitchcraft" single, the cover of which features a picture of the Virgin Mary with a rat on her lap. David Parvo argues that the case has the potential to move Slovenia toward forms of censorship which are even more severe than those endured during the years of Soviet domination. Here pop is acting as a barometer for Slovenian freedom of expression. Fortunately, Strelnikoff have managed to defend themselves and have secured a range of allies; indeed, the case has become something of a litmus test. The band's tactics, Parvo shows, have resonance beyond Slovenia.

Parvo's chapter leads into Part III of the book, "Up Against the State," which focuses on censorship by state agencies but includes instances of restrictive measures supported by progressive causes, international agencies, and even musicians themselves. Key themes which emerge here include the changing role of the state and the contested nature of state power, the importance of local as well as national censorship, and the controversial notion of cultural suppression as a progressive force. In the age of global communication, this section serves as a reminder of the continued power of the nation-state and of the resistance to that power which musicians have often helped to lead.

The section begins with Michael Drewett's review in Chapter 9 of the censorship of popular music in apartheid South Africa, concentrating on the dark years of the 1980s. Drewett surveys various forms of censorship and shows how many brave musicians resisted the apartheid regime. Crucially, South African musicians were divided among themselves about how best to counter apartheid and avoid censorship. Some saw exile from their homeland for the duration of apartheid as the only viable option; others saw remaining and recording messages of resistance—open or camouflaged—as more productive, a tactic that posits some form of self-censorship as a strategic and creative choice. The chapter also raises the question of whether censorship can be politically progressive, given that the resistance to apartheid was bolstered by a UN-sponsored cultural boycott of South Africa. In discussing the boycott, Drewett argues that the multifaceted nature of this policing effort prompted liberals and progressives to advocate forms of censorship. The chapter ends optimistically by noting how much freer South African musicians are in the postapartheid era, but it also serves as a stark reminder of how hard-won that freedom was.

Jeroen de Kloet's chapter focuses on the policing of pop in contemporary China. He begins by discussing the notion of a velvet prison which many observers use to describe the relationship between the artist and the state in communist societies. Drawing on his own field work within China, de Kloet shows that despite its superficial appeal, this notion fails to convey the complexity of the relationship between the Chinese state and popular musicians. He describes the ways in which popular musicians negotiate the various rules and regulations designed to police them. However, the fact that these negotiations take place is evidence, he suggests, that the Chinese state is not as all-powerful as is sometimes suggested. In addition, although rock's rebellious image can help to popularize it among fans, actual rebellious acts which lead the authorities to clamp down may be opposed by musicians who simply want to get on with making music. Once again, de Kloet raises the issue of self-censorship—in this case as part of a strategy for dealing with life in a one-party state. What emerges, he suggests, is not so much censorship as a set of strategies for exclusion, again illustrating the diversity of ways in which pop can be policed.

Whether censoring popular music can be politically progressive is one of the key questions raised by Alenka Barber-Kersovan in Chapter 11. The context here is the rise of neo-Nazi parties in Europe and the problems this poses for democratic states, especially with regard to protecting free speech while at the same time countering racism. Such issues are particularly fraught in Germany, which has the legacy of both a Nazi past and an eastern sector composed of a former communist state. Barber-Kersovan charts the rise of neo-Nazi rock, racist sentiments, and violence, as well as the reaction from the media, the government, and popular musicians. She suggests that at one level the neo-Nazi scene was inflated by media hype, which provoked a concerted reaction. Opponents staged Rock Against Racism concerts and distributed educational materials, while some neo-Nazi musicians were prosecuted as part of a more general state-sponsored clampdown. The result, according to Barber-Kersovan, was mixed: Some neo-Nazi musicians gave up their activities, but there was an increase in the overall number of bands and concerts. In many cases production simply moved abroad, and the range of activities widened. Repression did not crush the neo-Nazi scene; it simply led to a change of tactics, while the amount of neo-Nazi music available increases year after year. Ultimately, Barber-Kersovan concludes, the German case produces more questions than answers about how to police politically regressive pop.

In Chapter 12 José Roberto Zan examines the censorship of popular music in Brazil during the twentieth century, illustrating the changing nature of the state's involvement. Zan traces the development of Brazilian popular music and the Brazilian recording industry, charting two main periods of censorship—both during periods of political dictatorship. At such times, he argues, the portrayal of dissident lifestyles is likely to encounter official disdain and efforts to censor. By way of contrast, he also shows how the attempt by the Brazilian left to use popular music in the 1960s resulted in a form of censorship whereby indigenous music was exalted as the people's music and thus supported, while international pop was denigrated as part of international capital. Here self-censorship was urged in the name of politically progressive politics. Zan shows how changing social mores, political fortunes, and technology can alter the censorial climate. His story is essentially an optimistic one which charts a growing freedom of expression. The state's role as a censorial agent has declined. But this has left the field open to other forces, and it is clear that while Brazil's musicians are freer than before, that freedom will need constant vigilance if it is to survive.

The last chapter of *Policing Pop* concerns censorship in the United States. Here Paul D. Fischer shows that while freedom of speech is guaranteed under the First Amendment to the country's Constitution, the free expression of popular musicians has often been contested within American courts and legislatures. In this sense the First Amendment has proved to be less a guarantor than a frame of reference for contending parties. In fact, American courts have often granted exceptions to the First Amendment, as Fischer demonstrates through an examination of court cases, Senate hearings, state legislative moves, and the main agents in all these cases. His chapter ends with a rallying call to defend artistic expression in this new country and to shift the burden of proof to pop's accusers rather than its defenders. Fischer's ringing endorsement of the First Amendment's stipulation that Congress shall make *no* laws restricting freedom of speech ends *Policing Pop* on a strong note.

The collective impact of *Policing Pop* reveals the diversity of actors, agencies, and mechanisms that contribute to policing pop, including government officials, religious bodies, organized pressure groups, market forces, technological advances, copyright legislation and trade agreements, and, finally, musicians themselves. Concerns about the role of self-censorship and the problems inherent in trying to conceive of a politically progressive censorship also recur throughout these pages. What emerges is a complex picture in which the artist is but one player among contending forces whose collective might has the power to support, shape, or stifle artistic freedom.

While we recognize the social power of pop and generally celebrate artistic resistance to censorship, we also believe that simple pleas for artistic freedom must be balanced with calls for social responsibility. Overall, the chapters of *Policing Pop* endorse tolerance, but we also recognize that the peoples of the world come from a range of traditions with respect to the issue of freedom of expression. The task is to determine whether, where, how, and by whom lines can be drawn in politically progressive ways. The fact that not all the authors in this book offer the same answer to such vexing questions is further evidence, if any were needed, of the complexity of our subject.

Recognizing that pop will inevitably be policed, this book raises important questions about how such processes happen and in whose name they are carried out. *Policing Pop* will not always make easy reading, but we hope that it will provoke and enlighten, educate and entertain, and cause its readers to take sides. Let the music play.

Part I

Defining Issues and Themes

Martin Cloonan

---

1   Call That Censorship?
Problems of Definition

On 25 May 1977 Virgin Records in the United Kingdom released a single by the Sex Pistols entitled "God Save the Queen." This record was banned from airplay by every U.K. radio and television station and boycotted by a number of retailers. It was also allegedly denied its rightful place at the top of the June 1977 singles chart via chart fiddling (Savage 1991:364). However, there was no attempt by the U.K. government to suppress the single nor by the courts to prosecute it. It went on to sell hundreds of thousands of copies and became something of a rock classic.

The well-documented case of "God Save the Queen" (see Savage 1991) appears to offer an unambiguous example of popular music being censored. However, the case also raises a number of questions. Were the Sex Pistols actually censored? If so, how? By whom? At what level? If not, what *did* happen to the single? Such questions form a backdrop to this chapter and raise issues of concern for the rest of this book.

Policing Pop is about the ways in which popular music is censored, regulated, and controlled. It illustrates how complex the issue of policing popular music is, showing the wide range of policing activities to which pop can be subjected. Censorship is perhaps the most obvious way of policing pop. But to state this is again to beg some bigger questions. What *is* censorship? What forms does it take? How does it affect popular music? Above all, how can we tell if pop is being subjected to censorship?

What Is Censorship?

Many previous commentators have been somewhat blasé in their attitude toward what constitutes the censorship of popular music. It is striking that the majority of those who have written about popular music and censorship have failed to discuss what they mean by "censorship" and have tended to use the term almost indiscriminately (see, for example, Chastanger 1999, Jones 1991, McDonald 1989, Shuker 1994, and Sluka 1994). In a recent collection of nine articles (Winfield and Davidson 1999), only one writer bothers to define the term. This lack of precision leaves a vacuum in the analysis: Put simply, it is premature to claim that pop is being censored without knowing something about the nature of censorship.

One scholar who has ventured a definition, Paul O'Higgins (1972:12), describes censorship as "the process whereby restrictions are imposed upon the collection, dissemination and exchange of information, opinion and ideas." He identifies six forms: self, social, legal, extralegal, voluntary, and subterranean (ibid.: 12–13). Writing for *Index on Censorship*, Louis Blom-Cooper follows O'Higgins' definition word for word (Hampshire and Blom-Cooper 1977:55). For Michael Scammell (1988.10), censorship is "the systematic control of the content of any communications medium, or of several or all of the media, by means of constitutional, judicial, administrative, financial or purely physical measures imposed directly by, or with the connivance of, the ruling power or ruling elite." He emphasizes that in order to count as censorship such control must be *systematic*—that is, it must be carried out by governments which are determined to control *all* forms of communication.

Two key notions are articulated in the preceding paragraph—those of *process* and *restriction*. O'Higgins and Blom-Cooper both see censorship in terms of *process*. This raises the issue of agency and, in particular, whether censorship has to be a *deliberate* process carried out by active agents: In other words, must those carrying out the censorship have the intent (express or not) of restricting the material under consideration? I want to argue that censorship does *not* have to be a deliberate act; rather, it can result from processes which are not of themselves overtly concerned with restricting access to artistic works. In particular, as I will show below, there are ways in which the daily, market-informed, operations of the music industry act as forms of censorship (for evidence, see Mike Jones's report on the career of Latin Quarter in Chapter 6).

Importantly, both O'Higgins and Blom-Cooper see censorship in terms of *restriction*, suggesting that censored works do *not* have to be banned entirely, merely kept from being openly available to all. Perhaps the most familiar practices in this respect are the regulatory regimes which many countries have and which seek to deny certain audiences—most commonly children—access to certain materials. In the United Kingdom, for example, all videos must have certificates from the British Board of Film Classification (BBFC) before they can be sold legally. They are rated and given categories whereby some titles will be available only to adult buyers. This regulatory system is premised upon restricting the audience for some videos while reserving (and often exercising) the right to ban others entirely.

Among writers specifically concerned with the censoring of popular music, one of the few commentators to define censorship is Lindsey Fore (1999:95), who suggests that it is "the regulation or control of rock music." However, while it is clear that regulation can involve censorship (as the preceding paragraph shows), it is less clear that *all* regulation or control can be equated so easily with censorship. Regulation and control may be forms of policing, but they are not necessarily always forms of censorship.

Dave Marsh has provided perhaps the most systematic account of censoring pop. His analysis is based upon that of the American Library Association's Intellectual Freedom Committee. Marsh opts for what he describes as a "colloquial" definition of censorship, encompassing inquiries about the presence of certain material, expressions of concern, complaints, attacks, and outright censorship: "The removal of material from open access by government" (Marsh 1991:1). However, this approach seems simultaneously too broad and too narrow. It is hard to see how inquiries about materials can so easily be equated with censorship or why direct censorship can be carried out *only* by government. In fact, as the contributors to *Policing Pop* show, a range of agents can carry out direct censorship. Thus, a more precise definition is needed.

Having previously attempted to define the censorship of music (Cloonan 1995, 1996),[1] I am aware of the complexity of the issues at stake. The essence of the problem lies in drawing up a definition which is narrow enough to exclude apparently frivolous examples but broad enough to include incidents other than overt attempts by governments and other agencies to prevent musical expression. For me, censorship is the process by which an agent (or agents) attempts to, and/or succeeds in, significantly altering, and/or curtailing, the freedom of expression of another agent with a view to limiting the likely audience for that expression.

This definition aims to be broad enough to include processes ranging from market-based decisions within the music industry to the actions of official or state censorship agencies. It includes restrictions as well as outright bans. It is *not* predicated upon a belief that censorship has to involve a deliberate attempt to suppress, but there has be an effort to significantly alter. Here mere tampering is not enough. The definition has also been shaped by a desire to make it suitable for the particular art form with which I am concerned.

However, any definition has inherent limitations. It is clear that an attempt to provide a transhistorical definition of censorship is highly problematic, since judgments on what to censor generally rest upon prevailing norms. Thus, when EMI sacked the Sex Pistols in 1977 in a clear case of censorship (in that the intent was to limit the band's audience), EMI chairman Sir John Read spoke of the need to judge by "*contemporary* limits of decency and good taste" (Street 1986:93, emphasis mine). Similarly, a U.K. government report has noted that people judge questions of where to draw the line according to what they think is *currently* acceptable (Committee on Obscenity and Film Censorship 1979:30).

Matters are further complicated by the fact that there are competing traditions of free speech and thus of censorship. The U.S. tradition of the First Amendment has led to a system that has been described as "the most speech-protective in the world" (Strossen 1996:38). In contradistinction, the United Kingdom has a complex tradition of competing rules and regulations, obsessive secrecy in government, and some of the most restrictive censorship laws in western Europe, including at least twelve acts which restrict free speech (Collins and Murroni 1996:95) and, prior to the 2000 incorporation of the European Convention on Human Rights into U.K. law, none to protect it. These differing traditions lead to different approaches to questions of free speech and censorship, and suggest that attempts at transcultural definitions are also problematic.

Within popular music an additional complicating factor is that alleged examples of censorship are brought to commentators' attention through a variety of media which may have a vested interest in putting a particular slant on events. Some artists' publicity agents may deliberately mislead (Cloonan 1996:4), and writers (including this one) will bring their own prejudices to the topic. In addition the popular press is often keen to run censorship stories that may not bear closer scrutiny. For example, in December 1999 the United Kingdom's most important pop radio station, the BBC's Radio 1, decided not to play Cliff Richard's "Millennium Prayer" single, which set the words of the Lord's Prayer to the tune of "Auld Lang Syne." Despite the fact that the single rose to the top of the charts, the station refused to play it—on the grounds that it was not the sort of thing that its listeners tuned in for. This led to numerous stories in the press which equated Radio 1's aesthetic and editorial decision with a ban and thus censorship. However, since Richard's freedom of artistic expression was not significantly curtailed, the case falls outside my definition.

Similar erroneous stories appeared around a 1991 BBC decision to exercise restraint in playing some records during the Gulf War (ibid.:118–120). A list of records—many of which were unlikely to be played in any case—was compiled within the BBC, and it was suggested that care be exercised when broadcasting them, especially close to news bulletins about the conflict. Headlined in many places as a ban, in retrospect the list appears to have been a misguided attempt to show sensitivity to combatants' families at a time of national crisis.[2] The key point about both these cases is that some digging is required when censorship stories appear. As Scammell (1988:18) notes: "It is the resort of weak minds and vain egos to cry censorship whenever editorial judgment is being exercised." Some criteria for deciding whether artists are being censored need to be developed. Definitions are one element; another is to consider the sort of censorship that is taking place.

Levels of Censorship

The definition of censorship offered above is built on a realization that censorship can operate at a number of levels and can include both curtailing and suppression. The notion of levels of censorship recurs across the relevant literature. Three main levels can be identified: prior restraint, restriction, and suppression. For recorded popular music, the various levels of censorship may range from preventing recording to refusing to publish a song once it is recorded, to limiting a record's audience, and up to the outright banning of a disc.

Prior restraint has been the *bête noire* of anticensorship campaigners down the ages. For example, one of the greatest anticensorship tracts in English literature, Milton's *Areopagitica* (1644), is primarily an argument against governmental licensing of newspapers on the grounds that this would constitute a form of prior restraint. With regard to popular music, there are senses in which the music business's signing policies can be considered to be the equivalent of prior restraint: By not signing artists, record companies can effectively act as censors in the sense that, for whatever reason, they are acting to restrict an artist's audience. This is not to say that all decisions not to sign artists are acts of censorship, but rather that they can have censorial implications for the artists concerned. A related question here is whether censorship *has* to involve prior restraint. In fact, the most frequently cited examples of popular music censorship occur post-publication and only two forms of prior restraint appear to be at work in this field: not signing artists and thus denying them an effective voice, and refusing to release their material once they have been signed.

No state has developed a prior restraint system for the vetting of recorded popular music in the way that, for example, films, television, and plays have been regulated. Perhaps the nearest thing to such a system operated in the former Soviet bloc, where access to recording studios was policed by state functionaries and only officially approved musicians gained access (Wicke and Shepherd 1993). Furthermore, recorded music could be released only on the one state label, with a set number of recordings being pressed. Here the likely audience was inherently limited.

Richard Collins and Cristina Murroni (1996:98–99) define *restriction* as the imposing of certain conditions upon the placement or ownership of products. Perhaps the most important recent example for popular music is the refusal of U.S. retailers such as Walmart to carry stock which they regard as obscene, thus denying musicians an important market (<www.massmic.com/walmart.html>).

In western Europe and North America, the most frequently cited examples of popular music censorship—bannings of records from the radio—are examples of restriction. Here methods designed to censor other forms of media, such as spoken-word dramas and televised works, are used to restrict popular music. On occasion this has involved a deliberate attempt to limit the audience for this mass medium by such means as having a "watershed" time after which more adult material may be broadcast, since it is assumed that younger people will no longer be listening or watching. Once again the motivation here is to restrict, and thus limit, the potential audience.

It is apparent that the majority of attempts to censor pop in the west are at the level of restriction, rather than outright suppression. For example, in his report on censorship in the United States in the early 1990s, Jeffrey Sluka (1994:46) notes that the main aim of those campaigning against some forms of popular music was to promote *restrictions* on radio play and stickers on albums warning of "offensive" content. However, this campaign illustrates the easy transition which can be made from restriction to prior restraint, as one apparent result of this campaign appeared to be that Columbia Records edited Beastie Boys' tracks and dropped the band Slayer, allegedly because of their links to the occult (ibid.). Such campaigns were often led by the Parents Music Resource Center (PMRC), which argued for a more "responsible" attitude on the part of musicians and record companies. In other words they wanted both musicians and their labels to exercise forms of prior restraint or, failing that, for broadcasters and retailers to impose restrictions.

Such campaigners have filled a censorial gap in western liberal democracies, which lack state bodies dedicated to the censoring of popular music. This has left the field open for groups such as the PMRC in the United States and, to lesser effect, the National Viewers and Listeners' Association (NVALA—now known as Media Watch UK) in the United Kingdom. These pressure groups are often linked to religious organizations and are essentially restrictive in orientation, aiming to limit the audience for artistic works (often the stated goal is to protect children). However, their calls for artistic responsibility are effectively calls for prior restraint via self-censorship. Certainly they wish to significantly curtail artistic freedom of expression.

The most obvious and familiar level of censorship—*suppression*—tends to involve attempts by a government or legal system to enforce a moral and/or political code (chapters in Part III describe several attempts to suppress popular music by declaring various forms of it obscene under a country's legal system). But it may be that the power of nation-states to undertake such censorship has been fatally wounded by the arrival of the internet. One of the most interesting issues of future years will be to see how successfully governments will be able to police their electronic borders and how willing they will be to spend scarce resources suppressing material which is available on line, a theme that forms a backdrop to Chapter 2.

To reiterate the points made thus far, it is clear that there needs to be more rigorous consideration of what constitutes censorship and the level at which the alleged censorship is being carried out. In all cases it is important to determine whether the *claim* of censorship is justified before moving on to assess the level of censorship and the reasons behind it. It is also important to determine what *sort* of censorship is taking place. As Frederick Schauer (1982:122) notes, an individual may be censored if *The Times* refuses to publish his or her article, but he or she is censored in a somewhat different way if the government *tells The Times* not to print it. The former is a case of prior restraint (usually based on aesthetic or market considerations, or both); the latter is suppression based on political intervention. In pop terms there is a difference between not being played on the radio (restriction) and being threatened with prosecution (suppression). The difference is one of *levels* of censorship. Such levels are also bound up with the artistic form in question.

Popular Music: A Mass Medium

In order to make more precise judgments about the censorship of popular music, it is important to consider what popular music *is*, how it works, and what its key characteristics are. In other words, some understanding of the artistic form under discussion is necessary in order to understand the ways in which it can be censored. The key characteristics of popular music have been discussed previously in numerous places (see Frith 1983; Cutler 1985; Middleton 1990; and Wicke 1990), and it is not necessary to repeat old arguments here. It is sufficient to note here that both terms—"popular" and "music"—are contested and that their definitions are "never disinterested" (Middleton 1990:3). For the current discussion, the contested terminology is less important than the characteristics that mark out popular music from other artistic forms. Here there is some consensus that one of popular music's key distinguishing features is that it is a *mass* medium intended to reach a mass audience. For example, Simon Frith (1983:6) argues that, in distinction to other forms of music, "it is only pop music whose *essence* is that it is communicated by a mass medium" (emphasis mine), and Peter Wicke (1990:ix) describes rock as "a mass medium through which cultural values and meaning circulate." For Roy Shuker (1996:10), "Pop/rock's dominant characteristic is its . . . mass production for a mass, predominately youth, market."

   If the very essence of popular music is the intention to reach a mass audience, then it follows logically that the censorship of popular music must involve attempts to *prevent it* from becoming a mass medium. This can involve prior restraint, restriction, suppression, or some mixture of two or more of these, all of which fall within the definition given above. This has two important consequences. The first is that attempts to *prevent* popular music from becoming a mass medium are paradigmatic examples of its censorship. Despite recent interest in academic circles in local music and ethnographic portraits of popular music practice (see Finnegan 1989; Cohen 1991; Bayton 1998), most of pop's audience associates pop with stars and musicians signed to record companies who produce works which are sold as product. The fact that pop is intended to be a mass medium means that it may be the paradigmatic case in which the audience gives meaning to texts. Thus, to deprive a pop text of its audience is not only to engage in unparalleled censorship; it may also significantly alter the meaning of that text.

The second consequence is that consideration should be given to the idea that the creation of a mass medium is inherently censorious. There is a sense in which all artistic production for markets is potentially censorship-prone in that the artist, producer, or record company is constantly trying to second-guess what the audience wants. If popular music is about attracting a mass market, this means that the music industry—the means by which music becomes mass—is in a uniquely powerful, potentially censorial, position to alter artistic expression. Moreover, as both Reebee Garofalo (Chapter 2) and Steve Greenfield and Guy Osborn (Chapter 4) show, disputes over the *control* of recorded music have important implications for musicians' freedom of artistic expression.

Pop's status as an intended mass medium is predicated on its ability to reach a market, and it is the music industry which plays a key role in determining whether it does so. At one level pop is simply a commodity which has risen to become a mass product at the same time that a particular form of capitalism has emerged, so that pop is intertwined with the capitalist market. Indeed, as we have seen, many commentators base their definition of pop upon the market, in terms of its seeking a mass audience (see Middleton 1990:5). This has implications for the censorship of pop. While notions of the market are contestable, it can be seen as an artificial construct which informs the decisions of key players within the industry. In relation to the earlier discussion of what level of systemization is needed before a process is deemed censorial, it may be that the disorganized market censors most of all. Decisions about what is marketable inform daily practice within the music industry (Negus 1992, 1999), and while the market may not of itself be an agent, it is an imagined market which informs decision making by key agents within the music industry and which can lead them into undertaking censorial practices. Thus second-guessing about what will make a profit informs key actions. The intent is to secure a profit; the result may be a form of censorship. For example, one of the reasons why the Sex Pistols were sacked—and censored—by EMI in 1977 was that the band would not conform to customary promotional activities (Wood 1988). In essence, as far as EMI were concerned, the band had become unmarketable. They were thus censored.

Within popular music it is the music industry which has the power of prior restraint, and decisions about what to release—what to try to make into a mass art form—are normally taken with an imagined market in mind. Thus A&R (artist and repertoire) people will generally sign acts which they think will attract a market, and producers will aim to create a marketable sound. As a rule, popular music artists will initially be signed by a company on the strength of a notional market, and their subsequent work—or product—will be shaped by reference to that market. It is not necessary to agree with Schauer's (1982:119) assertion that in market conditions "all censorship is choice and all choice censorship" to see that the rise of free market capitalism has had implications for the censorship of musicians. I do not wish to argue that there exists some pure form of popular music which is corrupted by the market. Precapitalist societies were not free from censorship, and, as noted earlier, the "socialist" countries of the former Soviet bloc also exercised forms of censorship. Clearly, however, market conditions have censorial implications in that they can significantly alter the type of pop produced. There is a sense in which all art is censored in a market society, given that performers, producers, and companies involved in the creative process are *all* trying to work out how to modify—that is, significantly alter—the product for the market (cf. Negus 1999:114).

One of the most interesting discussions of the effect of this has come from Jacques Attali (1977). He argues that the onset of industrial capitalism meant that for musicians it "became almost impossible to have one's music heard without first being profitable. . . . It was necessary to sell oneself to have the right to create" (ibid.:70). Ultimately, Attali believes that the influence of industrial capitalism has left popular music "recuperated, colonised, sanitised" (ibid.:109). Although this analysis seems to fly in the face of the model of pop careers in which artists "pay their dues" creating music, playing clubs, and being unprofitable prior to being signed, Attali rightly draws attention to the constraints exercised by capitalist economic forces and the processes of commodification upon the creative process.

A number of commentators have observed that this particular set of economic relations has implications for artistic production. Richard Peterson (1972:236) identifies the potential for the profit motive to act as a censor of music, and Reebee Garofalo (1987:81) notes how the record industry, through promotional activities which treat pop's audience as segmented, "conspires to limit the range of musical styles available to a given segment of the consumer market."[3] In his polemic against censorship in the United States, Marsh (1991:1) argues that "the majority of censorship is *economic*, which forces artists to work day jobs to stay alive, and prevents them from creating freely, let alone acquiring the equipment to work with and the space to work in" (emphasis in original). The implication here may be that only via a change in the economic structure of society will censorship be overcome. However, as Walter Benjamin (1973) notes, such a change is likely to bring about a change in how art itself is viewed.

John Street (1986:107) has argued that censorship is exclusively the prerogative of the market and that the record industry censors artists *only* if the stock exchange is likely to be offended by their antics. This is what appears to have happened in

1995 when Time Warner decided to drop Ice-T, Snoop Doggy Dogg, and Nine Inch Nails from its roster. The decision to drop these "controversial" artists followed the "Cop Killer" episode, when Ice-T's track was withdrawn on a worldwide basis following a campaign against Warners by a number of powerful bodies in the United States, most noticeably the Los Angeles Police Department (*Guardian*, 7 June 1995; Ice-T 1994). In these cases concerns about market reaction led Warners to censor. "Censorship may take place in the decision not to sign a band, or not to release a particular track as a single," Street (1986:108) notes, again focusing our attention on decision making within the music industry.

Perhaps the best work on the daily operation of that industry has come from Keith Negus (1992, 1999), who has also noted the market's power to restrict (1992:69).[4] However, he argues that it is too simplistic to see the market as the sole determinant of which acts get signed and retained. Instead, he makes a persuasive case (1999:176) that such decisions are also likely to be shaped by the culture within particular companies, while also showing how "the music industry shapes the possibilities for creative practice" (ibid.:29). For example, in country and western music Negus notes that if artists do not produce suitable, radio-friendly material, companies may drop them or try to "fix" the problem:

> This may involve finding new songwriters, recruiting another producer and employing different musicians. If all this juggling, modification and rethinking does not lead to a "radio friendly" recording then it may ultimately result in a decision to drop an artist. (Ibid.:114)

Negus also illustrates the censorial implications of becoming a major international artist. He cites the case of Mari Hamada, who after years of independent commercial radio success in Japan was forced to sing in English and use a co-writer (ibid.: 159). A more familiar example is that of Celine Dion, who moved from singing in French to English in order to reach an international audience. Many British artists, Negus notes, are not now considered to sing in the right "international" English and so may be urged to sing in a more Americanized style in order to reach a wider market (ibid.:161).

The point is that the routine operations of a capitalist industry responding to market conditions have implications for the censorship of pop. Here there is a mixture of agencies which overlap and interact, notably those of market forces and the decisions of record company personnel who both react to and try to shape those forces. Within an unstable market, the industry's main aim is to exert as much control as possible. According to Avron Levine White (1987:175), this has led to a situation in which "the popular musician has been ensnared in a variety of agreements which are clearly unbalanced from the point of view of fairness to the artist." For example, music industry contracts are routinely based on exclusivity arrangements that limit potential collaboration and career moves (Greenfield and Osborn 1998: 74,

79). Attempts to be rid of such restrictions can lead to long court cases that sap both morale and creativity (ibid.:86, and see Chapter 4 below): "Legal developments over the past fifteen years regarding the law of copyright relating to songwriting and the recording of original material have imposed considerable constraints on the working habits of professionals and semi-professional musicians" (White 1987:164).

One key instrument in this battle for control is copyright. As Steve Greenfield and Guy Osborn (1998:61) note: "Copyright occupies a central role for the music industry being the vehicle by which artistic creativity can be commercially exploited." The music industry functions through copyright, which allows it to market and trade the artistic creations of others. Moreover, control of copyright within popular music also has censorial implications (see Sloop and Herman 1998), since it can be used to stifle creativity. Sue Curry Jansen (1988:75) has made the link explicit by noting that in Europe, historically, "Copyright law was an extension of censorship law."

Copyright holders can use ownership of the products of musicians' labor in order to prevent reuse by other musicians. Greenfield and Osborn (1998:65–66) cite as an example the Justified Ancients of Mu Mu's (JAMMs) "1987—What the Fuck Is Going On?" album. The album contains numerous samples, but was initially widely available. Then Abba became aware that its "Dancing Queen" was heavily sampled for the track "The Queen and I" and refused to allow this, asserting abuse of copyright. The album was effectively suppressed, remaining copies were burned, and the intended audience was not reached. In another example Oasis had to omit the song "Step Out" from their "(What's The Story) Morning Glory?" album because copyright clearance could not be gained in time (ibid.:65).

The fact that sampling now makes it easier to use old compositions but the copyright owners may object to the new versions leads Greenfield and Osborn to predict that the censorship issue will repeatedly resurface and that the outcome "will inevitably be a greater degree of self-censorship so that potentially costly consumer disputes can be avoided" (ibid.:71). It has also been reported that current copyright regulations would have precluded the making of such albums as De La Soul's "Three Feet High and Rising" and Public Enemy's "It Takes a Nation of Millions to Hold Us Back" because the cost of advance copyright clearance would have been too high (Lewis 1998:31). Once again we see the ability of one agent to impede another's freedom of expression via the exercise of copyright. Note also that copyright can censor at all three levels: prior restraint, restriction, and suppression.

In sum, while direct censorship of artists tends to grab the headlines, it is the more insidious forms of censorship which are of more importance on a day-to-day basis. Agents acting with an eye on an imagined market can significantly alter, restrict, and curtail free artistic expression at all of the levels cited earlier, while battles for the control of artistic product, especially around copyright, have censorial implications.

Is This Censorship?

Having examined the nature of censorship, popular music, and the routine operations of the music industry, we can now examine some alleged cases of pop censorship in order to see whether (1) they actually constituted censorship, and, if so, (2) at what level. The first example is drawn from within the industry.

Dick Hebdige (1990:80) describes how Chris Blackwell, producer of Bob Marley's 1972 album "Catch a Fire" and owner of Marley's record label, Island, added rock guitars that were not in Marley's original version. The lyrics were *not* changed, and the album achieved international success. In terms of the three levels of censorship examined earlier, this was neither prior restraint nor an attempt to restrict or suppress; rather, it was an attempt to achieve the mass status which many hold to be the essence of pop. However, the case also seems to be one of censorship. The original versions were not heard by their intended audience; instead, a form more acceptable to the mass market was produced. Moreover, the newly recorded music *was* significantly altered, bringing this case within my definition of censorship. However, the fact that this was done in order to achieve, rather than to deny, mass status renders the example problematic. It seems to fall between two stools, but ultimately I cannot escape the conclusion that Marley's music was censored in that his freedom of artistic expression was infringed—albeit for sound commercial reasons.

An apparently more straightforward example of censorship occurred in October 1988 when the United Kingdom's Home Secretary, Douglas Hurd, used his powers under the 1981 Broadcasting Act to forbid the country's commercial and television stations to broadcast statements from representatives of a number of organizations based in Northern Ireland. The main target for this ban was Sinn Fein, a legal political party closely linked to the Irish Republican Army (IRA). The following month the body with responsibility for commercial radio stations, the Independent Broadcasting Authority (IBA), banned from airplay on any commercial radio station in the United Kingdom the Pogues' "Birmingham Six." The song, taken from the album "If I Should Fall from Grace with God" (released January 1988), outlines the innocence of two groups of convicted "terrorists" known as the Birmingham Six and the Guildford Four. Members of both groups were convicted of Irish Republican bombings in the 1970s and spent many years in prison before determined campaigns resulted in their convictions' being overturned. At the time of the ban, the IBA stated: "The song alleges that some convicted terrorists are not guilty and goes on to suggest that Irish people are at a disadvantage in British courts of law. That allegation might solicit support for an organisation proscribed by the Home Secretary's directive" (Foley 1995:283).

In other words, the IBA decided that the song could encourage support for a terrorist organization. Even after the Guildford Four were released in October 1989, the IBA continued the ban, which was lifted only on the release of the Birmingham

Six in March 1991. The ban on broadcasting statements by "terrorists" remained in place until the announcement of an IRA ceasefire in June 1994.

The unusual decision to ban a track from an album which had been out for 10 months and was unlikely to feature in any commercial radio station's playlist can only be explained by the growing campaign to free both sets of prisoners, as well as the growing support for Sinn Fein. However, the case still needs to be approached with caution. Sluka (1994:60) uses this example to justify his claim that the United Kingdom has witnessed "the most blatant examples of political censorship." He attributes this to the country's sweeping security legislation and says that the ban was undertaken by the government for reasons of "national security" (ibid.). In fact Sluka's claims show the need for precision when dealing with censorship, as they are only partly true. The United Kingdom has *not* witnessed political censorship on the scale of, for example, apartheid South Africa, as is documented by Michael Drewett in Chapter 9. The ban was imposed by the IBA, *not* the government, and was undertaken because the song was believed to fall foul of Hurd's ban in that it might support terrorism, rather than because it threatened national security *per se.*

This was a political decision, but *not* one made by the British government, and it was a *restriction* rather than outright suppression. The album remained on sale throughout, and no attempt was made to prosecute the musicians. It was also an example of covert censorship. The government did *not* ban the song from the radio; rather, the IBA decided that the song fell under the jurisdiction of the Home Secretary's ban. The fact that this was *political* censorship does not mean that it was *state* censorship; rather, it was an instance of extralegal restriction. It was also a clear case of recorded pop being censored, since "Birmingham Six" was denied a potential mass audience. Thus, the case illustrates the need to get behind the headlines to examine the processes and actors involved.

My third example comes from autumn 1998, when the magazine *Index on Censorship* compiled a compact disc of banned music for a special issue on music and censorship. During this process it approached Virgin Records for permission to use the Sex Pistols' "God Save the Queen." Permission was refused, partly on the grounds that the record was not banned. It is well documented, however, that the record *was* banned from airplay in the United Kingdom in 1977, received very restricted play on the nation's most important station, Radio 1, and was boycotted by major retailers (Cloonan 1996). Moreover, the record company A&M had previously exercised prior restraint in March 1977 by melting down copies of the single that it had pressed before its decision to sack the band (who then moved to Virgin). Virgin presumably felt that only outright suppression constituted censorship, even though it is clear that in 1977 some broadcasters and retailers in the United Kingdom attempted to curtail the Sex Pistols' freedom of expression and deny them a mass audience by banning the record from shops and airplay.

My final example concerns information supplied on covers—often a key part of the marketing of recorded music for a mass audience. This is the PMRC-inspired practice of labeling or stickering albums which allegedly have "offensive" content. It arose because of the PMRC's campaign in the mid-1980s, and in particular the "porn rock" Senate hearings of September 1985 (Chastanger 1999:184).

In November 1985 the Recording Industry Association of America (RIAA) signed an agreement with the PMRC that albums containing explicit lyrics would carry an advisory warning. Subsequently, warning stickers saying "Parental Advisory Explicit Lyrics" started to appear on albums, and such labels continue to this day in and beyond the United States. Another of PMRC's tactics was to pressurize shops to stop stocking particular artists such as Mötley Crüe and Ozzy Osbourne. Some writers attach great significance to these cases. For example, Sluka (1994:52) argues that the PMRC is engaged in censorship because it uses the threat of legislation to enforce "voluntary" compliance from the record industry. He also suggests that the PMRC used legal action to tie up artists and labels so that they were unable to produce.

So, is labeling censorship? Many commentators have no doubt. Marsh cites the claims of the No More Censorship Defense Fund:

> Major music distributors have made it clear that they will not carry albums that bear warning stickers. Musicians who produce albums that do not fit the arbitrary criteria set by local censors will be shut out of the distribution system. Major labels won't release albums that they think might not be sold in major outlets. . . .
>
> Who will set the criteria for warning labels? How will the terms be defined? Most of the individuals calling for labels point to lyrics that they believe are "offensive" or "indecent." . . . If strictly enforced, record warning codes would require that almost every opera of the past three centuries bear a label. And if not strictly enforced, warning labels are even more outrageously undemocratic. (No More Censorship Defense Fund, quoted in Marsh 1991:43)

Similarly, Sluka (1994) has no doubt that labeling equals censorship, and Greenfield and Osborn (1998:71) argue that the "system has been used to identify those sound recordings that could be banned." Chastanger (1999:189) insists that "labeling can hardly be considered as anything but censorship," albeit disguised as consumer information.

However, somewhat reluctantly, I remain unconvinced that, *in and of itself,* labeling constitutes censorship. It does not significantly alter artists' freedom of expression. It is not a form of prior restraint, is only partially restrictive, and does not suppress. Although the PMRC certainly aimed to limit pop's audience and this falls within my definition, of itself the stickering campaign did not try to significantly alter the recorded texts. The fact that artists who are likely to get stickered may not be allowed to release certain tracks or may not even get signed in the first place reflects a form of prior restraint—*but* it is one performed by record companies under a fairly minimal amount of duress, not by the PMRC itself. I do not like the PMRC, but the fact remains that it is the music industry, rather than the PMRC, that has censored via exercising prior restraint by not signing potentially controversial artists. Although the RIAA refused other PMRC demands, such as a ratings system and a ban on explicit covers (Chastanger 1999:185), a general failure to stand up to bullying has characterized the PMRC saga.

Similarly, a case can be made that refusing to stock stickered albums is censorship at the level of restriction (rather than prior restraint or suppression). But it is the retailers who make such decisions, not the labelers or the PMRC. Anger should be directed at those who buckle easily, as well as those who campaign to restrict.

Final Thoughts

I began this chapter by arguing that more precision is needed when discussing the censorship of popular music. Hitherto, such discussions have tended to ignore the thorny issue of what actually constitutes censorship. Clearly pop's nature as a mass medium is a key to understanding censorship within it, but further consideration needs to be given to the parameters of censorship. The notion of levels of censorship is helpful in conceptualizing pop censorship and perhaps indicates a useful way forward. But the urge to cry wolf must be resisted, and the cases described here show how apparently simple cases become more complex on closer inspection. The need to dig deeper is a constant one. My contention that the PMRC's labeling campaign was not *of itself* a form of censorship is, I hope, a useful place to begin further debate. The rest of the chapters in *Policing Pop* serve to highlight and further other aspects of that debate.

Notes

1. In 1995 I wrote of censorship as "an attempt to interfere, either pre- or post-publication, with the artistic expressions of popular music artists with a view to stifling, or significantly altering, that expression" (Cloonan 1995:75). My intention then was to examine *deliberate* acts of censorship. In 1996 I broadened that definition by adding: "This includes procedures of marginalisation, as well as the overt banning, of such expressions. . . . this includes market, as well as moral, censorship" (Cloonan 1996:23).

2. A similar response followed the events of 11 September 2001 (see Introduction).

3. See Garofalo (1994) for more on this and related themes.

4. Elsewhere Negus also notes the influence of racism on censorship: "There is a strong sense, and a justifiable belief held by many in the industry, that the black divisions have not been allowed to develop a continuity and a sense of history that is consonant with the African-American contribution to US musical culture" (1999:89).

Bibliography

Attali, J. 1977. *Noise*. Manchester: Manchester University Press.

Bayton, M. 1998. *Frock Rock*. Oxford: Oxford University Press.

Benjamin, W. 1973. *Illuminations*. London: Fontana.

Chastanger, C. 1999. "The Parents' Music Resource Center: From Information to Censorship," *Popular Music*, 18:2, pp. 179–192.

Cloonan, M. 1995. "Popular Music and Censorship in Britain: An Overview," *Popular Music and Society*, 19:3, pp. 75–104.

———. 1996. *Banned! Censorship of Popular Music in Britain: 1967–1992*. Aldershot: Arena.

Cohen, S. 1991. *Rock Culture in Liverpool*. Oxford: Clarendon Press.

Collins, R., and Murroni, C. 1996. *New Media, New Policies*. Cambridge: Polity.

Committee on Obscenity and Film Censorship. 1979. *Report*. London: HMSO.

Cutler, C. 1985. "What Is Popular Music?" in D. Horn (ed.), *Popular Music Perspectives 2*. Exeter: IASPM, pp. 3–12.

Finnegan, R. 1989. *The Hidden Musicians*. Cambridge: Cambridge University Press.

Foley, C. 1995. *Human Rights, Human Wrongs*. London: Rivers Oram Press.

Fore, L. R. 1999. "*Rolling Stone*'s Response to Attempted Censorship of Rock 'n' Roll," in B. H. Winfield and S. Davidson (eds.), *Bleep! Censoring Rock and Rap Music*. London: Greenwood Press, pp. 95–102.

Frith, S. 1983. *Sound Effects*. London: Constable.

Garofalo, R. 1987. "How Autonomous Is Relative?" *Popular Music*, 6:1, pp. 77–91.

———. 1994. "Setting the Record Straight: Censorship and Social Responsibility in Popular Music," *Journal of Popular Music Studies*, 6, pp. 1–37.

Greenfield, S., and Osborn, G. 1998. *Contract and Control in the Entertainment Industry*. Aldershot: Ashgate.

Hampshire, S., and Blom-Cooper, L. 1977. "Censorship?" *Index on Censorship*, 6:4, pp. 55–63.

Hebdige, D. 1990. *Cut N Mix*. London: Comedia.

Ice-T. 1994. *The Ice Opinion*. London: Pan Books.

Jansen, S. C. 1988. *Censorship*. Oxford: Oxford University Press.

Jones, S. 1991. "Ban(ned) in the U.S.A.: Popular Music and Censorship," *Journal of Communication Inquiry*, 15:1, pp. 73–87.

Lewis, M. M. 1998. "Bad As Bad Can Be," *Index on Censorship*, 27:6, pp. 29–31.

Marsh, D. 1991. *50 Ways to Fight Censorship*. New York: Thunder's Mouth Press.

Martin, L., and Segrave, K. 1998. *Anti-Rock*. Hampden: Archon Books.

McDonald, J. 1989. "Censoring Rock Lyrics: A Historical Analysis of the Debate," *Youth and Society*, 19:3, pp. 294–313.

Middleton, R. 1990. *Studying Popular Music*. Milton Keynes: Open University Press.

Negus, K. 1992. *Producing Pop*. Cambridge: Edward Arnold.

———. 1999. *Music Genres and Corporate Cultures*. London: Routledge.

O'Higgins, P. 1972. *Censorship in Britain*. London: Thomas Nelson and Sons.

Peterson, R. 1972. "Market and Moralist Censors of a Black Art Form: Jazz," in R. S. Denisoff and R. Peterson (eds.), *The Sounds of Social Change*. Chicago: McNally, pp. 236–247.

Savage, J. 1991. *England's Dreaming*. London: Faber and Faber.

Scammell, M. 1988. "Censorship and Its History: A Personal View," in Article 19, *Information, Freedom and Censorship: The Article 19 World Report.* London: Longman, pp. 1–19.

Schauer, F. 1982. *Free Speech: A Philosophical Enquiry.* Cambridge: Cambridge University Press.

Shuker, R. 1994. *Understanding Popular Music.* London: Routledge.

Sloop, J., and Herman, A. 1998. "Negativland, Out-law Judgments and the Politics of Cyberspace," in J. Sloop and A. Herman (eds.), *Mapping the Beat.* Oxford: Blackwell, pp. 291–311.

Sluka, J. 1994. "Censorship and the Politics of Rock," *Sites,* 29, pp. 45–70.

Street, J. 1986. *Rebel Rock.* Oxford: Blackwell.

Strossen, N. 1996. *Defending Pornography.* London: Abacus.

White, A. L. 1987. "Popular Music and the Law—Who Owns the Song," in A. L. White (ed.), *Lost in Music: Culture, Style and the Musical Event.* London: Routledge, pp. 164–190.

Wicke, P. 1990. *Rock Music: Culture, Aesthetics and Sociology.* Cambridge: Cambridge University Press.

Wicke, P., and Shepherd, J. 1993. "'The Cabaret Is Dead': Rock Culture As State Enterprise— The Political Organization of Rock in East Germany," in T. Bennett et al. (eds.), *Rock and Popular Music: Politics, Policies, Institutions.* London: Routledge, pp. 25–36.

Winfield, B. H., and Davidson, S., eds. 1999. *Bleep! Censoring Rock and Rap Music.* London: Greenwood Press.

Wood, L. 1988. *The Sex Pistols Day by Day.* London: Omnibus.

Reebee Garofalo

2 I Want My MP3: Who Owns Internet Music?

At the dawn of cable television, the film industry ran a series of ads in movie theaters that proclaimed: "There's a monster in your TV set." At the time, the film industry was terrified that showing ad-free, first-run Hollywood movies on the small screen would seriously harm movie going. As we know, of course, the cable and film industries soon learned to co-exist without significant damage to either. Indeed, by the late 1990s, video rentals rivaled box office receipts as a source of revenue.

The music industry is currently in a similar position. Since the dawn of the new millennium—the digital millennium—the music industry has been trying to convince consumers that there is a monster in their computers: the monster of copyright violation. It has gone variously by the name of MP3, Napster, Gnutella, Freenet, Scour, and LimeWire, and already there are others such as Morpheus and KaZaA. These technologies are part of a digital revolution that is transforming the way music is produced and consumed. The music industry is terrified that computer users sharing and downloading music tracks for free over the internet will seriously cut into sales of compact discs, still the centerpiece of the industry's business model. In their attempts to curtail this development, the industry has adopted a two-pronged strategy of legislation and litigation, advocating for laws that extend the reach of copyright and filing lawsuits against alleged copyright infringers. To date MP3.com and Napster have been the prime targets of music industry litigation.

Rather than embracing the potential of the internet and taking the lead in developing convenient, affordable, easy-to-use methods of downloading music, the music industry has concentrated instead on protecting a business model whose core business revolves around the manufacture, sale, ownership, and possession of physical property. This strategy harks back to pre-internet days, when recording was in an analog format and copies deteriorated over successive generations. With the ascent of the digital compact disc, every release has become, in effect, a master recording. For a time the major labels felt secure because the CD was released as a read-only medium and all methods of copying were still analog. Then the advent of digital audio tape (DAT) allowed consumers to make a digital copy of a digital original, and the process has advanced with the introduction of recordable CD formats such as CD-R and CD-RW and the widespread adoption of MP3. To protect itself, the music industry has employed policing efforts that label anyone who tries to make creative use of these new technologies a pirate or a thief.

Although the policing of popular music is usually understood in terms of attempts to censor or otherwise regulate its content, these anti-"piracy" actions can be seen as policing of another sort—the attempt to control and regulate the form and use of popular music. As such this discussion necessarily takes us into the terrain of technological advances and copyright law and their relationship to commerce and public policy. For the sake of brevity and focus, my arguments about copyright are framed in terms of U.S. copyright, which, as we shall see, increasingly takes its cue from the imperatives of globalization. Where the internet is concerned, technological development is almost by definition global.

Technology

For the uninitiated, MP3 is file compression software that can shrink an audio CD file to one-tenth its original size without appreciable loss of quality, so that one can, for example, send a music track to someone as an email attachment. Online retailer MP3.com, once the self-described "premier music service provider," posted thousands of MP3 files on its website for easy download. This proved to be a particularly popular activity in areas with access to high-speed, high-capacity connections to the internet—namely, college campuses. Napster was designed as a combination search engine, communication portal, and file-sharing software that facilitated the sharing process by granting users access to all other Napster users and the MP3 files they choose to share. At its height, estimates of the worldwide Napster community ranged as high as 60 million users. While Napster was subsequently crushed under the weight of music industry litigation, newer technologies such as Gnutella and Freenet and second-generation services such as Morpheus and KaZaA have taken the process further. Whereas Napster required users first to log onto a central server to access other users' MP3 files, these newer networks allow direct user-to-user (peer-to-peer) connections involving multiple file types—audio, video, text, spreadsheets, databases, computer software, and so on. These innovations expand the universe of file-sharing activity and make it virtually impossible to track users or the files they choose to share.

In technological terms, these developments represent a change in the very architecture of the internet and a progressive decentralization of control. In the move from "content at the center" to "content at the edges," music files can be stored on and distributed from any computer in the world. It is easy to see why the music industry is concerned.

In its push toward globalization, the music industry has become significantly more concentrated at a time when technological advances demand a model of decentralization. With the merger of PolyGram and MCA into the Universal Music Group (currently owned by Vivendi), the AOL takeover of Time Warner, and EMI afloat as a major takeover target, what had been the "Big Six" in the early 1990s was moving toward becoming the "Big Four" as we entered the new millennium. These mergers were accompanied by a significant downsizing of staff, as the gigantic new companies moved to capitalize on economies of scale, and significant cutbacks in artist rosters, as they constructed a global marketing apparatus that demanded superstardom for success. Literally thousands of staff positions and hundreds of artists were dropped from the major labels as a result. In the merger that created Universal, for example, the artist roster at affiliated label A&M was cut from 90 to eight. The net effect for fans was fewer artists, fewer new releases, and a narrower range of musical offerings.

The internet, in contrast, had no such limitations, and MP3 held out the possibility of a business model linking consumers directly with the artists and music of their choice, bypassing the record companies completely. Further, MP3 is an unprotected format, which leaves the industry with no way to regulate its use. With articulate industry critics such as Chuck D and forward-looking artists such as Sheryl Crow leading the way, MP3 generated a momentum that the industry could ill afford to ignore. As early as 1999, *Wired* magazine reported: "About 846 million new CDs were sold last year. But at least 17 million MP3 files are downloaded from the Net *each day.* That adds up to almost 3 billion in the first six months of 1999" (Peraino 1999, emphasis in original). And that was before Napster was invented. A study by *Webnoise* estimated that Napster users downloaded 1.3 billion songs in September 2000 alone and that at any given moment there were 640,000 Napster users online together (Konrad 2000).

These developments signaled the death of an era in the music business and the dawn of a new one. Dying was the moment of music-as-product—the notion that music must be tied to a particular physical sound carrier, be it black vinyl, cassettes, or CDs. Ascending was the moment of music-as-content—a conception of music as free-floating digital files that could be accessed from and transmitted to anywhere in the world. In this new era, possession diminishes in importance, and use moves to center stage. It therefore becomes crucial to figure out which uses should be considered "fair use"—that is, uses that are allowed as exceptions to the limited monopoly of the copyright contract and are free to the user. And, conversely, if one believes, as I do, that artists should be able to make a living from their creativity, it is equally important to figure out which uses should be compensated, how should they be paid for, and what would be a fair price. At its root, this is what all the industry lawsuits have been about. And this is the tension that has always characterized copyright law.

Copyright

Since its inception, copyright has never simply been an exclusive contract to exploit the fruits of one's creativity, but rather a balancing act, weighing the legal protection of intellectual property against the public rights of access to information and freedom of expression. Inherited from British copyright law, this tension was first expressed in the United States in the Intellectual Property clause of the Constitution, which states: "The Congress shall have power . . . to promote the progress of science and useful arts, by securing for limited times to authors and inventors the exclusive right to their respective writings and discoveries."[1] According to the Harvard legal scholar William Fisher, the most popular school of thought holds that the promotion of learning was the primary concern of the Founding Fathers, while the protection of authors was a means to that end (Fisher 2000). This perspective has been reaffirmed over the years in provisions regarding the public domain, personal use, fair use, and rights of access. It was reiterated most recently in the House report on the Berne Convention Implementation Act of 1988: "The constitutional purpose of copyright is to facilitate the flow of ideas in the interest of learning. . . . The primary objective of our copyright laws is not to reward the author, but rather to secure for the public the benefits from the creations of authors" (cited in Patterson and Lindberg 1991:49).

From a legal standpoint, then, it can be argued that without the centrality of users' rights, copyright would be a violation of the First Amendment in that it limits free expression. From this perspective, concepts such as rights of access and fair use cannot be viewed as crumbs thrown to the public; they are the necessary conditions that enable copyright law to pass constitutional muster. Over the last century, however, users' rights have been steadily eroded in favor of corporate self-interest and the needs of the culture industry. This trend can be seen in a review of recent legislation, as well as in a comparison of the 1909 Copyright Act and the 1976 revision, the two major pieces of legislation that guided U.S. copyright law in the twentieth century.

Especially as regards music, the 1909 Copyright Act was clearly framed in terms of "public performance *for profit*" (emphasis mine).[2] In this context, all noncommercial uses of music were generally considered to be within the realm of fair use. In order to prove a violation of copyright under the 1909 law, a plaintiff was required to show evidence of commercial transactions on the part of the alleged violator.[3]

Again the notion of profiting financially was a key variable. Until 1976 such infringement was considered a misdemeanor.[4]

The 1976 Copyright Act is often cited as the revision that codified fair use, granting significant exceptions "for purposes such as criticism, comment, news reporting, teaching (including multiple copies for classroom use), scholarship, or research."[5] After a number of unsuccessful attempts to include fair use provisions in the 1909 Copyright Act and subsequent revisions, it was finally codified in 1976.[6] From this point of view, the 1976 revision is often seen as having extended and institutionalized the rights of the consumer.

There was, however, another significant feature of the 1976 revision that launched copyright law on a rather different trajectory. Section 106 dropped the language of "for profit," granting the exclusive right to "perform" or "display the copyrighted work publicly" to the copyright holder, whether profit was involved or not. In expanding the control of copyright holders into the new terrain of noncommercial use, this small change represents an erosion of user prerogatives that would have been allowable as a matter of course under the 1909 law and establishes a new logic for the application of copyright law. Thus, when President Clinton signed into law the No Electronic Theft Act of 1997, according to Mike Snider (1997), he made it "a crime to possess or distribute multiple copies of online copyrighted materials, for profit or not."

New Legislation

In the 1990s corporate capital further expanded its hold over intellectual property rights in at least three critical areas:

- extending the term of copyright;
- narrowing the arena for fair use; and
- creating new intellectual property rights.

Extending the term of copyright, the United States enacted the Sonny Bono Copyright Term Extension Act of 1998, a sweeping revision designed to bring the United States in line with changes in the European Community dating back to 1993. The move, spearheaded by Disney because under the existing law Mickey Mouse was about to enter the public domain, extends U.S. copyrights owned by corporations to 95 years and individually held copyrights to the life of the author plus 70 years. Such legislation obviously serves the interests of corporate capital over those of the general public by effectively postponing the entrance into the public domain of almost anything created in the twentieth century.

As noted above, the No Electronic Theft Act effectively diminishes fair use, even in noncommercial transactions. In its proposed sentencing guidelines for electronic copyright infringement, the U.S. Sentencing Commission made it clear that the No Electronic Theft Act was enacted to provide a statutory basis to prosecute and punish persons who, without authorization and without realizing "commercial advantage or private financial gain," electronically access copyrighted materials or encourage others to do so (Cohen et al. 1999:2). To drive the point home, the Justice Department secured a 1999 conviction of Jeffrey Gerard Levy, a 22-year-old University of Oregon student, for posting computer software programs, musical recordings, entertainment software programs, and digitally recorded movies on his website and allowing the general public to download and copy these copyrighted products, even though a Justice Department official said there was no evidence that Levy had made any profit from the freely available works (Reuters 1999).

The Digital Millennium Copyright Act of 1998 narrows the terrain of fair use still further by making it illegal to circumvent technological measures for protecting sound recordings and other copyrighted material. Title I prohibits the circumvention of any effective technological protection measure (e.g., a password or any form of encryption) used by a copyright holder to restrict access to its material, as well as the manufacture of any device, or the offering of any service, primarily designed to defeat an effective technological protection measure. Such measures, seemingly in the interest of creative artists, create, in effect, a new owners' right to control access, which compels us to revisit the diminishing terrain of fair use. "If data can be protected by code—and it's illegal to break the code," argues Robert J. Samuelson (1998), "then 'fair use' for anything that arrives digitally may vanish."

One of the main avenues through which the international music industry currently seeks to protect its interests is the World Intellectual Property Organization (WIPO). Established in 1970 and currently representing 171 member nations, WIPO is charged with developing treaties for protecting the rights of intellectual property owners. These agreements are, in turn, codified in national legislation. Passage of the Digital Millennium Copyright Act, for example, was a direct result of pressure from WIPO: The United States was a signatory to the WIPO treaties negotiated in Geneva in 1996, which required member nations to update their copyright laws to account for the requirements of the digital environment.

At that same conference, WIPO proposed (but did not ratify) the creation of a completely new intellectual property right to protect the owners of electronic databases. "The general objective of this right," according to the treaty, "is to protect the investment of time, money, and effort by the maker of a database, irrespective of whether the database is in itself innovative" (WIPO 1996). This "right" is envisioned as a new copyright-like protection that could be renewed perpetually with no exceptions for fair use or other noncommercial uses. In the United States, it has been a long-term, court-backed concept of intellectual property law that protection is offered for ideas but not facts—that is, for creativity rather than the "sweat of the brow" labor of data entry. In practice, this has meant that the data stored in large databases—from the telephone directory to the *Billboard* charts—could not gain copyright protection for facts. In 1998, however, Senator Rod Grams (R-Minn.) introduced S. 2291, the Collections of Information Antipiracy Act, which sought to re-establish the same "sweat of the brow" protection for compilations that the Supreme Court found unconstitutional in 1991. Such legislation remains on the political agenda. If it is passed, it may not only be illegal to duplicate a record; it may also be illegal to quote its chart position without permission.

Litigation

Armed with an array of new legislation, the music industry launched its first legal salvo against online music in October 1998, targeting Diamond Multimedia's Rio, a portable, Walkman-like digital MP3 player capable of downloading, storing, and playing back 60 minutes of music. The Rio caused the music industry to stand up and take notice because it was the Rio that first moved MP3 beyond the computer desktop. Fearing piracy on a grand scale, the Recording Industry Association of America (RIAA) was quick to seek an injunction against the Rio, claiming a violation of the Digital Audio Home Recording Act of 1992. This act was itself the result of a compromise between manufacturers of audio recording hardware and record companies; it imposes levies on blank digital audio recorders and media to compensate the music industry for revenues allegedly lost because of home taping. Significantly, the law permits home taping, effectively taxing consumers for the privilege. In the Rio case the courts came down on the side of users' rights, but in this instance it was because Diamond squeezed through a loophole by successfully arguing that the legislation targeted only recording devices, whereas the Rio was a storage device. Once the injunction was quashed, other portable MP3 players were rushed to market. With the introduction of hard-drive-based players such as Apple's stylish iPod, MP3 has become the preferred format for portable music.

Undaunted by this setback, the RIAA trained its sights on MP3.com, then the best-known source of MP3 files. As an online retailer, MP3.com's core business involved allowing unsigned recording artists to post their own CDs and MP3 files on the website for sales and self-promotion. But in late 1999, having constructed an online database of some 60,000 commercially available CDs, MP3.com inaugurated two new services in conjunction with the company's My.MP3.com personalization initiative—"Beam-It" and "Instant Listening." "Beam-It" software allows a customer to insert a CD she or he already possesses into the CD drive on a computer and communicate the contents of the CD to MP3.com. MP3.com then registers the track information and places a copy of the CD into the customer's password-protected account on the My.MP3.com website. Similarly, "Instant Listening" allows any customer who purchases CDs from MP3.com partners to gain immediate access to digital versions of the music contained on those CDs from their personal online accounts. These services allow users to listen to the music of a given CD on any web-enabled computer, anywhere in the world.

"Beam It" and "Instant Listening" got an instant response from the music industry. In January 2000 the RIAA brought suit against MP3.com, alleging that the two services infringed the copyrights of all the major label recordings in the database. Since MP3.com had failed to negotiate permissions or licensing arrangements to construct the database in the first place, it was almost a foregone conclusion that it would lose the suit. Still, its use argument was interesting and would be advanced in other cases. In its defense, MP3.com argued that once a consumer buys a recording, the music industry should no longer have control over how it is used. If that person chooses to upload the contents of that CD to an online database, he or she should have the right to do so, since the Audio Home Taping Act allows copying for personal use. MP3.com claimed that the "Beam It" service simply facilitates that process. The RIAA countered that the database was unlawful to begin with and that the service encouraged piracy.

Artists themselves are divided on the question. While Paul McCartney actually sued MP3.com and Sean "Puffy/Puff Daddy/P-Diddy" Combs spoke out against services like Napster that facilitate MP3 file swapping, unsigned artists have turned overwhelmingly to the internet as an alternative vehicle for self-promotion. Appearing at the July 2000 Senate hearings on digital music, Roger McGuinn, founder of the Byrds and veteran of 25 albums on four different labels, testified: "In most cases a modest advance against royalties was all the money I received for my participation in these recording projects" (McGuinn 2000). Regarding his experiences with MP3.com, in contrast, he stated:

> They offered an unheard of, non-exclusive recording contract with a royalty rate of 50% of the gross sales. . . . MP3.com not only allowed me to place these songs on their server, but also offered to make CDs of these songs for sale. They absorbed all the packaging and distribution costs. So far I have made thousands of dollars from the sale of these folk recordings on MP3.com, and I feel privileged to be able to use MP3s and the Internet as a vehicle for my artistic expression. MP3.com has offered me more artistic freedom than any of my previous relationships with mainstream recording companies. I think this avenue of digital music delivery is of great value to young artists, because it's so difficult for bands to acquire a recording contract. When young bands ask me how to get their music heard, I always recommend MP3.com. (Ibid.)

Music industry fears about piracy came to a head in a series of lawsuits involving Napster. Although the RIAA filed suit against Napster on behalf of 18 powerful record companies in December 1999, alleging "contributory and vicarious" copyright infringement, it was the suit brought by the heavy metal group Metallica (which was joined by rapper Dr. Dre) that thoroughly polarized an already tense situation. Upset by reports that unfinished tracks from the soundtrack to *Mission Impossible II* were already being traded over the internet, Metallica hired NetPD to monitor three days of Napster activity. Drummer Lars Ulrich then hand-delivered the results—60,000 pages of screen names, documenting 330,000-plus Napster users who had downloaded 1.4 million Metallica songs during the three-day period (Harris 2000; Morse 2000). The group demanded that Napster remove the viola-tors from its service in a lawsuit that also named Yale, Indiana University, and the University of Southern California.

The Metallica suit was somewhat neutralized when Napster complied, in keep-ing with its own antipiracy policy, and removed all 330,000-plus users. As required by law, Napster also issued a disclaimer stating that any users who felt that they had been falsely identified could petition the company and be reinstated. Within days 30,000 users were reinstated, placing Metallica in the position of having to ini-tiate 30,000 individual lawsuits against some of the band's most ardent fans. More "creative" solutions for getting back onto Napster were posted on message boards (including Napster's) and in chat rooms all over the internet. A group of unnamed open source developers went so far as to charge that the method Napster used to remove users—forcing changes to their Windows operating system registry files—constituted "criminal trespassing and vandalism." They threatened to sue Napster, ironically naming Metallica as a criminal accessory, and promising to drop the suit if Metallica agreed to indemnify Napster and if Napster agreed to reinstate all of the banned users. At the same time, these developers posted a public domain soft-ware patch that allowed banned Napster users to get back on the system immedi-ately. Metallica's alienated Napster-using fans then struck a final blow by making Metallica's entire back catalog available on the internet.

In July 2000 the RIAA succeeded in persuading U.S. District Judge Marilyn Hall Patel to issue an injunction against Napster. That same week—with the addition to the Napster legal defense team of David Boies, the government's lead attorney in its antitrust case against Microsoft—Napster won a stay of the injunction on appeal. The legal arguments in the case had to do with interpretations of other landmark cases: whether the noncommercial copying permitted in the Rio case according to provisions of the Audio Home Recording Act would also permit Napster-style copy-ing; whether the outcome of *Universal* v. *Sony*, the "Betamax" case, which held Sony blameless for the actions of Betamax users in a suit brought by Universal Studios, would protect Napster; or whether the "safe harbor" provision of the Digital Mil-lennium Copyright Act, which protects service providers against the actions of their subscribers, would apply to Napster (Heilemann 2000). In addition, Boies raised the issue of copyright misuse, arguing that because the record companies have cre-ated a "copyright pool that dominates an industry" and have used that power to "disable the competition," the industry should lose the ability to sue to protect its copyrights (Borland 2000a).

Perhaps more interesting than the legal arguments was the way the sides lined up on the issue. In September 2000 the government (as represented by the Justice Department, the Copyright Office, and the Patent and Trademark Office) filed an amicus or friend of the court brief on behalf of the RIAA, saying that, unless enjoined, "Napster's users would be permitted to engage in digital copying and public distribution of copyrighted works on a scale beggaring anything Congress could have imagined when it enacted the [Digital Millennium Copyright] Act" (Borland 2000c).[7] The technology industry, realizing that peer-to-peer technology could save its members billions of dollars through the increased efficiency of not having to rely on central servers, weighed in heavily on Napster's side. Closing ranks were an impressive array of industry associations whose memberships included Sony Electronics, Apple Computer, Cisco Systems, Yahoo, America Online, Amazon.com, Excite@Home, and the then-leading online music companies such as Listen.com and EMusic.com.[8] In two separate amicus briefs, these groups argued that Judge Patel had misapplied copyright law that protects technologies with "substantial non-infringing uses" and that the "safe harbor" provisions of the Digital Millennium Copyright Act protected Napster as a "service provider" (Borland 2000b).

As 2000 drew to a close, Napster was still in court facing major suits from Metallica, Dr. Dre, and all the major labels. In the midst of all this, it announced an alliance with one of the plaintiffs, BMG, to develop a new, secure subscription service as a joint venture. Under the terms of the deal, Bertelsmann, parent of one of the five major music companies suing Napster, agreed to withdraw its lawsuit once Napster successfully introduced the membership-based service. The other majors, however, showed little interest in the concept, perhaps preferring to make an example of Napster. By summer 2001 Napster had been effectively shut down.

In the campaign that led to winning this legal battle, the major labels had declared war on consumers, and they paid a price for their victory. As P. J. Huffstutter (2000) reported in the spring of 2000 in the *Los Angeles Times:* "The industry's crusade to block technological innovation has been taken as a declaration of war against young music fans, traditionally its most fervent customers. Fighting back, computer-savvy kids have united and are turning a business dispute into a holy war." In demonizing its core fan base as pirates and thieves, the music industry as a whole and groups like Metallica in particular lost the good will of the most dedicated segment of the record-buying public. This loss was reflected in sales, but apparently not because of file swapping.

Conventional music industry wisdom is premised on the notion that internet music file swapping adversely affects CD sales. The data suggest otherwise. According to the industry's own figures, the U.S. market for recorded music climbed 6.3 percent (to $14.6 billion) in 1999, the year Metallica filed suit against Napster (Waller 2000). Indeed, according to a RIAA press release from mid-2000—a period of heavy Napster activity, "The number of full-length CDs . . . is at an all-time high, growing 6.0% from this time last year . . . which suggests once again, that consumer demand for music in the form of a CD remains the mainstay" (RIAA 2000). Interestingly, these figures show that in the period leading up to the July 2000 injunction against Napster, CD sales rose steadily. In the period following the Napster injunction, however, sales decreased. After an initial surge in sales, the year 2000 finished with an overall 1.5 percent decline (International Federation of Phonographic Industries [IFPI] 2001a). The industry fared even less well in 2001, with a projected 5 percent decline in overall sales (IFPI 2001b). Faced with the backward thinking and outright hostility of the music industry, as well as a sluggish economy, consumers simply voted with their wallets.

Piracy and Theft

Loaded terms such as "piracy" and "theft," of course, cannot simply be taken at face value. In the campaign leading to the passage of the Audio Home Taping Act, the music industry persuaded Congress that it was entitled to be compensated for the loss of sales due to home taping. Yet the industry was never required to produce convincing evidence that home taping actually cut into sales. Indeed, a 1989 study by the Office of Technology Assessment showed precisely the opposite:

- Tapers are buyers—that is, tapers buy more records than nontapers;
- the majority of nontapers do not listen to recorded music;
- tapers tend to tape their own collections for their own personal use;
- 75 percent of all taping is recording something other than music (U.S. Congress Office of Technology Assessment 1989).

In the case of online music, the music industry has tried to make the case that file swapping and digital downloading are different. But a study conducted by the Norman Lear Center at USC in June 2000, in the wake of the Napster hearings, showed essentially the same pattern as the 1989 study: namely, that MP3 usage does not reduce students' CD consumption patterns. Fully 73 percent of students who download MP3s reported that they still bought either the same number of CDs or more (Latonero 2000:2).

The music industry's projection of terms like "piracy" and "theft" onto consumers has tended to deflect attention from its own less than ethical practices. In May 2000 the Federal Trade Commission settled a suit against Universal, Sony, Time Warner, BMG, and EMI involving a price-fixing scheme known as minimum advertising price programs (MAPS), whereby these majors routinely paid a store to advertise a particular CD in return for specifying a required minimum retail price in the ads. Referring to what the FTC called "coercive agreements," FTC Chairman Robert Pitofsky stated: "There was no plausible business justification for this other than to get prices up" (*Bloomberg News* 2000). According to the suit, consumers were overcharged $500 million for CDs in a two-and-a-half-year period. While the majors admitted to no wrongdoing, the terms of the settlement obligated them to refrain from imposing MAPS-like requirements on retailers for seven years, resulting in potential savings for consumers of an estimated $17 million per month.

While the music industry often casts its policing actions in terms of legal protection for creative musicians, the evidence suggests that corporate bottom lines are a much higher priority. Aside from a long history of one-sided contracts—low royalty rates, unfair publishing arrangements, multiyear renewals that keep artists tied to a particular label, and advances-against-royalties that keep them perpetually in debt—the music industry clearly revealed its economic self-interest with the 1999 "Work for Hire" amendment. At the behest of the RIAA and unbeknownst to Congress, Mitch Glazier, then majority counsel to the House Judiciary Subcommittee on Intellectual Property, slipped into an omnibus appropriations bill a three-line amendment that made all recordings works for hire, reducing all artists, in effect, to hired hands of the record companies. Master recordings, which previously reverted to artists after 35 years, became the property of the record companies forever. The bill was signed into law by President Clinton without debate. Mitch Glazier then left his post to become the RIAA's chief lobbyist. (The law was reversed the following year under intense pressure from artists themselves.)

Such behavior calls into question the uncritical acceptance of music industry logic and reinforces the notion that "piracy" and "theft" are relative terms to begin with. Using such language also has the effect of putting a narrowly negative spin on issues that are considerably more complicated. If "piracy" and "theft" are replaced by phrases such as "file sharing" and "community building," for example, a very different picture emerges—one that emphasizes the more positive aspects of the Napster community. Indeed, Napster displays any number of features that the music industry simply has to incorporate if it is to survive.

In the first place, the Napster interface makes the process of locating and downloading a song so easy that even a neophyte can do it. In this way Napster set a standard for user friendliness that the industry must match. More important, Napster and other similar services offer users a music library that cuts across categories of artists, songs, and labels, an eclecticism that individual labels—organized and divided by imprint, genre, race, language, etc.—cannot duplicate. Music fans typically have no label loyalty. In most cases they neither know nor care what label an artist records for. They know that they like a particular song, and they want access to it as easily as possible. File-sharing services like Napster enable users to construct their own customized compilation CDs of exactly the music they want. Record companies, as currently structured, cannot duplicate such a service. Finally, Napster users do not simply trade music files; they communicate with each other. They share ideas and feelings, argue passionately about music, and turn each other on to new sounds. In short, they self-select into communities of taste, which, without spending a dime, constitute a better promotional vehicle than anything the music industry currently has at its disposal.

There is a sense in which the major labels may have used their legal muscle to buy the time to figure out how to enter the online record business on their own terms. Key to this prospect has been the industry's search for a secure format to use for commercial music downloading—the Secure Digital Music Initiative (SDMI), interestingly headed by Leonardo Chariglioni, founder of the Motion Picture Experts Group (MPEG), which certified the MP3 format in the first place. SDMI is a standard that would encode a sound file with a digital "watermark" identifying its owner and origin as a way of discouraging piracy on the internet. Years of experimentation with various types of watermarks bore little fruit. A challenge issued by Chariglione in September 2000, offering up to $10,000 to anyone who could crack the SDMI code, was flatly refused by the hacker community (Brown 2000). Then, in October, Princeton computer scientist Edward Felten and a team of researchers claimed to have defeated all four watermarks (Bray 2000). As an interesting aside, Felten was threatened with a lawsuit by the music industry when he announced plans to discuss his research at a public symposium on the topic. As a result, he later joined forces with the Electronic Frontier Foundation to challenge parts of the Digital Millennium Copyright Act. As for SDMI, more than two years after the initiative began, there was still no music being produced with the watermarking technology included.

What Next?

Faced with the disappointing results of SDMI and the prospect of declining sales, by late 2001 the music industry began to take the need for a meaningful online presence more seriously. Gearing up for the holiday season, the major labels inaugurated two online music services. Pressplay, a joint venture of Sony and Vivendi Universal, included deals with Yahoo, Roxio, the Microsoft Network (MSN), and, interestingly, MP3.com. MusicNet, a project of AOL Time Warner, BMG, and EMI, partnered with RealNetworks and reportedly agreed to allow Napster itself to license its catalog. At launch, both services were restricted to the catalogs of the participating labels and offered limited access to digital music for a monthly fee. For $24.95 a month, Pressplay, for example, allowed a user to stream 1,000 songs, download 100, and burn 20, but no more than two by any given artist. Industry analysts were quick to point out that both services were likely to enjoy little success as long as they offered limited catalogs and restricted how music could be used. Meanwhile, the U.S. Department of Justice launched an antitrust investigation of MusicNet and Pressplay to determine whether the major labels had been colluding illegally to set rates and terms for the use of their music.

A more troublesome limitation arose from the fact that the two services aligned themselves with bitter internet rivals Microsoft and RealNetworks, which could only hamper collaboration and cross-licensing. Pressplay is based on Microsoft's Window's Media Player, whereas MusicNet uses RealNetworks' RealOne Player. "It's a crying shame that the Microsoft-RealNetworks rift has spilled over to the major labels," said Aram Sinnreich of Jupiter Media Metrix. "The end result is that it will be a longer time before consumers will have access to a music-subscription service that offers them enough music" (Hu 2001). Not surprisingly, a number of next-generation Napster clones jumped in to fill the void left by the major labels. For the first week of January 2002, for instance, the RealOne Player was downloaded 18,000 times from software library Download.com, compared with 1.5 million downloads for Morpheus and 1 million for KaZaA (Reuters 2002).

In an online future, reorienting music industry practices toward licensing agreements and subscription services holds out the possibility of creating a business model that can deal equitably with artists, record companies, and consumers. Still obsessed with copyright protection and centralized control at the expense of user-friendly services, however, the major labels tend to lag far behind the third-party services that they should be trying to emulate rather than eliminate. For all the music industry rhetoric about consumer piracy and theft, the overall pattern has been unmistakably clear: The public domain has been all but eliminated, fair use has been narrowed almost to extinction, and the industry itself has engaged in any number of anticompetitive practices. By inflating CD prices, demonizing the record-buying public and the online community, and failing to offer a convenient, afford-able method of accessing music online, the music industry has repeatedly given consumers all the incentive they need to take matters into their own hands and feel righteous in doing so. Throughout this period its strategy has been tied to an enforcement mentality, when a model of providing better service would be far more appropriate to the task.

Notes

1. U.S. Consitution, Article 1, section 8, clause 8.

2. See, for example section 1e, which states that the copyright holder shall have the exclusive right: "To perform the copyrighted work publicly for profit if it be a musical composition and for the purpose of public performance for profit."

3. In cases of infringement, section 25b stated that an infringer shall be liable: "To pay to the copyright proprietor such damages as the copyright proprietor may have suffered due to the infringement, as well as all the profits which the infringer shall have made from such infringement, and in proving profits the plaintiff shall be required to prove sales."

4. Section 28 stated: "That any person who willfully and for profit shall infringe any copyright secured by this Act . . . shall be deemed guilty of a misdemeanor."

5. Section 107: "Limitations on exclusive rights: fair use. Notwithstanding the provisions of sections 106 and 106A [17 USCS Sects. 106, 106A], the fair use of a copyrighted work, including such use by reproduction in copies or phonorecords or by any other means specified by that section, for purposes such as criticism, comment, news reporting, teaching (including multiple copies for classroom use), scholarship, or research, is not an infringement of copyright. In determining whether the use made of a work in any particular case is a fair use the factors to be considered shall include:

(i)   the purpose and character of the use, including whether such use is of a commercial nature or is for nonprofit educational purposes;
(ii) the nature of the copyrighted work;
(iii) the amount and substantiality of the portion used in relation to the copyrighted work as a whole; and
(iv) the effect of the use upon the potential market for or value of the copyrighted work."

6. See Hilliard (1998) for a well-researched discussion of fair use.

7. Senator Orrin Hatch, chairman of the Senate Judiciary Committee, which helps make copyright law, broke ranks with the Department of Justice and the Copyright Office and sent a terse letter to the court saying that the government brief did not represent the opinion of the full U.S. government.

8. The list of trade associations included the Consumer Electronics Association, Net-Coalition, a lobbying group based in Washington, D.C., the Digital Media Association, the Ad Hoc Copyright Coalition, the U.S. Internet Industry Association, the Information Technology Association of America, the Commercial Internet Exchange, the United States Telephone Association, and the Computer and Communications Industry Association.

Bibliography

Bloomberg News. 2000. "FTC slam record labels on CD sales practice," 10 May. <yahoo.cnet.com/news/0-1005-2001.851819.htm?pt.yfin.cat_fin.txt.ne>.
Borland, J. 2000a. "Napster lawyer turns antitrust experience on RIAA," CNET News.com, 20 July. <news.cnet.com/news/0-1005-200-2295301.html>.
———. 2000b. "Tech giants slam Napster injunction," CNET News.com, 25 August. <news.cnet.com/news/0-1005-200-2612001.html>.
———. 2000c. "U.S. sides with RIAA against Napster," CNET News.com, 8 September. <news.cnet.com/news/0-1005-200-2731198.html>.
Bray, H. 2000. "Hackers Go One Up," Boston Globe, 26 October.
Brown, J. 2000. "Crack SDMI? No thanks!" Salon.com, 14 September. <www.salon.com/tech/log/2000/09/14/hack_sdmi/index.html>.
Cohen, K., et al. 1999. No Electronic Theft Act: Policy Development Team Report. Washington, D.C.: United States Sentencing Commission, February.
Fisher, W. 2000. "Theories of intellectual property," draft of 11 April. <www.law.harvard.edu/Academic_Affairs/coursepages/tfisher/iptheory.html#_ftnref10>.
Harris, R. 2000. "Metallica to Napster: Cut Users," Boston Globe, 4 May.

Heilemann, J. 2000. "David Boies: The Wired interview," *Wired,* October. <www.wired.com/wired/archive/8.10/boies_pr.html>.

Hilliard, K. B. 1998. *Music Copyright Laws: Implications for Music Educators.* Ph.D. dissertation, Columbia Teachers College.

Hu, J. 2001. "Web, music giants march to different tunes," CNET News.com, 13 July. <news.cnet.com/news/0-1005-200-6561339.html?tag=dd.ne.dtx.nl-sty.0>.

Huffstutter, P. J. 2000. "Music Makers at Wits' End in Battle with Internet Takers," *Los Angeles Times,* 29 May.

International Federation of Phonographic Industries (IFPI). 2001a. Press release: "Recording industry world sales 2000: CD albums up, overall unit sales down 1.2%," London, 19 April. <www.ifpi.org.uk/index.html>.

————. 2001b. Press release: "Global recorded music sales down 5% in first half of 2001," London, 28 September. <www.ifpi.org.uk/site-content/press/20010928.html>.

Konrad, R. 2000. "Napster among fastest-growing Net technologies," CNET News.com, 5 October. <news.cnet.com/news/0-1005-200-2938703.html>.

Latonero, M. 2000. *Survey of MP3 Usage: Report on a University Consumption Community.* Los Angeles: Norman Lear Center, Annenberg School for Communication, University of Southern California.

McGuinn, R. 2000. Statement to Senate Judiciary Committee Hearing on the Future of Digital Music: Is there an upside to downloading? 11 July. <www.senate.gov/~judiciary/7112000_rm.htm>.

Morse, S. 2000. "Napster Strikes Dissonant Chords," *Boston Globe,* 5 May.

Patterson, L. R., and Lindberg, S. W. 1991. *The Nature of Copyright: A Law of User's Rights.* Athens: University of Georgia Press.

Peraino, V. 1999. "The Law of Increasing Returns," *Wired,* August, p. 144.

Recording Industry Association of America (RIAA). 2000. Press release: "Compact disc shipments at all-time high," Washington, 25 August. <www.RIAA.com/PR_Story.cfm?id=312>.

Reuters. 1999. "Copyright Troubles." Washington, D.C., 20 August.

————. 2002. "Music industry still in first gear online," CNET News.com, 7 January. <news.com.com/2100-1023-802359.html>.

Samuelson, R. J. 1998. "Meanwhile Back on the Hill . . . ," *Washington Post,* 17 September.

Snider, M. 1997. "Law Targets Copyright Theft on Line," *USA Today,* 19 December.

United States Congress, Office of Technology Assessment. 1989. *Copyright and Home Copying: Technology Challenges the Law.* OTA-CIT-422. Washington, D.C.: U.S. Government Printing Office.

Waller, D. 2000. "Dance to the music: RIAA celebrates record profits in 1999," *Variety,* 22 February. <www.variety.com/index.asp?layout=story&articleid=VR1117776600&categoryid=16&cs=1>. Posted 22 Feb. 2000.

World Intellectual Property Organization (WIPO). 1996. "Basic Proposal for the Substantive Provisions of the Treaty on Intellectual Property in Respect of Databases to Be Considered by the Diplomatic Conference," Geneva, 30 August, notes on Article 1.07.

Vanessa Bastian and Dave Laing

---

3   Twenty Years of Music Censorship Around the World

The policing of popular music can take many forms. In this chapter we consider the censorship and oppression on a global scale of musicians, fans, and others involved with popular music during the last two decades of the twentieth century (1980–1999). We look at the geographical distribution of that censorship, the causes of censorship and oppression, and the punishments suffered by the victims—and also some instances where censorship has been lifted or moderated.

The source of our data is the journal *Index on Censorship*. Founded in Britain in 1972 as a response to the persecution of writers in the Soviet Union, *Index* is dedicated to the exposure and critique of censorship of all kinds and in all areas, from politics and religion to journalism and the arts. In the journal's first issue, the poet and critic Stephen Spender wrote that its role would be

> to study the situation of those who are silenced in their own countries and to make their circumstances known in the world community to which they spiritually belong . . . (especially) the ever more jealous surveillance by governments and police of individual freedom. (1:1, p. 3)[1]

A regular feature of *Index*, a country-by-country listing of instances of censorship, has provided the details upon which this chapter is based. It should be said that the 214 incidents of music censorship considered here are a small proportion of the total number listed by *Index*. Most of the others involve actions taken by governments and other authorities against print and broadcast journalists, writers, poets, and filmmakers. Moreover, the 214 incidents are by no means a comprehensive list of acts of music censorship during these two decades. Additional cases have been discussed in articles in the *Index* itself or reported in other media. Although we sometimes refer to these additional acts of censorship, for reasons of consistency our statistics refer only to the 214 incidents.

Index has from time to time focused on music censorship, notably in its 1998 special issue entitled *Smashed Hits: The Book of Banned Music* (27:6). This included articles detailing acts of music censorship in more than twenty countries on four continents. A compact disc containing examples of "banned music" from Mauritania, Nigeria, South Africa, Tibet, and the United Kingdom accompanied the special issue. Also of interest are a leading article from 1983 entitled "Music Is Dangerous" (12:2, p. 8), a 1989 interview with the late Fela Kuti (18:9, p. 12), and "Pop Go the Censors" by David Holden, a 1993 comparison of music censorship in the United Kingdom and the United States (22:5–6, pp. 11–15).

Some commentators and readers might regard the implicit definition of censorship adopted by *Index* as relatively narrow. As the quotation from Spender states, the primary concern is with state-sponsored suppression of free speech. Therefore, almost all the reported incidents involve the use of force (judicial or otherwise) to prevent the dissemination of certain songs or to punish those who have created, disseminated, or merely listened to music the censors or oppressors disapproved of. In most, but not all, cases the censors were state or quasi-state bodies. Thus, the *Index* listing includes no cases of "self-censorship" and only a few cases where such nonstate bodies as religious organizations, vigilantes (such as terrorist groups), or businesses (such as retailers) have acted as censors.

With these provisos in mind, we have collated the *Index* data under the following headings: the country and the continent where the censorship took place; the victims; the censor; the motivation; and the punishment. We have analyzed the data in some of these categories in quantitative form and presented the results as tables. In all categories we have looked at the 20-year period both as a whole and as divided into two decades: the 1980s and the 1990s.

Geopolitical Locations of Censorship

The 214 separate incidents of censorship reported in *Index* were distributed almost equally between the two decades. We have analyzed these incidents by the nation-state and the geographical region in which each occurred, using the regional definitions provided in the *Encyclopedia of Popular Music of the World* project, found in *Popular Music Studies: A Select Bibliography* (Shepherd et al. 1997). The resulting numbers are given in Table 3-1.

The region with the greatest number of incidents comprises the Middle East and North Africa, with 54 over the 20-year period, divided almost equally between the two decades. This region includes the country with the greatest number of reported incidents: Turkey (23). The remainder are distributed among a further 11 countries, of which Israel and the Occupied Territories (10) and Algeria (8) are the most significant in terms of censorship and the persecution of musicians. The region with the second-greatest number of reported incidents (42) is Eastern and Southeastern

TABLE 3-1. Censorship Incidents by Region

Region	1980s	1990s	Total
Africa (sub-Saharan)	18	11	29
Asia	8	18	26
Caribbean	4	1	5
Eastern and SE Europe	32	8	40
Latin and Central America	19	2	21
Oceania	0	0	0
Middle East and N Africa	24	30	54
North America	3	15	18
Western Europe	2	19	21
Total	110	104	214

Europe. This region includes all the countries that had communist regimes until the late 1980s, including the USSR. The collapse at the end of the 1980s of the communist regimes, along with their established state censorship systems, explains the dramatic fall in the number of reported incidents of music censorship here in the 1990s—only eight compared with 32 in the 1980s.

After those two regions come five whose numbers range from 29 (sub-Saharan Africa) and 26 (Asia) to 21 each for Latin and Central America and Western Europe and 18 for North America. Almost half the incidence of censorship in Africa involved the apartheid regime in South Africa, but incidents were reported from nine other countries. Censorship was reported in 13 countries in the Asian region, where the most incidents took place in China (five) and Vietnam (four), countries still controlled by authoritarian communist parties. In Latin and Central America, 10 incidents of censorship were reported from Chile, and the remaining 11 were split among seven other countries. Here almost all the acts of censorship were taken by right-wing military dictatorships, notably that of Augusto Pinochet in Chile. With six incidents each, France and the United Kingdom had the most reported incidents among the seven countries of Western Europe where music censorship occurred, while all the incidents in the North American region took place in the United States.

Africa and Latin America saw a fall in the number of incidents between the 1980s and 1990s. In the case of Latin America, this can be attributed mainly to the ending of the Pinochet dictatorship. In the other three regions, however, the numbers grew considerably in the latter decade. The reasons are not immediately apparent, although hostile responses to rap music account for some of the 1990s incidents in both North America and Europe.

Five incidents were reported in the Caribbean region. The countries involved were Barbados, Haiti, Jamaica, and Puerto Rico.

TABLE 3-2. Censorship Incidents: The Top Ten Countries, 1980–1999

Country	1980s	1990s	Total
Turkey	6	17	23
USA	3	15	18
South Africa	7	6	13
Israel/Occupied Territories	10	2	12
Chile	10	0	10
USSR and CIS	8	2	10
Czechoslovakia	8	1	9
Algeria	4	4	8
France	1	5	6
UK	1	5	6

Finally, no incidents were reported in Oceania, although the *Smashed Hits* issue gives details of a 1998 case of broadcast censorship in Australia. The song involved, "I'm a Backdoor Man" by Pauline Pantsdown, was a political satire by a gay activist on Pauline Hanson, leader of the racist One Nation party (27:6, p. 152).

If we turn to individual countries, we find that the oppression of musicians and others was reported in some 69 countries during the 20-year period. Other *Index* articles referred to music censorship in at least three other countries. The 10 nation-states with the greatest number of acts of censorship are listed in Table 3-2 and discussed individually in the following sections.

Turkey

A total of 23 incidents of censorship or oppression were reported in Turkey. In 1986–1987 *Index on Censorship* reported on the country's adoption of a new and more oppressive system of censorship targeting artistic works (including songs) that offended against "the state interest, national sovereignty, the public interest and national morality" (15:4, p. 40). The supervisory council responsible for administering the censorship regime includes representatives of the ministries of culture and foreign affairs and the national security council, and "one artist" (16:1, p. 44).

The level of oppression rose markedly in 1990–1991, when 12 incidents were reported as against six in the whole of the 1980s. The majority of these incidents were the result of attempts by successive Turkish governments to suppress the language and culture of the Kurdish people. Typical incidents included the withdrawal from sale of a cassette of songs by Yzan Cugdis for being "against law and order" (19:10, p. 39) and the arrest of Ahmet Kaya for causing "political incidents" during one of his performances (ibid.). The *Smashed Hits* issue included an interview with the Kurdish singer and songwriter Shivan Perwer, who has lived in exile since

1976. He has produced almost 30 albums in that time and tours all over the world, performing to Kurdish and Turkish community organizations and at multicultural solidarity gigs, which, he says, "gives me the opportunity to get Kurdish culture across to other communities" (27:6, p. 126).

In order to facilitate the country's entry into the European Union, the Turkish regime gave assurances that it would improve its human rights record. Yet as recently as 1999 Turkey's 1998 Musician of the Year, Ahmet Kaya, was again put on trial for saying that he wished to compose songs in Kurdish (28:5, p. 145).

United States

In contrast to such countries as Turkey and South Africa, acts of censorship or attempted censorship in the United States are instigated more often by institutions or individuals in civil society than by organs of the state. The few incidents reported in the 1980s included the Boston Symphony Orchestra's cancellation of a contract with the actress Vanessa Redgrave because of her pro-Palestinian views (17:10, p. 40) and MTV's banning in 1988 of Neil Young's video "This Note's for You," which satirized musicians who advertised drinks (ibid.). Ironically, the highly commercialized MTV gave as the reason for its censorship the fact that Young's song included brand names. MTV's role as censor was not limited to this case, of course. David Holden's article "Pop Go the Censors" reported that the network had edited out of a Paul McCartney concert film the pro-environmentalist song "Big Boys Bickering" because it referred to "the fucking ozone layer." MTV had also drawn accusations of racism in the early 1980s when it excluded videos by black artists from its programming.[2]

The arrival of rap as a major music genre in the 1990s dramatically increased the quantity of actual and attempted censorship in the United States. Much of the action by various "citizen" and police groups in the early 1990s centered on two *causes célèbres:* the album "As Nasty As They Wanna Be" by 2 Live Crew and Ice-T's track "Cop Killer." The range of those caught up in the subsequent moral panic was considerable. It included record store owners, warehouse packagers, police unions, television evangelists, board members of Time Warner, members of the U.S. Congress, and, of course, lawyers and judges (19:9, p. 40; 20:2, p. 40; 21:9, p. 48; 22:5–6, pp. 13–14).

In an article about the antimusic campaigns of the religious right for the *Smashed Hits* issue, Jim d'Entremont listed five ways in which these "theocratic organizations" had attempted to circumvent the First Amendment to the Constitution, which guarantees the right to freedom of speech (27:6, pp. 37–38): "harassment and intimidation directed at artists in an effort to promote self-censorship"; "prosecution of artists, retail outlets, broadcasters and record companies"; parental advisory labels and ratings; legislation; and boycotts. Examples of oppressive legislation include the Louisiana state law of 1990 that forbade sales of albums with "explicit lyrics" stickers to "unmarried minors" (19:9, p. 40) and a Texas law that prohibits public agencies from investing in any concern that is itself an investor in a corporation that produces music that "describes, glamorizes or advocates violence, drug abuse or sexual activity" (27:6, p. 38).

South Africa

All 13 incidents reported from South Africa were the direct result of the apartheid policy pursued with varying degrees of rigor until the election of President Nelson Mandela in 1994. However, there were also strong pressures to ban material deemed offensive to religious sensibilities. The South African state operated an ambitious censorship policy that sought to prevent the publication, performance, or broadcasting of any political, journalistic, or artistic material that criticized or opposed apartheid.

The government's Publications Control Board issued lists of newly banned cultural products at frequent intervals. Examples in the music category included the album "Change Is Pain" by the Sowetan dub poet Mzwakhe Mbuli (16:10, p. 38), Brenda Fassie's song "Good Black Woman" (19:2, p. 39), and songs by foreign artists such as Tracy Chapman, Stevie Wonder, Pink Floyd, and Bruce Springsteen (see Chapter 9 in this volume for more details of censorship under the apartheid regime).

Israel and the Occupied Territories

The case of Israel may be compared with that of Turkey in that the majority of reported instances of music censorship concern the repression of the artistic expression of an ethnic group, in this case the Palestinian Arabs. In 1981 the Israeli authorities closed Bir Zeit University after students held a four-day festival of Palestinian culture (10:2, pp. 75–76). In 1984 the musician Jamil Asa'ad was ordered not to sing in public or private without permission from the security services (13:5, p. 44), and in 1983 the Jerusalem police arrested seven men for distributing cassettes of Palestinian national songs (12:2, p. 45). Jewish singers were punished for showing sympathy for the Palestinians: Nurit Airon's song "After the Deluge" was banned by Israeli state radio in 1989 for this reason (18:8, p. 38).

Chile

Although Latin America contained other military dictatorships during the 1970s and 1980s, the most oppressive of these in terms of censorship of the arts seems to have been the Pinochet regime in Chile, which seized power in a 1973 coup d'etat that overthrew the elected government, led by President Salvador Allende. Pinochet and his military junta showed their recognition of the power of music early on through the brutal murder of singer-songwriter Victor Jara and the enforced exile of many other members of the Chilean new song movement. Foreign artists were also refused entry to the country, although the banning in 1982 of the French singer-songwriter Gilbert Becaud, who was due to perform at a song festival, was later said to be result of an error by the Chilean authorities, who confused him with the actor Yves Montand, a vocal critic of the Pinochet regime (11:3, p. 43).

USSR and Commonwealth of Independent States

Artistic expression was subject to extremely strict controls in the Soviet Union. The story of popular musicians' attempts to evade censorship and arrest has been told by the critic Artemy Troitsky, who describes conditions "at the peak of the Chernenko-era anti-rock campaign" (Troitsky 1990:38). In 1986 the Soviet authorities issued a ban on music that "depicts our life in a distorted way and makes propaganda for ideals and attitudes alien to our society." At the same time, 41 bands were forbidden to perform in public (27:6, p. 50).

Those who attempted to circumvent the banning order were dealt with severely. Members of the Georgian group Phantom were arrested after performing private concerts in apartments in 1985 (14:5, p. 69). The brothers Grigori and Isai Goldstein from Phantom were eventually allowed to leave the country after 15 years of attempts to emigrate (15:6, p. 41).

Czechoslovakia

All the satellite states of the USSR in Eastern Europe operated restrictive censorship regimes, but Czechoslovakia seems to have been the most enthusiastic in its pursuit of alleged political infractions by musicians. It was the site of two widely publicized cases involving the avant-garde band Plastic People of the Universe and the officials of the Jazz Section of the Musicians Union, an organization with 7,000 members. The persecution of Ivan Jirous, artistic director of the Plastic People, began in 1978, when he was found guilty of making "antistate" remarks at the private opening of an art exhibition and imprisoned (5:4, p. 66). He was again arrested with three other members of the group in 1982. On this occasion, Jirous was sentenced to three and a half years in prison for publishing "antistate" material in the underground magazine *Vikno* ("Window") (11:5, p. 34).

The Jazz Section officials were arrested in September 1986 for "illicit trading," the culmination of a long campaign of harassment caused by the section's success in "promoting dubious bourgeois culture" among Czech youth (15:9, p. 47).

Algeria

Although only eight incidents were reported from Algeria, three of these involved the murder of musicians. These were among the numerous victims of the civil war between the military government and Islamist militants during the 1990s. Details of the killings are given later in this chapter.

Leading factions of the fundamentalist Front Islamique de Salut (FIS) opposed all musical expression. In his book *Men and Popular Music in Algeria* (1999), Marc Schade-Poulsen reports the views of a FIS supporter and former rai music aficionado: "They (the FIS) sent a delegation to Saudi Arabia to consult the real learned men ('ulama') and they said it is not only rai that is forbidden. All music is hr,m (illicit)" (Schade-Poulsen 1999:87).

Following their victory in local elections in 1990, Islamists prevented all public concerts in Oran (ibid.:10). In 1992 the army seized power in order to prevent the election of a government led by the FIS. Subsequently, musicians found themselves attacked and victimized by both sides. In 1994 an armed Islamist group threatened to burn down schools unless music lessons and gymnastics lessons for girls were abolished (ibid.:196). On the other side, state persecution of musicians took place in the 1980s, as when the popular Berber singer Louns Ait-Menguellet was sentenced in 1985 to three years imprisonment for organizing a concert in support of Islamic resistance (15:1, p. 33), and the singer and human rights activist Farahat Mehenni was given three years for "undermining state authority" (14:5, p. 64).

France

The perpetrators of the acts of censorship reported in France have been a mixture of state and nonstate bodies. The two members of the rap group NTM were convicted in 1996 of "insulting people in authority" after they made remarks about police at their 14 July concert (26:1, p. 113), while in 1994 the interior minister Charles Pasqua banned a concert by Ashraf Marziah, an Iranian singer opposed to the Islamic fundamentalist regime in Tehran. Pasqua said that the concert would be "in reality a demonstration of support for the Mujahideen," an exiled opposition movement (24:1, p. 239).

The Islamic faith was involved in an incident in 1989 when the singer Veronique Sanson withdrew the song "Allah" from her repertoire after receiving anonymous threats against her life (18:4, p. 37).

United Kingdom

As in France the censors involved in the six reported incidents from the United Kingdom came from both the state and civil society. During the Gulf War conflict in

1991, the state broadcaster BBC urged DJs to treat with care such tracks as John Lennon's "Give Peace a Chance" and Lulu's Eurovision Song Contest song, "Boom Bang a Bang," for the duration of the conflict. Carter USM's "Blood Sports for All" (about a racially abused black soldier in the British army) was banned. The group Massive Attack had to abbreviate its name to Massive (22:5–6, p. 14; 27:6, p. 184). In addition to these incidents, Holden's "Pop Go the Censors" refers to the campaign against "offensive" pop music waged by the chief constable of Greater Manchester, which included the seizure of recordings by Morrissey and Flux of Pink Indians (22:5–6, p. 12).

In 1991 the Island record company was unsuccessfully prosecuted for obscenity for distributing the album "Efil4zaggin" by the rap group NWA (21:2, p. 48). Other incidents included the shooting of hip-hop DJ Tim Westwood by unknown attackers in 1999 (28:5, p. 146) and the sacking of a black DJ, Steve Jackson, by London station Kiss FM, which led to Jackson's claim that he was unfairly dismissed (28:6, p. 254). More detailed discussion of music censorship in Britain can be found in Martin Cloonan's *Banned!* (1996).

Victims

Who were the victims of these 214 incidents of music censorship? The vast majority were, of course, performers, but some were broadcasters, retailers, or even members of the audience.

In 1999 the authorities in Serbia blacked out the broadcast of the MTV Europe Awards by the independent station B52. The reason was that B52 itself was to receive a special freedom award (28:1, p. 99). The Florida music retailer Charles Freeman was victimized in 1991 when he was fined $1,000 for selling an album by 2 Live Crew to a teenager (20:2, p. 40). The album had previously been declared "obscene" by a Florida judge.

To be a fan of certain types of music has been an offense in many countries. In 1988, for example, the Serbian authorities in the province of Kosovo arrested two men of Albanian ethnic origin for possessing cassettes of Albanian music (17:9, p. 40). In 1996, 28 teenagers in Iran were arrested for possessing "obscene" CDs and cassettes (25:6, p. 175), and the following year Egyptian police rounded up heavy metal fans in an incident reported in the *Smashed Hits* issue (27:6, p. 169).

In the era of communist regimes, music fans were frequently persecuted. Frank Noetzeld, an East German, was imprisoned for 18 months for allowing his friends to make copies of banned records by the exiled singer-songwriter Wolf Biermann. Police dispersed a 1981 gathering of several hundred in Moscow to commemorate John Lennon (10:2, p. 78). Nine pacifist demonstrators were arrested and fined after demonstrating at a Rock for Peace concert in Gdansk, Poland, in 1986 (15:2, p. 38).

In 1987, 20 people were arrested in East Berlin after chanting, "The Wall must go," while gathered at the Wall to hear a rock concert taking place on the western side (16:8, p. 37). A British woman, Rachel Goldwyn, was arrested and imprisoned in Burma in 1999 for singing a freedom anthem in the street (28:6, p. 234).

There is no noticeable trend in terms of the styles or genres of music which have been targeted, although rap has been censored in both the United States and France, punk in both Hungary and Germany, and various types of folk music in a number of countries where the expression of a particular cultural identity was forbidden: Kurdish music in Turkey, Palestinian music in Israel, Albanian music in Kosovo, and Chinese lyrics in Indonesia.

The rollcall of artists whose works were banned during the 20-year period is an impressive one. Among Anglo-American artists, Madonna has suffered censorship in Ireland, Japan, South Africa, and the United States; Tim Rice and Andrew Lloyd Webber were censored in India and Uruguay; Sheryl Crow, Paul McCartney, k. d. Lang, and Neil Young in the United States; Tracy Chapman, Bruce Springsteen, Steven van Zandt, and Stevie Wonder in South Africa; and John Lennon and Lulu in the United Kingdom. Among other victims were the Cuban jazz pianist Gonzala Rubelcaba in Puerto Rico, the Spanish singer-songwriter Joan Manuel Serrat in Chile and Uruguay, and the rai singers Cheb Hasni and Cheb Aziz in Algeria.

Censors

A wide range of organizations, institutions, and individuals instigated or carried out acts of music censorship and oppression. Most of the reported incidents involved the judicial and military organs of the state—the police, the armed forces, and the courts. But a considerable number were perpetrated by broadcasters, usually those controlled or financed by the state. Such incidents were reported from France in 1990 (20:4–5, p. 54), Egypt in 1996 (25:4, p. 101), Greece in 1981 (10:5, p. 44), Israel in 1989 (18:8, p. 38), Pakistan in 1990 (20:1, p. 37), Sierra Leone in 1981 (10:6, p. 109), South Africa in 1986 (15:1, p. 35), Thailand in 1986 (16:2, p. 40), and the United Kingdom in 1990 (20:4–5, p. 52). The censorship system of the South African Broadcasting Corporation (SABC) included weekly meetings of a Censor Board Committee after which "restricted" records were defaced and made unplayable by being scratched with a nail (27:6, p. 85).

Censorship of teen pop music by South Korea's state broadcaster KBS in 1997 went unreported by *Index*. This censorship applied to both music and clothing: KBS announced that "entertainers who wear outfits which may harm the sound emotional development of youth will be banned" (Howard 1997). In Sierra Leone, the banning order against songs "not in the public interest" coincided with a protest against price rises and food shortages. In Thailand, the song "Prachapapipathai"

("Democracy") by the group Carabgo was banned because of its satirical attitude toward the country's political system.

In the private sector there was censorship by commercial broadcasters in South Africa, the United Kingdom, and the United States, where a number of radio stations in the Midwest refused to play records by k. d. lang after she appeared in an advertisement for People for the Ethical Treatment of Animals (20:1, p. 40). In South Africa, a station called Capital 604 announced in 1985 that it would play "Free Nelson Mandela" only if it judged the song to be "extremely wonderful" (15:1, p. 35).

Two festival directors acted as censors under authoritarian regimes. In 1988 the head of the Vina del Mar song festival in Chile excluded a Peruvian song that allegedly called for a plebiscite on the future of the Chilean head of state (17:10, p. 36). In Czechoslovakia in 1989 the director of the Bratislava Festival pulled the plugs on the singers Ivan Hoffman and Vladimir Merta, who were appearing alongside Joan Baez (18:8, p. 37).

Direct censorship by state bodies has been enforced on an *ad hoc* basis by police and politicians or more systematically by specialized censorship organizations. The latter appear in various guises across the world. In the former communist states, official unions of artists were often employed to silence or punish dissidents. In the Soviet Union it was decreed in 1983 that no music group could perform in public unless 80 percent of its song lyrics were written by a member of the Union of Composers (27:6, p. 50). Since this union denied membership to "underground" or radical rock musicians, the requirement amounted to an outright ban.

In many countries, forms of prior censorship of lyrics were, and remain, institutionalized. In the 1980s and 1990s, Singapore's Controller of Undesirable Publications regularly prevented record companies from issuing "hardcore" rap tracks and also prevented the release of two greatest-hits albums by TAFKAP (formerly and subsequently known as Prince) because three tracks had lyrics with "sexual connotations." The Philippines has a Videogram Regulatory Board that controls the release of sound recordings and has the power to censor any that are "immoral, indecent, libelous, contrary to law or good customs, or injurious to the prestige of the Republic of the Philippines or its people" (Fitzgerald 1995:40). The Ministry of Information of Saudi Arabia checks all proposed record releases, and it was reported that recordings by Julio Iglesias were banned because "Iglesias" means "churches" in Spanish. In addition, lyrics considered "offensive to the Islamic religion, to have a sexual content or featuring any Zionist sentiments are prohibited" (*Music and Copyright* 1997:8).

China has a similar regime: No local recording can be made and no foreign recording imported until the lyrics have been approved by government censors. Industry professionals are expected to work to the implicit guidelines and cut out anything that might introduce "spiritual pollution" (see Chapter 10 in this volume for more on China).

TABLE 3-3. Motives for Music Censorship

Motive	1980s	1990s	Total
Political	84	59	143
Cultural	11	17	28
Moral	6	14	20
Religious	4	12	16
Sexual	1	11	12
Aesthetic	3	1	4
Other	11	10	21

In countries without such forms of prior censorship, the agents of censorship and oppression include both state officials and organizations from civil society. The state officials mainly operate by applying laws ranging from those intended to curb obscenity or race hatred to those designed to promote state security.

In the United States, especially, the use of civil law by pressure groups has been a feature of censorship campaigns. Thus, in 1992 various police organizations sought to sue Time Warner over its release of Ice-T's "Cop Killer" (21:8, p. 41). A more informal pressure group assembled in Israel in 1981, when a violent and noisy crowd protested against the decision by Zubin Mehta and the Israel Symphony Orchestra to perform Wagner's Prelude to the opera *Tristan and Isolde* (11:1, p. 44).

Motives

Why did these acts of censorship take place? We divide the apparent motives of the censors into six broad categories (Table 3-3). Because some acts of censorship seem to involve a combination of motives, the totals add up to more than the number of discrete incidents (214). We found 21 incidents to be unclassifiable because insufficient information was given in the reports in *Index on Censorship*; these are listed as "Other" in the table.

Political

We estimate that political motives were involved in 143 incidents of music censorship, or almost three-quarters of the total. In nearly all of these cases the censorship was carried out by agents of the state, such as the police or courts, enforcing laws that prohibited the expression of political opinions contrary to those of the government of the day. It is notable that the numbers of such cases fell by about one-quarter, from 84 in the 1980s to 59 in the 1990s. This reflected the ending of a number of authoritarian regimes in Europe and Latin America and the subsequent collapse of systems of strict control of artistic matters.

In the communist states of the 1980s, the reported charges included the phrase "antistate" in Czechoslovakia, "anti-Soviet slander" and "treason in the form of espionage" in the Soviet Union, and "attacking Communism and the Soviet Union" in Hungary, where members of the punk rock band Coitus were jailed for two years in 1985 for performing a song opposing nuclear weapons. In Yugoslavia a female singer in a hotel was arrested after refusing a request to sing a number called "Comrade Tito, We Pledge to You That We Will Not Swerve from Your Path" (17:1, p. 41).

Burkina Faso's ruler, Captain Thomas Sankaro, closed down nightclubs in 1983 and announced a ban on "anti-popular, reactionary and bourgeois music." The clubs were to be replaced by popular music and dance "meetings" (13:1, p. 46).

Within the broad "political" category, many acts of censorship can be understood either as attempts by communist regimes to stifle dissent from "socialist" norms or as an attack by right-wing regimes on their left-wing or centrist critics. In a small number of cases, however, the objects of censorship have been musicians expressing racist or fascist sentiments. Such incidents were reported in Germany in 1993, where authorities banned the music of neo-Nazi Oi! groups (22:3, p. 35); in the Czech Republic in 1994 (24:3, p. 173); in post-Communist Russia, where *Rokopop*, a Tatarstan television show, was taken off the air in 1994 when it carried an interview with a musician who expressed pro-Nazi views (24:1, p. 239); and from Sweden, where attempts to convict members of a neo-punk movement called White Noise had, as of 1998, so far failed (27:6, pp. 153–155). After pressure from Jewish organizations, in 1998 the authorities in Bavaria also prevented the actor and director Ekkehard Schall (the son-in-law of Bertolt Brecht) from releasing a CD with antifascist motives on which a reading of Hitler's *Mein Kampf* was accompanied by sounds that undermined its message (27:3, p. 109).

Purely nationalist motives lay behind censorship in South Korea, Pakistan, Indonesia, and Syria. Any music construed as expressing favorable attitudes toward hated neighboring countries was strictly suppressed. In South Korea songs were banned in 1996 for "praising" North Korea (25:2, p. 102), while the Pakistan rock band Junoon was banned from performing after touring India and singing, "We have no nationality" (27:6, p. 165). From 1965 to 1995, no Chinese-language songs could be broadcast in Indonesia (26:1, p. 178), and in 1980 the Syrian regime banned all performances by the Lebanese singer Sabah because she was alleged to have associated with pro-Israel elements (10:1, p. 78).

Cultural

By "cultural" censorship or oppression we mean the persecution of a segment of society for expressing its cultural identity through the use of a particular language or musical genre associated with that identity. The principal example analyzed here is the Turkish state's attempt to eradicate the cultural identity of the Kurds.

From Yugoslavia and from Israel and the Occupied Territories came reports of authorities' breaking musical instruments used to perform forbidden songs. In 1984 the instruments belonging to the Palestinian singer Mustafa Kurd were seized and destroyed by the Israeli security police when he arrived in Jerusalem to give a concert (13:5, p. 44). In 1993 soldiers of the Serb-led Yugoslav army assaulted members of the Kosovan Albanian folk group Xhelil Reshiti and destroyed their instruments; they also arrested Hysen Sadik in Prestina for selling cassettes of Albanian folk music (22:5–6, p. 47).

Moral

The rhetoric of moral decay was frequently used by communist regimes and as such was coterminous with their acts of political repression. For example, in 1986 the Vietnamese authorities announced a crackdown on cassettes that contained "reactionary and decadent" western pop music (15:1, p. 36). "Decadent" pop music from the west was banned in 450 Bulgarian discotheques in the same year (15:3, p. 38). In 1983 a Chinese actress was criticized by Zhon Wezi, a vice-minister of culture, after she had appeared dressed in "Hong Kong clothes" and thrown herself into a man's arms while singing a duet. Zhon called for a ban on plays that spread "feudal ideas and bad taste" (12:6, p. 44).

The imposition of conservative morality was equally a feature of the military regime in Chile. In 1980 seven Spanish performers were accused of "immoral" behavior and expelled because male actors had impersonated female singers in their show (9:5, p. 61). Two years later the regime prohibited the sale of "reactionary, pornographic or vulgar" music tapes (11:3, p. 43).

In the United States, pressure for censorship on moral grounds has come from religious and political groups rather than the state itself. In 1985 the Parents Music Resource Center (PMRC) was set up by Tipper Gore, wife of Senator Al Gore, the future vice-president. PMRC promoted court actions against recordings by the Dead Kennedys and Judas Priest. Those efforts were unsuccessful, but in the mid-1980s the PMRC persuaded the record industry to place stickers on albums whose lyrics were offensive to PMRC's conservative moral code (22:5–6, p. 12). The spokespersons of the campaign against Ice-T's "Cop Killer" in the 1990s were William Bennett, a former official in Ronald Reagan's administration, and C. Dolores Tucker, a sometime activist in the African American civil rights movement (24:5, p. 191).

Religious

Religiously motivated censorship may focus on either music's irredeemably secular character or its association with religious beliefs outlawed by the state. The antimusic censors of the late twentieth century were principally, though not

exclusively, Islamic. In the 1970s the spiritual leader of the Iranian revolution, Aya-
tollah Khomeini, denounced music as "no different to opium." To broadcast or perform it was, he said, "a treason to the country, a treason to our youth" (8:5, p. 67).

During the 1990s at least two countries enacted stringent laws against music and
dance. In 1991 Pakistan's parliament brought the religious Sharia law into force.
Among other things, this gave police the power to prohibit any music or dancing
that "directly or indirectly incites sexual pleasure" (20:8, p. 54). Five years later the
Taliban regime in Afghanistan banned all music from radio and television (25:5,
p. 80).

Islamic antipathy to music and dance was also blamed for the death in 1994 of
a Sudanese musician who was killed in the aftermath of a ban on women and men
dancing together (24:1, p. 250) and the murders of several rai performers in Algeria in the 1990s.

In the same era the Vatican delivered a counterblast against pop through a statement delivered by its chief moral watchdog, Cardinal Ratzinger, in 1996. He urged
young people not to listen to rock music that was "an instrument of the devil." He
spoke of the "diabolic and satanic messages" of some heavy metal music but warned
also of the "subliminal" satanic influence exercised by more traditional groups such
as the Beatles, the Rolling Stones, and Pink Floyd (26:1, p. 127). In keeping with
this approach, the lyrics of songs by Bob Dylan ("Blowin' in the Wind") and John
Lennon ("Imagine") were changed to eliminate atheistic sentiments before they
were performed for the pope in Bologna in 1997 (26:6, p. 114).

Accusations by Christian religious leaders that *Jesus Christ Superstar* presented a
"tarnished image of Christ" caused the banning of a school production in Kerala,
India, of Andrew Lloyd Webber and Tim Rice's musical (20:2, p. 37).

Communist regimes were responsible for acts of repression against Christian
music. Christian rock musician Valery Barinov was detained in the USSR in 1984,
and in 1986 it was reported from China that security police in Hebei Province had
beaten up Roman Catholic nuns and priests when they began to sing hymns (16:1,
p. 39).

Sexual

Perhaps this category should be labeled "antisexual," since it includes incidents
where the object of censorship was sexual expression. One particular target of such
censorship has been Madonna, whose book *Sex* was banned in countries ranging
from Japan to Ireland and South Africa (22:1, p. 37; 22:2, p. 37; 22:4, p. 40). The
book was not concerned with music, however. The songs of Prince were also a focus
for sexual censors in the United States and elsewhere. Rap has encountered censorship problems in the United States because of sexual references in songs by
artists such as 2 Live Crew.

In Ireland the actor Tom McGinty was arrested and charged with "public indecency" in 1991 after appearing in the street in his *Rocky Horror Show* stage outfit of black corset, feather backpiece, fishnet tights, and G-string (21:1, p. 38).

In such African countries as Togo, Kenya, Ivory Coast, Burkina Faso, Niger, and Cameroon, the authorities condemned the erotic nature of the dance craze of 1999, variously known as Mapouka and Ndombolo. "The dance is sexually suggestive and drives many Kenyans to casual sex, leading to the spread of Aids," claimed the permanent secretary to the Kenyan Ministry of Health, Professor Julius Meme (Duval-Smith 1999:23).

Aesthetic

Our sample contained only a few reports of censorship based solely or primarily on artistic grounds (the charge that the music was too bad to be distributed). One occurred in Swaziland in 1984 when broadcasts of reggae, disco, and rasta-type music were banned (13:6, p. 48). The attack on a stage show in China in 1983 alleged that it was in "bad taste" (13:6, p. 44). In 1994 Montenegro's Ministry of Culture denounced the turbo folk music emanating from Serbia as "cultural kitsch" (23:6, p. 248). Other examples were the banning of an Iron Maiden concert in Lebanon in 1995 (24:6, p. 179) and the public burning of Western musical instruments in Libya in 1985. The latter was organized by the People's Committee of Information and Culture, which stated that the use of such instruments "distort[ed] authentic Arab culture and heritage" and "posed a threat to public standards of good taste" (14:5, p. 66).

Some of these attacks could equally be regarded as religious or political in nature, with the object of censorship in Swaziland being the Rastafarian religion and the China and Montenegro cases motivated by dislike for the political implications of the music. It seems that few if any acts of censorship are undertaken against music *qua* music; rather, they are stimulated by the perceived connotations of a particular song or genre. In the terms developed by Lucy Green (1988), censorship is aimed at music's delineated meanings, not its inherent meanings.

Punishments

The 214 incidents reported in our survey led to imprisonment, fines, expulsions, and the murders of seven musicians and one radio worker. Those killed were:

Michael Smith, reggae poet, murdered in Jamaica in 1983 by persons unknown (12:6, p. 45);

Pat Lewis, musician and political activist, killed in Jamaica in 1985 by police (14:3, p. 51);

A. G. Marquez, composer, killed in Colombia in 1988 by persons unknown (17:4, p. 36);

Cheb Hasni, rai singer, killed in Algeria in 1994 by persons unknown (23:6, p. 230);

Khojali Osman, musician, killed in Sudan in 1994 by an Islamic mob (24:1, p. 250);

Lila Amara, Berber singer, killed in Algeria in 1995 by persons unknown (24:5, p. 169);

Cheb Aziz, rai singer, killed in Algeria in 1996 by persons unknown (25:6, p. 166);

Felix Haro Rodriguez, radio DJ, killed in Peru in 1999 by the Sendero Luminoso guerrillas (28:5, p. 136).

All were killed illegally. But in 1982 a government committee set up to determine how to make Pakistan an Islamic state proposed that the death penalty be introduced for anyone involved in ballroom dancing (12:1, p. 46).

The imprisonment of musicians was widespread during the last two decades of the twentieth century. In 1985 the Nigerian military jailed Fela Kuti for five years, of which he served 20 months before being released following the overthrow of the military dictatorship. In the same year two Algerian singers were given three years in jail (15:1, p. 38; 15:2, p. 38).

Other cases of imprisonment included the members of the Jazz Section and the Plastic People of the Universe in Czechoslovakia. In Turkey, three singers were imprisoned for a year for singing in the Kurdish language at a Youth Festival in Izmir in 1999 (28:5, p. 144). The USSR was notorious for detaining dissidents in psychiatric hospitals: The previously mentioned Christian pop musician Valery Barinov of the group Trumpet Call was punished in this way in 1984 (13:2, p. 49).

A favorite method of punishing artists and musicians in authoritarian states has been to exile them or to force them to flee the country. Numerous musicians left Latin American countries for Europe in the 1980s and earlier. The Chilean group Illapu attempted to return home in 1982 but were refused entry under a law that permitted the president to send any citizen into exile without the chance to appeal (11:1, p. 42). The East German poet and singer Wolf Biermann had been expelled in the 1970s, and Karel Soukup of the Plastic People of the Universe was sent into exile by the communist regime in Czechoslovakia in 1982 (11:3, p. 43). Alternatively, governments punished musicians by preventing them from traveling abroad to fulfil professional engagements. This is what happened to the Russian singer Reni Penkova in 1980 (9:1, p. 74).

Dictatorships also routinely expelled or denied entry to foreign musicians. The Spanish singer-songwriter Joan Manuel Serrat was turned away from Uruguay and Chile in 1983 (12:4, p. 44), and the U.S.-born, East German–based singer Dean Reed was expelled from Chile in 1983 (12:6, p. 43). The Guyana-born calypsonian and label owner Rudy Grant was turned out of Barbados in 1983 after he released songs that satirized Prime Minister Tom Adams (12:6, p.43).

Music itself was used as a punishment in Czechoslovakia, Guatemala, and Paraguay. In the Old Town Square in Prague in December 1987, police played Christmas songs through loudspeakers to disrupt a meeting of antigovernment protestors (17:2, p. 38). Latin American radio stations critical of authoritarian regimes were ordered to change to music formats. In Guatemala the military dictatorship imposed censorship in 1983 and ordered all radio stations to play only martial music (12:5, p. 43), while in 1986 the Paraguayan talk station Radio Nanduti, which had reported on opposition to the Paraguayan dictator Alfredo Stroessner, was made to broadcast only music and "noncontroversial" news (15:7, p. 43).

The Lifting of Censorship

This account of music censorship in the latter part of the twentieth century would be incomplete without an acknowledgment of the defeats suffered by the censors. These were largely due to the crumbling or overthrow of the various authoritarian governments that had imposed strict censorship regimes—dictatorships of the communist left and the militaristic and racist right. In addition to the Soviet-dominated regimes in 10 or more European countries and the apartheid state in South Africa, military governments fell in Greece and in a number of South American and African countries.

The methods by which censorship was lifted varied considerably. Most dramatically, in 1985 the new civilian government in Brazil "unbanned" 4,560 songs that had been forbidden during the 21 years of military government (14:6, p. 55). Three years later, the Chilean folk groups Illapu and Inti-Illimani returned for a triumphant tour of their homeland after 15 years in exile (17:10, p. 36).

In South Africa, the censors' actions were often inconsistent during the late 1980s and early 1990s. In 1985, for example, the South African Broadcasting Corporation imposed a six-month ban on music by Stevie Wonder after he had dedicated his Oscar to Nelson Mandela. This had to be swiftly reversed when the SABC realized that it could not broadcast the charity record "We Are the World" while the ban on Wonder remained! Seven years later, the SABC lifted restrictions on three albums by the exiled activist Miriam Makeba and, at the same time, banned the video of the song "No Apartheid" by Carlos Dje Dje (21:1, p. 47).

In Russia, the ending of state censorship after 1989 left some musicians feeling disoriented. An article by Flemming Rose in the *Smashed Hits* issue of *Index* quotes Slava Butusov of the rock band Nautilus Pompilius:

> If somebody puts up road signs with prohibitions, it's easy; you just have to find a way round the signs to move forward. But from an artistic and existential point of view the most difficult thing is to end up in an open space, where you have to make your own choice without any interference from outside. (27:6, p. 51)

Despite these successes, at the start of the twenty-first century there are still many countries where music censorship remains implacable. While state censorship for political reasons is now less common, the remaining examples of systematic state censorship are mostly to be found in those countries of Asia or the Middle East with strict Islamic regimes. But even here the prohibition can be evaded. A contribution by Rahimullah Yusufzai to the *Smashed Hits* issue describes how one taxi driver "played a cat-and-mouse game with Taliban guards." While driving he played a cassette of Urdu film music, but "whenever a road-block came into view, the cassette would be slipped into one of his numerous pockets, only to reappear as soon as the danger was past" (27:6, p. 135). Thus in Afghanistan censor and music lover played out the game illustrated by other examples in this chapter and throughout *Policing Pop*.

Notes

1. References to *Index on Censorship* indicate volume, issue, and page numbers: Thus, "1:1, p. 3" indicates page 3 of issue 1 of volume 1.
2. See Banks (1996) for a discussion of MTV's racism.

Bibliography

Banks, J. 1996. *Monopoly Television: MTV's Quest to Control the Music*. Boulder: Westview.

Cloonan, M. 1996. *Banned! Censorship of Popular Music in Britain 1967–92*. Aldershot, U.K.: Arena.

Duval-Smith, A. 1999. "Dance-Crazy, Bottom-Wiggling Africans Alarm Moral Minority," *Independent on Sunday*, 31 October.

Fitzgerald, J. 1995. "Naked Truths," *Music News Asia*, December, p. 40.

Green, L. 1988. *Music on Deaf Ears: Musical Meaning, Ideology, Education*. Manchester: Manchester University Press.

Howard, K. 1997. "Pop Ordered to Clean Up Its Act," *Times Educational Supplement*, 12 September, p. 10.

Music and Copyright. 1997. "Market Survey: Middle East," no. 122, 8 October, p. 8.

Schade-Poulsen, M. 1999. *Men and Popular Music in Algeria*. Austin: University of Texas Press.

Shepherd, J., et al. 1997. *Popular Music Studies: A Select Bibliography*. London: Mansell.

Troitsky, A. 1990. *Tusovka: Who's Who in the New Soviet Rock Culture*. London: Omnibus Press.

Steve Greenfield and Guy Osborn

4 Remote Control: Legal Censorship of the Creative Process

The concept of "policing pop" goes beyond censorship to cover all the ways in which artistic output can be regulated and controlled. Traditionally, analysis of the legal aspects of music censorship tends to concentrate on the broad area of state control over "obscene" material: the ways in which product[1] can be regulated by the law on the basis that its content is somehow unsuitable. Various aspects of music may infringe both statutory and common law regulations that govern the protection of public morality and decency. Within the United Kingdom (on which this chapter focuses), liability is generally based on the Obscene Publications Act 1959, although the older common law offenses such as outraging public decency may still have effect.[2]

The application of legislation and other legal measures to control artistic works raises important civil liberties questions. Even outside the legal framework, however, a self-regulatory regime may be imposed via gatekeepers such as shops, pressure groups, and the media. This can severely curtail the ability of the public to gain access to certain types of music and material (see Cloonan 1996).[3]

Although the application of state censorship is of both academic and practical importance, in this chapter we examine a different type of regulation. We are concerned with the ways in which legal controls may be exerted over, and affect, the creative process of musicians—first, through restrictions on the subsequent use of copyright material, and second, through contractual terms that may place limits upon what an artist may produce. These two controls are not, perhaps, seen as censorship in conventional terms, but both may have fundamental importance for artistic freedom and the development of popular music. Aside from censorship, they also raise interesting side issues concerning the nature of creativity and the commodification of artistic production. In this chapter we analyze some of these issues, primarily from the perspective of the situation in England, although much of the discussion will be applicable, in a broader sense, to other jurisdictions and practices. In looking at these elements of control, we also seek to highlight some of the crucial ways in which creativity can be fettered, and provide ideas as to how artists might combat these elements of control.

Copyright Control and the Creative Process

Copyright is the bedrock on which the modern music industry is based, the vehicle by which rights in material are created, allocated, and distributed throughout the music business. Indeed, without copyright protection for artists' work, the industry could not have developed commercially in the way it has done.

Despite its value, however, the concept and application of copyright are frequently misunderstood. This point is well illustrated by considering the issue of home taping. Intellectual property is different from physical property in that it more easily permits contemporaneous use by more than one person. Technology allows a piece of musical work to be easily reproduced and used by different people at the same time without any limitations on the original owner. Physical property does not have the same flexibility, and this is one rationale for some people's apparent indifference toward legal "abuse" of intellectual property. To the person who tapes a compact disc, there is no obvious interference with property rights—the CD can be returned to the original owner and the copy retained. The "rights" that exist in the song and its recording are less apparent than the rights to a piece of physical property.

Edwin Hettinger (1989) illustrates this distinction through an example: Only one person at a time can borrow a piece of physical property (such as a lawnmower), whereas I can give my intellectual property (such as a recipe for guacamole) to all of my friends, who can copy it and, theoretically, all make it at the same time. The CD and the lawnmower are both pieces of physical property, and both have underlying intellectual property rights. It is physically far more difficult to infringe the underlying rights that may relate to the lawnmower's patents and designs than to infringe the copyright of the material on the CD. Ease of infringement is an important element. Advances in hardware and the introduction of digital recording allow for high-speed reproduction without loss of quality. Furthermore, there is no formal attempt to police such domestic infringements, and the use in some countries of a tape levy is an indication that the practice is well established and impossible to prevent. This problem is exacerbated by the distribution and reproduction of music via the internet. For the music industry, the fundamental problem is that copying a CD just doesn't *feel* like a property infringement.

In England and Wales copyright does not need to be formally registered; it exists once a new piece of work is fixed in some form. Once copyright exists in a work—a process involving "originality," "fixation," and "authorship," among other requirements—the question arises as to what ownership of such copyright permits. A number of distinct copyrights may exist with respect to the same piece of "work." Even at the point of creation, separate copyright exists in the lyrics and the music. This multiplication of rights continues with a third copyright in the sound recording of the song. In order to produce a sound recording, therefore, a performer will require a license from the other copyright owners. In addition, certain noneconomic rights may also have to be considered.

Below, we outline how such rights are bought and sold, but the first stage is establishing what rights exist in copyright work or, perhaps, the reverse—what acts are prohibited through copyright ownership. In the United Kingdom the protection of copyright is governed by the Copyright, Designs and Patents Act 1988. Copyright is a statutory creature, and new Acts of Parliament have been required as new technological developments have affected both the creation and the reproduction of works (see Greenfield and Osborn 1997). The crucial part of the Act as regards future use of work is contained in section 16, which allows the copyright owner the sole ability to:

(i)   copy the work;
(ii)   issue copies to the public;
(iii)   rent the work to the public;
(iv)   perform the work in public;
(v)   broadcast the work (and include it in a cable-program service);
(vi)   adapt the work.[4]

It can therefore be seen that copyright allows the owner of a copyright work certain exclusive rights. Potentially this may extend to control over how the original work can be used by others, including new artists. Moreover, copyright can be bought and sold to varying degrees, which means that control may well pass from the original creator to a third party who may view the copyright as an economic investment and treat requests to use the work accordingly. This may have implications for the integrity of the original creator, who may not wish to see the work used in particular ways (perhaps, for example, in an advertisement for "objectionable" goods). Once copyright ownership has passed, the only means of redress in this situation is to try to harness the concept of moral rights. Moral rights have been developed to protect artists' integrity and reputation. The idea that there is more to a piece of artistry than its economic value has a distinguished history in many European countries. The development of international conventions has led to attempts to standardize such rights across different countries, with varying degrees of success. The concept has not fitted in particularly well in common law systems, though limited provisions are now contained within sections 76–80 of the Copyright Designs and Patents Act 1988. Unfortunately for musicians, the two most important jurisdictions, England and the United States, have historically sought to resist the introduction of greater protection, and those provisions that do exist have been watered down.

One problem with the system of copyright is that it does not acknowledge the "practical" aspects of creation but instead adopts a highly theoretical approach. If the work is not a copy of a previous work and basic requirements are met, the work is protected. Previous works and artists whose influence has helped form the background to the work are not "legally" credited, even though artists may acknowledge their creative roots. Copyright law assumes creation in a vacuum and ignores the reality that a work may be developed through a "building block" process. If a work closely resembles a former piece, then there is the potential for an infringement action. But how many times have we heard a new song that reminds us of an older one? The question for the law is how to judge when a "new" work is a copy. In order to demonstrate that the work is a "copy," it does not have to be shown that it is an exact reproduction, and there does not need to be any intent to copy. This latter point is well illustrated by the case of *Francis, Day and Hunter v. Bron* [1963] Ch. 587, where it was argued that the defendant's song "Why" was an infringing copy of the original, "In a Little Spanish Town." The court held here that copying need not always be a conscious act and could take place subconsciously. There was insufficient evidence to demonstrate copying in this case, but the fact that a court could decide that a work was subconsciously copied represents an important step forward. If the new work is not legally a "copy," then there is copyright in this new piece, and influences and inspirations are unrecognized in legal terms.

Means of (Re)production: Copying, Adapting, and Sampling

An artist who wishes to record a song must seek permission from the owner of the copyrights in the music and lyrics. Thus, before a cover version of a song can be recorded, a license to use the work is needed. Each "new" rendition of, for example, "My Way" will need permission from the current owner of the copyright in the words and music.[5] To facilitate what might otherwise be an arduous process, collective licensing systems have been developed and have at times been put on a statutory footing. For example, in the United Kingdom the Mechanical Copyright Protection Society (MCPS) is able to grant licenses to reproduce those songs (legally the musical and literary works) within its portfolio.[6] A performer wishing to cover a song approaches the MCPS, which will either grant permission with details of the fee payable or refer the application to the copyright owner.

Some copyright holders do not subscribe to the blanket licensing system and will require direct authorization, and there are strict limits as to what reproduction may be licensed. This has led to instances of "copyright censorship," such as that affecting Carter the Unstoppable Sex Machine's "After the Watershed" in 1992. The owner of the copyright (which had changed hands from the original writers) in "Goodbye Ruby Tuesday" had to be contacted in order to get permission to use the original in the new composition. According to reports on the case, permission would be granted only if 100 percent of the publishing royalties for the new work were vested in the original owner. Carter USM refused, pulled the song from their album, and reputedly never played it live again. Here the problematic area of ownership and authorship comes to the fore. Mick Jagger, for example, was reported to have said:

> Whether it's a painting or a song, whatever, as soon as it comes out, it belongs to everybody. . . . I think that as soon as you've recorded a song it doesn't belong to you any more. It just goes out and everyone can sing it, everyone can do it if they want. They can change it. You know what I mean? It's not yours. *(New Musical Express [NME]*, 7 March 1992, p. 3)

More recent cases involving artists as diverse as Kevin Rowland and Spiritualised show that work may in certain circumstances be fettered by the copyright in previous work. If the work is an adaptation, further problems are encountered. Although the MCPS may be able to give licenses for copies, it cannot give licenses to artists who wish to adapt the original. Kevin Rowland, formerly of Dexy's Midnight Runners, recorded a cathartic collection of songs entitled "My Beauty." These were his personal takes on classic songs that had helped him through a difficult period in his life. He wanted to use Bruce Springsteen's "Thunder Road," but, despite a personal plea from Rowland, Springsteen would not approve the adaptation. Consequently the song did not appear on the album; as Rowland noted:

> It wasn't meant to be. Had I chosen to re-record the vocal, staying true to Springsteen's lyrics—which was an option—I would have felt I'd compromised the whole record. The whole thing about this album is that they are my interpretations, not covers, and that would have rendered it artistically invalid. (*NME*, 2 October 1999)

Rowland's experience illustrates how future work can be curtailed by copyright owners, and even personal pleas and exhortations might not be sufficient to allow the work to proceed. However, it is far better to attempt to obtain permission before releasing any product than to run the risk of later legal action for breach of copyright, which might entail withdrawal of released material. It is worth contacting the owners directly on the off chance that an appeal to artistic sensibility might succeed. The Beta Band's use of lyrics from the classic "Total Eclipse of the Heart" is a case in point. Jim Steinman, lyricist for Bonnie Tyler and Meat Loaf collaborator, apparently refused to allow the use of the lyric "Once upon a time I was falling in love / But now I'm only falling apart" in the Beta Band song "The Hard One," from their eponymous debut album (*NME*, 12 May 1999). Shortly after the refusal was recounted in the music magazine *NME*, however, it was reported that Steinman had read the *NME* story, heard the song, loved it, and had a change of heart, allowing the lyric to be used after all.

The area of copyright is problematic enough as it is; when the practice of sound sampling is added to the equation, it becomes even more complicated. In sampling, a chunk of a previous sound recording is utilized within the new work (see Bently and Sherman 1992; Durant 1993), requiring another level of permission:

> The arrival of digital music technology has manifestly altered the way in which music is produced for consumption; with the advent of digital samplers and sequencers we have seen the dawning of a new culture that is able to appropriate sound recordings and utilise them in new "creative" ways as part of new compositions. These new technologies have heralded a new type of music culture, a culture that records changing relationships between performers, audiences and the forms of representation. (Greenfield and Osborn 1998:65)

If the sound recording is used, the artist must contact the owner of the work, usually the record company. Yet the recording is also a derivative work, predicated upon the mechanical copyrights that exist in the song itself (as detailed above). The whole area of sound sampling is contentious, including questions about whether it is a legitimate method of creation and whether samplers should have any entitlement to use previous work. Much of the debate has centered on what is meant by the term "substantial part," since a sample that amounts to a "substantial part" will constitute an infringement. Usually this boils down to an argument about the quality, length, and centrality of the work taken, although there is little in the way of legal definition.[7]

One of the earliest and most controversial sampling cases concerned the Justified Ancients of MU MU (JAMMs) and their LP "1987: What the Fuck Is Going On?" The album used samples from popular artists such as Sam Fox and the Sex Pistols along with clips from soundtracks and television shows. One track—"The Queen and I," based upon Abba's "Dancing Queen"—proved to be particularly problematic. The composer and lyricist of "Dancing Queen," Benny Andersson and Bjorn Ulraeus, objected vehemently to its use. The JAMMs attempted to justify their use of the song and their interpretation of it:

> I sat down and started writing this whole thesis on the defence of what we were doing, artistically, and creatively, saying that if machines were going to be invented like samplers, you can't stop them. . . . So our whole idea was to go over, meet up with Benny and Bjorn, sit down with them, artist to artist, and sort of go through it. They were singing in English for a start, which was taking our language, they were taking a form

that was American popular music, and making it into something their own and selling it back to the world. I just thought that there was no difference in what they were doing, to what we were doing. (Bill Drummond, quoted in Robinson n.d.:7)

In the event the case was put in the hands of their lawyers, and the MCPS notified the JAMMs in August 1987 that Abba was not prepared to grant a license for the track. The letter ordered the JAMMs to: (1) cease all manufacture and distribution; (2) take all possible steps to recover copies of the album, which were then to be delivered to MCPS or destroyed under its supervision; and (3) deliver up the master tape, mothers, stampers, and any other parts commensurate with manufacture of the record (letter from MCPS to JAMMs, cited ibid.:8). All masters were surrendered,[8] and the album was re-released in "sample-free" format later in the year, with long gaps of silence and details of how to recreate the original LP:

> If you follow the instructions below you will, after some practice, be able to simulate the sound of our original record. To do this you will need three wind-up record decks, a pile of selected discs, one T.V. Set [sic] and a video machine loaded with a cassette of edited highlights of last week's *Top of the Pops*. (Quoted in Frith 1993:5)

The crucial issue is that a new work, irrespective of the fact that it used a copyright work as its fulcrum, was prevented from being released. This is how copyright exerts censorial control over music. Due to the existence of property rights, future use can be fettered on the grounds that someone owns the original work and can therefore control its reuse. It is certainly arguable that this aspect of copyright deters creativity, notwithstanding the traditional view that copyright promotes creative endeavor by acting as an incentive.[9] Given the current legal position, the only solution is to obtain permission from the owners before commercial release, perhaps through an appeal to their artistic sensibilities—although, as Kevin Rowland's letter to Bruce Springsteen shows, even impassioned pleas are not always successful.[10]

An alternative to legalistic conflict has been mooted, although with little success to date, via the creation of a Sampling Disputes Panel. Initiated by the Music Publishers' Association (MPA), the panel was "set up on a trial basis for rights owners of musical works involved in sampling disputes, to enable submissions to be put forward to a specially constituted Disputes Panel, who will recommend (albeit on a non binding basis) what they perceive a fair split of royalties should be" (MPA n.d.). This U.K. initiative has thus far not been replicated in other jurisdictions, but it was a useful attempt to adopt alternative dispute resolution (ADR) within the music industry. The ADR movement, active within both the United States and the United Kingdom, attempts to prevent costly and time-consuming legal battles; clearly such a panel would operate only in a situation where a work's owner is prepared to negotiate a price (i.e., a royalty split), as opposed to a situation of outright rejection.

Stifled by Contract: Artistic Warranties, Commercial Suitability, and Other Censorial Practices

Within the music business artists enter into three key agreements: publishing, recording, and management contracts. It is the first two, and in particular their implications for artistic freedom, that concern us here. Both contracts reflect the different copyrights that exist in a work. The publishing contract is concerned with the rights in the songs themselves and their subsequent exploitation, whereas the subject matter of recording contracts is the creation of sound recordings. The contracts will contain a number of obligations that can affect the artist's ability to control the work. The extent of these restrictions may well depend on the relative bargaining strengths, or leverage, of both parties. A number of key contractual clauses are likely to be covered in all agreements, although their extent may vary according to individual leverage. These contractual clauses can themselves create regulatory conditions that impose a censorial role over the creative process.

Contractual theory is based upon the exchange of obligations, and it is the obligations placed upon artists within these contracts that can operate to restrict artistic freedom.[11] The company will also have a number of positive obligations with respect to the treatment of the artist and exploitation of the product.[12] Music contracts will often be in quasi-standard form, with the same basic constituents, although the details may differ in each case.[13] In terms of censoring the artist's output, a number of key artist warranties may be included, notably clauses that indemnify the publisher or record company against claims arising from delivered work that is defamatory or obscene. The law of defamation permits actions against anyone who "publishes" the work, and clearly a large company is a more attractive financial target than an artist who may have few assets. Such a clause allows the company to pass on any costs associated with actions against it and would cover financial losses in cases where records are withdrawn after release because of their subject matter. By inserting such clauses the company both puts the onus on the artist to clear material prior to delivery and also provides itself with a possible means of redress for any loss suffered.

Similarly, artists may be required to deliver work that does not infringe any third-party rights. Recording and publishing companies do not wish to be faced with claims for copyright infringement. The worst scenario is the one in which an artist uses works without prior permission and omits to tell the company: Once the work is released, the original copyright owner is in a strong bargaining position, given the costs associated with withdrawal. Indemnity clauses are designed to protect the company from copyright and other infringements by the artist. The company will often, because of its financial position, be in the legal firing line, and such clauses will at least draw an artist's attention to the need for care. The record company may also wish to set controls over the quality of the work produced under the contract. Consider the following fairly typical clause, taken from a recording contract:

Each master recording made by you shall be subject to our reasonable approval as being commercially and technically satisfactory for the manufacture of records and tapes therefrom and you shall at our request repeat any performance until master recordings acceptable to us as aforesaid are obtained. Instrumental recordings and recordings other than in a recording studio will not be acceptable unless we have previously agreed to the contrary.

Here the creative artist faces a number of potential problems. First and foremost, the record company is able to reject material on the basis that it does not meet the criterion of being "commercially and technically satisfactory." The technical aspect is less contentious, although it could conceivably thwart an artist who wanted to adopt a low-fi approach on artistic grounds. However, the commercial aspect is potentially far more problematic. What if an artist wishes to produce work that is different from that previously delivered?

This issue was part of the dispute between George Michael and his record company, Sony Entertainment (UK) Limited.[14] Michael launched a claim that his original contract was unduly onerous and constituted an unjustifiable restraint of trade (see Greenfield and Osborn 1998). He was reportedly upset by Sony's failure to support the artistic direction he wanted to take and his wish to become a "serious artist" appealing to a more adult audience. This goal precluded both his appearance in promotional videos and marketing based solely on his image. The potential for a clash with his record company is clear. Michael had, after all, been a phenomenal commercial success, and the company might well want more of the same. In a sense this type of dispute is between the wish for artistic freedom on one hand and the desire of the company for maximum market penetration on the other. Michael's immense popularity in every phase of his career to date might lead one to expect the company to accommodate his desire to shift emphasis. Given the structure of the music industry, with the very high percentage of groups who fail and therefore cause losses, however, it is easy to see why companies would wish to stick with a tried and trusted formula.

Some artists, such as Elvis Costello, have successfully changed styles, and an artist who enjoys a good relationship with the record company may be allowed this type of development. If the artist is in a strong position, legal advisors can try to adapt such clauses so that they become less of a hindrance. But the ultra-competitive ethos of the record industry, where many agreements are underpinned by a "take it or leave it" philosophy, means that few artists have strong leverage. Similarly, the contract might empower the record company to choose a producer for the work, the songs that will appear as singles, the artwork to be used, and other features. All of these are potentially severe censorial restrictions and should be resisted, at least as far as the individual leverage allows, by the artist who wants to maintain some degree of artistic control.

Cases such as *Silvertone* v. *Mountfield* (the Stone Roses case) have highlighted the postcontractual restraints that might prevent artists from re-recording, or even playing live, material that they had delivered during the contract period.[15] Furthermore, music contracts are invariably *exclusive* agreements, and this in itself places a restriction on collaborative projects, as approval will be needed to appear with other artists. This desire to retain exclusive control over artists is most keenly felt with publishing agreements. Songwriters may wish to write jointly, encouraged by the simple division between music and lyrics, and there are many famous examples of such duos, including Leiber and Stoller, Jagger and Richards, and Lennon and McCartney. A publisher will be happy to encourage writers to work with others, provided that the copyright in the joint work is assigned to it. This can cause problems if the other party has his or her own individual publishing contract.

For the songwriter (and particularly for the writer who is not a performer), an important aspect of publishing contracts is the company's obligation to exploit the work. Since a publishing contract will be an exclusive agreement for the writer, he or she will be unable to offer the work to other companies, though the company will have other writers under contract. The restrictive nature of such agreements has led to litigation. The most important of these cases concerned the songwriter Tony Macaulay,[16] who counted Elvis Presley among the artists who performed his compositions. Macaulay signed an onerous publishing agreement in 1966 without seeking independent advice, and later attempted to free himself from the agreement with a groundbreaking use of the doctrine of restraint of trade. The case ended up in the House of Lords, the highest domestic court in England and Wales. A key issue was the fact that there was no contractual obligation on the part of the publisher to exploit the work. As Lord Reid pointed out:

> The respondent (Macaulay) is bound to assign to the appellants (the publishing company) during a long period the fruits of his musical talent. But what are the appellants bound to do with those fruits? Under the contract nothing. If they do use the songs which the respondent composes they must pay in terms of the contract. But they need not do so. As has been said they may put them in a drawer and leave them there. (*Schroeder Music Publishing* v. *Macaulay* [1974] 3 All ER 621)

Since this case was resolved in Macaulay's favor, the issue has been addressed by some companies in the United Kingdom via the use of a nonexploitation clause providing that if songs are not exploited by publishers after a certain period, then the rights in them will revert to the songwriter (see Biederman et al. 1992).

Contracts, Copyright, and Creative Expression

Music contracts and the copyright in songs and sound recordings are intimately bound together. The purpose of the contracts is to provide a vehicle for the exploitation of the copyright that exists. Without copyright protection the economics of the music business change drastically. Work that is not protected can be freely copied without payment, thus making the economic value of the work negligible. In a sense copyright is essential for writers and performers, providing a bedrock for income generation. A strict regime of copyright control, however, can interfere with creativity. Artists who wish to draw significantly upon the work of others may find themselves infringing that original copyright. There needs to be a balance between the rights of copyright owners and those who wish to use the work. The role of law is to develop a system of regulation that allows both to coexist.

This tension was highlighted in the United States during the litigation over "Oh, Pretty Woman."[17] The U.S. rap group 2 Live Crew used Roy Orbison and William Dees's co-authored work "Oh, Pretty Woman" as the basis for their own composition, which was a parody. The rights in the work had been assigned to Acuff-Rose Music, and the question was whether the parody amounted to a copyright infringement. Ordinarily there would have been no question, since a substantial part of the original was used. However, in this instance it was argued that the utilization of the original piece fell under the heading of fair use. This case was portrayed as a dispute between freedom of speech—the right to make a parody—and the existing rights of copyright owners to decide how "their" work can be used. Although a defense existed in this case through the very limited fair use provisions, this would not apply to sampling or other uses that do not have a freedom-of-speech element.

Composing and recording is a precarious business for the overwhelming majority of aspiring pop stars, and the economics and cultural features of the industry have led to the construction of austere agreements. The lure of stardom and, usually, the lack of any bargaining power often lead musicians to sign very restrictive contracts that offer little in the way of artistic freedom, at least at the outset. In turn the music industry claims that it needs a strict hold over artists to compensate for the high failure rate. Even apart from the contractual areas that artists usually concentrate upon (length of term, number of albums, royalty rates), it is crucial that they appreciate some of the other restrictions that may be placed upon them. As we have shown, these problems are not always insurmountable, but are dictated to a large degree by artists' position within the industry and their willingness to concede economic benefits in the quest to maintain some degree of control over output.

At the heart of the issue concerning future (ab)use of copyright lie advances in technology. Sampling has become a contentious matter, since the principles of copyright protection were established before the widespread copying and dissemination of material became relatively easy. Use of existing works has dramatically increased in recent years through the emergence of the internet as a means to copy and distribute music:

> The movement towards the digital distribution of music could fundamentally alter the music industry. Digital distribution offers the potential for efficient access to broader

consumer markets with negligible distribution costs. At the same time, however, the extent to which music piracy exists on the Internet is threatening the value of the intellectual property rights held by the industry. (Selby 2000:4)

The debate about the legality of sites such MP3 and Napster has already begun (see Chapter 2). In the near future, legal provisions will need to be enacted to deal with some of these problems. Additionally, although this chapter focuses upon the U.K. position, the rise of the internet makes the need for an international standard of provisions even more pressing. It remains to be seen whether the internet will allow artists to seek alternative methods of distributing work and lessen the need to be so strictly tied via contracts into contemporary industry structures.

Notes

1. "Product" is industry slang, and we use it here to denote all aspects of musical creation: the music, the artwork, the advertisements, and potentially the musicians themselves.

2. See, for example, *R. v. Gibson* [1991] 1 All ER 439 (All England Law Reports).

3. The myriad examples of this range from radio bans on output such as Frankie Goes to Hollywood's "Relax" and the Sex Pistols' "God Save the Queen" to Woolworths' refusal to stock the Smiths' eponymous first LP to Channel 4's cutting a live Pogues performance of "Streets of Sorrow."

4. For an accessible and detailed exposition of the law relating to copyright and intellectual property more generally, see Bainbridge (1999).

5. Copyright does not continue indefinitely, and statutory limits are imposed. Permission to use works will be required only while such works are within the period of copyright protection.

6. Whereas the MCPS deals with the mechanical rights to copy work, the Performing Right Society (PRS) is concerned with public performance (on radio, in concert, etc.). The two bodies' work may be said to be complementary, but their areas of focus are separate.

7. On substantiality see, for example, *Hawkes* v. *Paramount* [1934] 1 Ch 593.

8. The JAMMs issued the following advertisement in the aftermath of the furor: "WARNING: We interrupt this page to bring you the following warning. Anyone in possession of the Justified Ancients of Mu Mu album '1987' could be breaking the law. If you own a copy please return it to PO Box 283, HP22 5BW" (*Sounds,* 12 September 1987, cited on sleeve of "Shag Times").

In fact some copies of the LP were ceremoniously burnt (the event was captured for posterity by the *NME*), and the rest thrown into the North Sea during their return trip to England. Five copies that the JAMMs later found in a second-hand record shop were offered for sale in *The Face* for £1000 each; allegedly three of these were sold.

9. This incentive is often cited as a key reason for copyright's existence. Others include the idea that people who create something are entitled to own it and also to exploit their creations, and therefore they should be able to exercise control over the reproduction of their work.

10. The letter was quoted in *Q* as follows:

18 August 1999

Dear Bruce,

My name is Kevin Rowland. I was in a group called Dexys Midnight Runners who had a hit with Come on Eileen in '83. I've covered "Thunder Road." I've done an album of songs that helped me out of my drug addiction. I've been completely free from drugs for nearly six years now. I'd done "Thunder Road" because it helped me in my early recovery. I've sung each song to myself, visualising myself at different ages as I sung. This was the greatest thing I could give myself. In order to communicate truthfully, I've changed words where they didn't fit my own experience and I've changed a few on "Thunder Road." All of these songs are completely relevant to me. I needed to sing them. It's not a cash in, it's my story told through these songs. These are my interpretations, how I hear them.

Please allow me to sing this song, my way. I love your version but this is my version. I was told your management won't allow me to have it on the album as it stands. But I can't change it. It makes artistic sense as it stands to me. Please listen to it and listen to your heart.

Best Wishes

Kevin Rowland.

11. For a general work on the law of contract, see Beatson (1998). For contract law as it applies to the entertainment industry, see Greenfield and Osborn (1998).

12. See Passman (1998) generally on the U.S. position and typical U.S. clauses.

13. For example, all contracts will have terms concerning length (duration), royalties, territory, etc., but the specific length, royalties, and territory will depend upon the individual contract.

14. *Panayiotou and others* v. *Sony Music Entertainment (UK) Limited* [1994], Entertainment and Media Law Reports 229 (EMLR).

15. *Silvertone Records Ltd.* v. *Mountfield and others* [1993] EMLR 152.

16. *A. Schroeder Music Publishing* v. *Macaulay* [1974] 3 All ER 616.

17. *Campbell* v. *Acuff-Rose Music, Inc.*, 114 S. Ct. 1164 (1994).

Bibliography

Bainbridge, D. B. 1999. *Intellectual Property.* London: F. T. Pitman.

Beatson, J. 1998. *Anson's Law of Contract.* Oxford: Oxford University Press.

Bently, L., and Sherman, B. 1992. "Cultures of Copying: Digital Sampling and Copyright Law," *Entertainment Law Review,* 3:5, pp. 158–163.

Biederman, D.; Pierson, E.; Silfen, M.; Glasser, J.; and Berry, R. 1992. *Law and Business of the Entertainment Industries.* New York: Praeger.

Cloonan, M. 1996. *Banned! Censorship of Popular Music in Britain: 1967–1992.* Aldershot: Arena.

Durant, A. 1993. "A New Day for Music? Digital Technologies in Contemporary Music Making," in P. Hayward (ed.), *Culture, Technology and Creativity in the Late Twentieth Century.* London: John Libbey, chap. 10.

Frith, S. 1993. "Music and Morality," in S. Frith (ed.), *Music and Copyright.* Edinburgh: Edinburgh University Press, chap. 3.

Greenfield, S., and Osborn, G. 1997. "Good Technology? Music and the Challenge of Technology Towards the Fin de Siecle," *Information and Communications Technology Law,* 6:1, p. 77.

———. 1998. *Contract and Control in the Entertainment Industry: Dancing on the Edge of Heaven.* Aldershot, U.K.: Dartmouth.

Hettinger, P. 1989. "Justifying Intellectual Property," *Philosophy and Public Affairs,* 18, pp. 31–52.

Music Publishers' Association. No date. Press release: Sampling Disputes Panel.

Passman, D. 1998. *All You Need to Know About the Music Business.* London: Penguin.

Robinson, P. No date. *Justified and Ancient History: The Unfolding Story of the KLF.* East Grinstead: Self-published.

Selby, J. 2000. "The Legal and Economic Implications of the Digital Distribution of Music—Part 1," *Entertainment Law Review,* 1, pp. 4–10.

Part II

Controlling the Artistic Process

Keith Kahn-Harris

5 Death Metal and the Limits of Musical Expression

The act of music censorship implicitly or explicitly assumes that music is in some way socially significant. That significance may be viewed as lying in music's ability to produce negative social consequences to which censorship is perceived to be the answer. More cynically, one might say that the significance of music lies in the possibilities for asserting and maintaining power through its suppression. It does not follow, of course, that opposition to censorship necessarily involves a belief that music is insignificant. Indeed, one possible argument against censorship is that musical expression is *too* socially significant to be suppressed. Nor does opposition to censorship necessarily imply that all musical expression is somehow "harmless." Belief in music's significance tacitly implies that it is at least possible that some music may be socially harmful in some way, even if censorship is not seen as the answer to this harm. It follows, then, that however one views music censorship, if one believes that music is at the very least potentially socially significant, it is necessary to "evaluate" music that might be seen as socially problematic in some way.

The evaluation and discussion of music is a common social activity; indeed, the practice is part of the pleasure that music affords (Frith 1996). Yet the evaluation of music that might be considered harmful has an urgency that leads to two difficult problems. One problem is how to decide the basis on which a particular form or piece of music may be judged harmful. The second problem is what to "do" about such music. The second problem is particularly difficult if censorship is rejected as an acceptable "solution."

In this chapter I explore these twin difficulties through an investigation and evaluation of a particular piece of music—the song "Fucked with a Knife" by the American Death Metal band Cannibal Corpse. This investigation is motivated by my own concern about the song and the larger body of the band's work of which it is part. Searching for an effective basis from which to evaluate it, I analyze the song from a variety of perspectives—lyrics, music, social context, and so forth. Having arrived at highly ambiguous conclusions, I then consider what to "do" with the analysis produced by my investigation.

The investigation presented in this chapter is a form of policing of popular music. "Policing" here implies a kind of intellectual vigilance based on the belief that individuals have a responsibility to think hard about the music that they themselves or others are troubled by. More specifically, this chapter "polices" the limits of what can be explored musically without wider social harm. Policing is a metaphor that implies the exercise of some kind of power. I ultimately reject the exercise of power represented by censorship as a response to the song that I investigate. This does not mean, however, that the intellectual policing in this chapter is somehow not implicated in the exercise of power. At the end of this chapter, I discuss the dilemmas and dangers that my analysis of "Fucked with a Knife" presents in the context of this book.

A Horrific Text

Directions for accessing the lyrics to Cannibal Corpse's song "Fucked with a Knife" are shown in Appendix A. They unambiguously catalog, from the protagonist's perspective, the rape, genital mutilation, and murder of a woman, associating this with her own sexual pleasure. When I first encountered these lyrics during my research on the global Extreme Metal scene, I had an inchoate feeling that such lyrics "must" in some way be harmful and "must" contribute to misogyny in male listeners. My concern led me to an examination of Cannibal Corpse's wider body of work.

Cannibal Corpse was formed in the late 1980s in Florida and has released seven studio albums. "The Bleeding," from which the song is taken, was the fourth, released in 1994. Cannibal Corpse's lyrics have dealt virtually without exception with the manifold ways in which the body can be destroyed and mutilated. In "Fucked with a Knife" the protagonist is an obsessive rapist/stalker. His ability to cause physical harm is compounded by his ability to control the perspective through which that assault is seen. To describe in detail the victim's assault and claim that "She liked the way it felt inside her" is to exercise a voyeuristic power to control ways of seeing. This first-person perspective dominates the lyrics of Cannibal Corpse. Yet although this kind of protagonist is overwhelmingly concerned with mastery over a female Other, it is an ambiguous kind of control. Many lyrics depict being taken over by some greater force that impels the protagonist to murder and mutilate:

> Temptation to kill again
> The sensation comes over me
> An addiction to murdering
> I can't stop murdering
>
>> ("Pulverised," from "The Bleeding")

Horror is often expressed at the protagonist's own actions:

> I was once a man before I transformed
> Into this molester . . .
>> ("Necropaedophile," from "Tomb of the Mutilated")

A small number of lyrics apply these detached descriptions of bodily decay to the protagonist's own body. In the song "I Cum Blood" (on "Tomb of the Mutilated"), a decaying male corpse, neither alive nor dead, commits sexual murder on women alive and dead and in doing so willingly exacerbates his own moral and physical decay. Moreover, the male protagonist does not appear in all lyrics, nor are all the protagonists male and all the victims female. For example, "Split Wide Open" (on "Tomb of the Mutilated") deals with infanticide by a woman, and the song "Meat Hook Sodomy" (on "Butchered at Birth") describes the violent sodomizing of victims whose gender is indeterminate.

Cannibal Corpse lyrics articulate a powerful desire to "Return to Flesh" (on "The Bleeding") through some combination of sex, mutilation, and murder. Although this desire does not always involve misogynistic murder, lyrics in which a male mutilates and destroys a female have become increasingly common in Cannibal Corpse's work.[1] Moreover, when women do appear in the lyrics, they are predominantly constructed as the objects of sexualized assault. But not all of Cannibal Corpse's work deals with sexual violence against women. "Fucked with a Knife" is part of a broader body of work that is not simply reducible to misogynistic violence. Knowing this opens up the possibility of unexpected complexities in the analysis of an apparently simple song.

Music and Lyrics

The complexities of analyzing "Fucked with a Knife" are reinforced when the lyric is put into the context of its music. As Johan Fornäs shows, evaluation of problematic texts can be particularly difficult where music is concerned: "Deciding the meanings and functions of sounds and images might be more difficult than with spoken or written words, which complicates the issues of free expression" (Fornäs 1998:186).

Separating music and lyrics is an analytical strategy much criticized by popular music scholars (see Frith 1983). Yet in this case considering lyrics in isolation and then turning to the music forces us to eschew simple readings of the song. For, as with most Death Metal, the lyrics are almost totally indecipherable without a lyric sheet. The vocals are grunted and screamed rather than sung clearly. The musical backing is extremely fast and dexterous, with complex tempo changes. The guitars are highly distorted, and the speed and complexity of the riffs make the songs dense and difficult to follow. Given that such sounds are generally coded as harsh and unpleasant, they seem utterly suited to the subject matter of the lyrics. The interpretation of lyrics is always problematic, but how might we understand them when they are indistinct? Moreover, for reasons discussed later, the lyrics are not actually printed on all Cannibal Corpse compact discs. Yet whether the lyrics are available or not, the song titles generally are, and they leave little room for ambiguity. A title like "Fucked with a Knife" creates such a horrific image that it may determine the "meaning" of the song to the point where lyrics are virtually superfluous. The title may hide and counter possible divergent and ambiguous readings.

The issue of song titles raises the question of what exactly a musical "text" is. As Fornäs (1997) argues, the distinction between music and words is not a clear one. Is "Fucked with a Knife" an agglomeration of music and lyrics? Is it just the sounds themselves? Could there be a number of "versions" of this text—a sonic one and a written one? This is a crucial issue: If we do not know for sure what the text is, how can we form any kind of response to it? Even a consideration of the "use" of the text does not solve the problem. If we were to criticize the song, would it be necessary to confine that critique to instances where the listener follows along with the lyric sheet? Would it apply to hearings when no lyrics and song titles are available? There is a real danger of being paralyzed by the sheer uncertainty brought about by a sustained consideration of the status of "Fucked with a Knife" as a text. In escaping crude readings, the text may also escape *any* reading.

The Aesthetics of Death Metal

A more productive way of examining the text in question is to consider it in relation to the aesthetics of Death Metal. Cannibal Corpse is one of a large number of bands playing Death Metal. In the early 1990s it was one of several Florida-based bands that were highly influential in the development of this emerging genre. Their sound is characterized by extremely "clean," compressed, distorted guitar sounds, intricate riffs, few guitar solos, and complex speed and tempo changes. It is a highly controlled sound characterized by Deena Weinstein (1991) as musical "fundamentalism." Death, gore, and mutilation were very common lyrical themes, although few bands ever dealt with sexualized violence with Cannibal Corpse's explicitness. The work of Cannibal Corpse is part of a systematic lyrical exploration of the "darker side of life."

This kind of aesthetic agenda has been taken seriously and advocated by a number of critically minded theorists, some of whom have argued that the "transgression" of the boundaries of what it is acceptable to represent and to practice is a fundamental human need. For example, both Mikhail Bakhtin (1984) and Peter Stallybrass and Allan White (1986) discuss the medieval carnival, showing how it inverted the everyday symbolic order to produce a temporary escape from the oppressive conditions of everyday reality. Victor Turner describes as "liminal" the transgressive behavior that occurs "in the gap between ordered worlds" (Turner 1974:13). For Turner liminal behavior occurs in all societies. It questions the symbolic order by showing the arbitrariness of boundaries and as such is a source of concern to authorities. It is legislated against or restricted to the margins of society or specific periods of time.

Transgression allows people to escape power and authority, if only for a time. In societies with strict taboos about sex and death, carnival revels in the body and in sex, death, decay, and excretion—things that are usually strictly controlled. Carnival and other forms of transgression produce "excess," an overpowering of limits. George Bataille (1985) argues that transgression may exceed language itself. For Bataille, transgression is based on an engagement with mortality and/or eroticism, the two most vivid and powerful ways of testing being and authority. Experiences of mortality and eroticism are somehow beyond words and excessive. Exceeding language allows us to experience "sovereignty" over our being.

Yet transgression, while challenging authority, affirms and creates boundaries even as it challenges others. Carnival was often the occasion for pogroms against Jews. The reason is that transgression is based on an ambivalence toward the "abject," that which is formless, disgusting, terrifying, and threatening. Abjection is associated with "vile" bodily fluids and excesses but may be displaced elsewhere— to women, to Jews, to animals, and so on. The abject has to be removed from orderly society, destroyed, or both. Yet as Stallybrass and White (1986:191) argue, "Disgust always bears the imprint of desire." The abject's allure is based on a desire to return to the primal formlessness of the mother–child union (Kristeva 1982). This desire may be intolerable, particularly for men in societies that emphasize the importance of self-control over the body (Theweleit 1987). This is why transgressive behavior, although it revels in the abject, also displaces abjection elsewhere. In turn, those who transgress boundaries may themselves be treated as abject. Murderers and child abusers may be treated as so intolerable that they, and all trace of them, have to be removed from society as completely as possible (Jenks 1998). Yet, at the same time, they exert a strange fascination over those who do not indulge in this kind of behavior (Jenks and Lorentzen 1997).

The idea that art should purposely set out to transgress the limits of what is socially acceptable and that this exploration is socially necessary is well established. The question is whether we can make this sort of claim for "Fucked with a Knife."

Some of the concepts discussed above are applied in one of the few pieces of serious criticism of Death Metal—the analysis presented by Simon Reynolds and Joy Press in their book *The Sex Revolts* (1995). Reynolds and Press draw on feminist criticism, particularly the work of Julia Kristeva, in order to understand the construction of sexuality in contemporary popular music. They analyze the work of the "Grindcore" band Carcass through the concept of the abject (Grindcore is a subgenre of Death Metal featuring extremely fast tempos and a less distinct and controlled sound than is found in conventional Death Metal). Reynolds and Press see the simultaneous attraction to and repulsion from the abject as a key theme in rock music. Carcass's lyrics are a catalog of bizarre and disgusting things that can happen to the human body.[2] They are often lengthy and use extremely explicit medical terminology. Their "Cadaveric Incubator Of Endo-Parasites" (Appendix B) deals with a dead body infested by maggots. Accompanying the highly detailed medical descriptions are sections of bizarre comedy. Sickening descriptions of a particular act are juxtaposed with a ludicrously bathetic word or phrase, often likening the body to food—their first two albums contain words such as "giblets," "doggy bag," and "munch."

The majority of Carcass's lyrics deal with processes beyond human control. Some, however, deal with murder and mutilation, but in a totally different way from the Cannibal Corpse approach. For one thing, such murders are as a rule totally ungendered (at least in the Cannibal Corpse sense).[3] But the main difference is the use of humor. "Forensic Clinicism/The Sanguine Article" (from "Necroticism: Descanting the Insalubrious") depicts a surgeon dismembering an anesthetized patient on the operating table. He is not a man driven by forces that he cannot control, but a gleeful performer, aware of the lunacy of what he is doing:

> Welcome to my theatre, the stage upon which I act
> Turning in a sumptuous performance, heinously I hew and gash.

Clearly, as Reynolds and Press (1995:95) put it, such lyrics are "beyond self parody." They treat the body and its manifold constituents as ludicrous but endlessly fascinating and are "a testament to the threat and the almost voluptuous allure posed by the abject" (ibid.). As with Cannibal Corpse, the lyrics are incomprehensible without a lyric sheet, but the music is in key respects different. Whereas Cannibal Corpse songs are focused, structured around repetitions and clear riffs, and pursued at speed, with Carcass "any sense of organic musical flow [is] brutally ruptured by tempo changes and gear shifts" (ibid.:94). So while Carcass musically and lyrically revels in fantasies of losing oneself in the abject, Cannibal Corpse musically and lyrically presents fantasies of mastering and dominating it. Although both bands explore transgression, Cannibal Corpse in fact reinforces certain limits through its emphasis on control. That control is achieved partially through extreme musical discipline and partially through obsessively constructing images of dominant masculinity.

Carcass's work shows that Death Metal and Grindcore offer radical aesthetic possibilities for exploring the boundaries of the body. The work of Cannibal Corpse, and specifically "Fucked with a Knife," exploits these radical possibilities—but only up to a point. The song (like the body of work of which it is part) reinforces certain boundaries even as it transgresses others. From this perspective, it is possible to argue that "Fucked with a Knife" is equally undeserving of critical approbation and condemnation. Rather, it is a demonstration of how easily a radical transgressive project that questions the boundaries of the gendered body can be transformed into a more sinister project that strongly affirms both gendered bodies and the violent forms of power through which gender is affirmed.

The Response to Death Metal

Transgression is not a purely textual matter; it is a response to forms of power and authority and frequently attempts to provoke hostile reactions. Death Metal and Cannibal Corpse have been implicated in occasional public criticisms and successful and unsuccessful attempts at censorship. Martin Cloonan (1996) recounts some attempts to censor Death Metal in the United Kingdom. In 1991 police seized stock of the Metal label Earache Records in an ultimately unsuccessful attempt at prosecution. In the same year customs officials tried and failed to prevent the importation of an album by the Swedish band Dismember on the grounds that the lyrics of the song "Skin Her Alive" would incite the listener to violence.

Cannibal Corpse has faced censorship problems throughout the world.[4] In Germany, government censors banned the first three albums because of their covers and lyrics. There have been similar problems in Australia, New Zealand, Canada, Taiwan, and South Korea. However, "censored" versions of these albums, with different cover art and no lyric sheet (but with song titles shown inside the CD booklet), were subsequently produced and are freely available. For subsequent albums, the record company practiced self-censorship and produced a version with less offensive cover art and without a lyric sheet (although lyrics sheets are easily available on the internet). The uncensored versions are available only in the United States and South America. Moreover, even in areas where the uncensored versions are available, certain record stores may stock only the censored versions, or no version at all.

Media interest in and publicity campaigns against Cannibal Corpse have been sporadic and unsystematic. During their 1995 German tour, one Christian schoolteacher made a concerted attempt to ban Cannibal Corpse from playing certain venues, with limited success. The band has since toured Germany without problems. In 1996, in a speech that received some media coverage, U.S. presidential candidate Bob Dole referred negatively to Cannibal Corpse, among others. The attack rebounded when Dole admitted that he had never heard the band (Carter 1998).

In 1994 Cannibal Corpse and others were mentioned as inspirations by the four perpetrators of a brutal armed robbery in Eugene, Oregon; the record label settled out of court (without admitting guilt) in a civil suit brought by the victims' families (Moynihan and Søderlind 1998). All of these cases were covered by the mass media, yet none of them resulted in sustained interest or campaigns to ban such music or any of the other responses that characterize "moral panic" (Cohen 1987; Thompson 1998).

Cannibal Corpse is clearly transgressive in the sense that the band has offended a number of people in authority. Yet it remains largely unknown in the wider public sphere, compared with such infamous artists as Marilyn Manson. Indeed, Death Metal is comparatively little known. In the 1980s Heavy Metal—a genre with little of the lyrical or musical severity of Death Metal—was the focus of moral panics and concerted attempts to control it in the United States and elsewhere (Miller 1988; Walser 1993). In contrast Death Metal and other Extreme Metal genres remain relatively "invisible," despite producing material that would probably be censored if it were exposed to public scrutiny. How is this relative invisibility produced, and how might it affect an analysis of "Fucked with a Knife"? The answer lies in the "scene."

The Extreme Metal Scene

"Scene" is a concept increasingly deployed in academic discussions of popular music culture (Shank 1994; Straw 1991). The concept is similar to "classic" definitions of subculture (Hebdige 1979; Willis 1978) in that scenes are generally visible to their members and cohere around texts that present a transgressive challenge to the dominant symbolic order. Yet the concept is also designed to capture a heterogeneity, opacity, and complexity not present in subcultural theory. From this perspective, the Extreme Metal scene consists of a set of closely related, overlapping, and interlocking local, regional, and global scenes that cohere around a cluster of related Metal genres (Black Metal, Death Metal, Doom Metal, etc.).

Compared with other youth cultures, the Extreme Metal scene rarely comes to public attention, and in this way it has escaped the worst consequences of state and media surveillance. As Angela McRobbie and Sarah Thornton (1995) point out, in recent years moral panic has become an increasingly complex process, rather than simply the monolithic assault of authority on a defenseless subculture (Cohen 1987). Scenes are far more reflexive about potential threats, and the strategy that protects the Extreme Metal scene is relative secrecy—a strategy that Michel Maffesoli (1996) identifies as crucial to the survival and coherence of such "tribes" in contemporary society. Extreme Metal practice is reproduced through decentralized networks of small peer groups and individual fans and bands. Fanzine writers, tape traders, and record label owners may never meet other scene members face to face, interacting instead through the telephone, the postal system, and e-mail. Scenic institutions may be based in countries or towns with very weak local scenes. There are large numbers of almost identical-sounding bands worldwide and very few real "stars." There are few concerts, and some major Extreme Metal acts have never even played live. The scene may produce highly transgressive texts, but its institutions ensure that it does so through mundane, decentralized networks of reproduction. The scene does not resemble "classic" subcultures—little "resistance" or "spectacle" is produced by a scene with such limited visibility.

The details of everyday scenic interaction have the same mundane quality. In my own ethnographic and interview research into the Extreme Metal scene, members were in the main keen to stress their normality. Interviews in Extreme Metal fanzines tend to be dominated by the detailing of such matters as a band's relationship with its record label and jovial bantering, rather than intense aesthetic explorations. Lyrics are rarely discussed in the Extreme Metal media or in everyday interaction. When I interviewed (now-ex) Cannibal Corpse singer/lyricist Chris Barnes about his new band Six Feet Under (Harris 1997b), he emphasized his distance from his own lyrics and talked as much about his fondness for smoking cannabis, restoring VW Beetles, and the British cartoon series *Dangermouse*.

It is hard to reconcile this mundanity with much recent work in popular music studies. It has become increasingly popular to ground work on popular music on pleasure and the experiencing of music in the socialized body (Frith 1996; Middleton 1990). Within the Extreme Metal scene, unambiguous demonstrations of pleasure occur in "moshing" (a vigorous form of slam-dancing) at gigs and in delirious fan talk in fanzines and magazines about a particular band. Certainly the joy of moshing at a good gig or hearing and raving about a favorite CD may help keep the enthusiasm of scene members going. Yet we cannot ignore either those morose, sparsely attended gigs where no one moshes or the huge numbers of bored fanzine reviews of mediocre bands. It may be that the most common type of pleasure in the Extreme Metal scene comes from participating in reciprocal exchange networks and exercising "subcultural capital" (Thornton 1995) through learning to distinguish hundreds of nearly identical-sounding bands. Transgressive bodily pleasures are, for most Extreme Metal scene members, a rare treat.

The Extreme Metal scene may be a space in which transgressive themes are explored textually, but not necessarily one where texts are experienced in a transgressive manner. Some scene members attempt to live transgressive lifestyles, of course: Michael Moynihan and Didrik Søderlind (1998) detail murders and terrorist activities by Extreme Metal musicians and fans. However, nearly all of these were associated with Black (Satanic) Metal rather than Death Metal, and even here such practices tend to be confined to particular times and places, such as the early 1990s in Norway. Scenic practice and scenic texts can be disengaged: For most scene members, there is a dramatic gulf between the transgressive texts that they produce and consume and their everyday practice. I am not arguing that music can ever be totally "autonomous" from the social conditions of its production and consumption, but certainly within the Extreme Metal scene members attempt to keep music and practice at arms length from each other.

That is not to say that scene members do not have a relationship with the music they produce and consume. Clearly, texts like "Fucked with a Knife" offer them something: powerful fantasies with deep unconscious resonances. Psychoanalytic criticism has been used to explore "slasher" horror films—films that feature themes similar to that of "Fucked with a Knife." Linda Badley (1995) argues that they productively explore contemporary post-Freudian anxieties about the body in spectacular and fantastic ways. Carol Clover (1992) uses feminist psychoanalysis to show how slasher films dealing with violence against women allow male viewers to explore alternate genders through nightmarish violence.

Whether the fantasies offered by "Fucked with a Knife" can be seen as "healthy" and valuable or not, the tendency within the scene to disengage text and practice means that most scene members refuse to discuss such issues, or even how music affects them in general. Sequences such as the following are common:[5]

Interviewer: Right. OK. So . . . how—what d'you, what d'you think made you get into this sort of music?

Respondent: What made me [get] into it?

I: [Yeah]. Why?

R: [Inaudible]

I: Why d'you think it appeals to you?

R: Hh. I don't think there is a reason it appeals to me. It's just I like it, you know? It's not the sort of thing you can say, I like it because . . .

I: Hm. Hm.

R: It's just, it's just there.

There is no evidence whatsoever that Cannibal Corpse or its fans have engaged in rape, murder, or genital mutilation, nor is there evidence that they have advocated such activities. Other than this, there seems little we can say about the "effects" of "Fucked with a Knife" on its listeners. The scene actively resists this sort of inquiry. We can only speculate on how the text relates to scene members' unconscious fantasies. Perhaps it provides a "fantastic" outlet for male hatred of women. Perhaps it allows male listeners to vicariously identify with the victim in a complex, homo-erotic, sado-masochistic fantasy. Only sustained interviews of the sort that psychoanalysts conduct could ever provide satisfactory answers to this question.

But perhaps this sort of inquiry is not the most productive way of approaching the relationship between the text in question and those who listen to it. Scene members distance themselves from the texts they consume and produce. This is not necessarily a matter of obfuscation. Maybe the disengageability of relationships to musical texts is the source of the pleasures that the scene offers. The scene allows members to produce and consume highly transgressive texts, yet the scene itself never becomes unequivocally transgressive. Members can "play" with transgression, but they are rarely exposed to state and media surveillance. They can play with transgression, but never to the point where transgression becomes self-destruction. In order to understand "Fucked with a Knife," we need to understand the politics of a scene that produces this opaque relationship between text and practice.

The Politics of "Fucked with a Knife"

Mundane practice is not necessarily benign practice. The Extreme Metal scene is dominated by men, and this dominance is reproduced through unspoken everyday practices. Although there is a sizable minority of female fans, few women are involved in an institutional capacity (as label owners, fanzine editors, etc.), and there are virtually no female musicians. Sexist and sometimes overtly misogynistic language is commonplace within scenic conversations. Yet it is by no means clear whether the scene is any more sexist than many other music scenes. The exclusion of women from scenes and from popular music making has been well documented by feminist researchers (Bayton 1989, 1997; Clawson 1999; Cohen 1991, 1997). The practice of popular music making (and in particular rock) appears to exclude women endemically.

Yet, as in other scenes, women *do* become involved in the Extreme Metal scene. Indeed, some women have very prominent positions within scenic institutions. For example, Cannibal Corpse's U.K. press officer is female. Such women are generally vociferous in claiming that they are not offended by bands that use misogynistic lyrics. The following example comes from an interview with a British female scene member and band manager. She is discussing a CD called "Her Gash I Did Slash" by the British Death Metal band Gorerotted:

> "Her Gash I Did Slash"—that was reviewed in a magazine and it's, the magazines are saying: "Oh they won't be getting a lot of female buyers." It's like, the magazines are like making up this hatred, to make females isolated. It's like, I as a female would buy that CD, I don't find that insulting at all. . . . People are just too sensitive towards things like this, you've got to have open mindedness.

This quotation effectively represents the point at which the disengagability of text and practice is converted into an active refusal to engage with questions of power and textual politics within the scene. As I have argued elsewhere (Harris 1999), the scene is oriented toward a rejection of "politics" and reflexive change. Although women can and do get involved in the scene, that involvement depends on not questioning the overall dominance of men. Women who enter the scene cannot be committed to any overt and reflexive challenge to the male domination of the scene. This means that female scene members cannot criticize or question texts like "Fucked with a Knife." Furthermore, it is more difficult for women to get deeply involved in the scene than it is for men, and most tend to take highly passive roles as girlfriends and low-key fans. Texts *may* reinforce female marginality through lyrically dramatizing masculine dominance, especially given the lack of texts that endow women with any kind of agency. Furthermore, lyrics making discourses of horrific misogyny commonplace contribute to the normalization of sexist everyday discourse.

Yet the dominance of men within the scene is also an outcome of processes having nothing to do with sexist lyrics. It might be thought that such texts would alienate women from the scene. In fact, the insulation of the scene is so well developed that any prospective female member would have to make a considerable effort to enter the scene in the first place before "discovering" such a text. The alienation of women happens prior to this. For reasons that are unclear, the harsh, distorted sounds of Metal and Extreme Metal are repulsive to many women, regardless of lyrics. One piece of research showed that Metal is the form of music that adolescent women most hate (Shepherd 1991). Robert Walser (1993) shows that female Metal fans tend to prefer more melodic Metal subgenres. For reasons that are beyond the scope of this chapter, it seems that most women are predisposed to reject certain sounds as pleasurable. There is nothing "natural" about this process, but it is nonetheless rigid. The reasons why women do not like Extreme Metal are deeply rooted in society as a whole, rather than exclusively within the scene. The disinclination of women to enter the scene creates such an overwhelming numerical male dominance that there is little counterweight to the development of sexist practice. The scene might well be overwhelmingly sexist even in the absence of any misogynistic lyrics. "Fucked with a Knife" reinforces a misogyny that was already in place before it was written.

Responding to "Fucked with a Knife"

My investigation into "Fucked with a Knife" to some extent mollified my concern that the song was directly implicated in intense misogyny within the Extreme Metal scene. But although it is a problematic text and definitely implicated in sexist practices, we cannot identify exactly *how* it is connected to them. Moreover, there are also persuasive arguments that such a transgressive text may be a (flawed) part of an important aesthetic project. Is there a danger that the methods of analysis presented here might simply encourage a critical paralysis when faced with a text like this one?

The use of contemporary methods in cultural investigation make this paralysis more likely. My analysis is based on the assumption that meanings are never fixed and are ultimately the result of the active efforts of those who produce and consume texts within certain social formations. This assumption tends to make *all* texts into chimera: The more one analyzes them, the less clear their meanings become. Investigation and evaluation of texts such as "Fucked with a Knife," for which an effective analysis is an urgent matter, may lead to highly ambiguous conclusions, inhibiting effective responses to such texts, particularly with regard to censorship. Even if one does not *a priori* reject censorship as an "answer" to harmful texts, contemporary methods of textual investigation make arguments for censorship all the more difficult, since an unambiguous reason for censorship can rarely be pinned down. To a certain extent, then, serious analysis of texts is the enemy of censorship. In most cases arguments for censoring a particular text have to ignore its context and the potential variability of readings.

The ambiguity that undermines any consistent case for censorship also makes it harder to formulate any other response to a problematic text such as "Fucked with a Knife." If power resides in multiple locations, how important is it to tackle the ambiguous kind of power wielded in practices centered on this text? If the exercise of sexist power within the Extreme Metal scene is not entirely reliant on this text or others like it, how important is it to deal with such texts? Is one text really important enough to be subjected to sustained political and analytical attention?

One way of dealing with such issues might be to begin to formulate a kind of "textual politics" appropriate to the Extreme Metal scene. Such a politics would be based on a recognition of the importance of transgressive forms of representation in contemporary society—including songs like "Fucked with a Knife" that may carry unpleasant things along with that transgression. From this perspective, the text in question is an incomplete form of transgression that upholds certain forms of power, when compared with the more radical form of transgression practiced by Carcass, for example. Judith Butler (1997) holds out the possibility of recontextualizing problematic forms of representation as a progressive form of textual politics. Comparing the work of Cannibal Corpse with that of Carcass is one possible way of doing this, raising the issue of how to pursue transgressive aesthetics without reinforcing misogyny and power.

Ultimately, though, such a textual politics may be impossible. The texts that the Extreme Metal scene produces may not be the most effective fulcrum for change. The scene is so effective in disengaging texts from practices that even a radical change in the texts that the scene produces would not necessarily change the dominance of men within it. Change has to happen in the scene's practices of exclusion and male power—the lack of female musicians and the normalization of everyday sexist discourse. These structures of domination are prior to and exceed texts such as "Fucked with a Knife."

It is extremely difficult for outsiders to influence changes in scenic practices. The scene is so insulated that change can happen only through the efforts of scene members themselves—possibly bolstered by outsiders who are also able to move within it. In addition, the wider exposure of the scene by intellectuals (Berger 1999; Walser 1993; Weinstein 1991) may help to break its isolation and force it into a more effective engagement with critical discourses. Yet this process is at a very early stage, and right now opportunities for dialogue with critically minded intellectuals are extremely limited.

The concern that motivated the study of "Fucked with a Knife" has gradually dissipated into a concern about the exercise of power within the Extreme Metal scene itself, which in any case ultimately derives from the wider society. Ironically, the analytic attention paid to one text in the hope of formulating a practical response has led to vague and generalized prescriptions for change. Even if sustained investigation is a better response to worry about a specific musical text than censorship, it may not necessarily be the best way of formulating a practical political response. Perhaps one reason censorship is attractive to some as a response to certain musical texts is that it is a satisfying negation of the threatening ambiguity of music and the critical political paralysis that music may engender.

At the start of this chapter, I referred to the investigation presented here as a kind of "policing" of popular music. "Policing" here implied intellectual vigilance and an interest in exploring the limits of musical expression. As I pointed out, the word also implies some exercise of power. For all the ambiguity of my investigation and all my intended sensitivity, we cannot ignore the forms of power that this chapter might be implicated in and the fact that it exposes the Extreme Metal scene and Cannibal Corpse to a scrutiny that would otherwise not have occurred. This wider scrutiny may have consequences that I cannot control or that I may not approve of. Sustained attention to this obscure scene—whether by critically minded academics or censorship-minded politicians—may have unforeseen consequences. This chapter may, for example, draw "Fucked with a Knife" to the attention of parties who might actively want to censor it. Policing is never innocent.

Yet sustained intellectual policing of problematic forms of popular music remains the most appropriate way of responding to them. The consequences may never be entirely predictable or satisfactory, and certainly it is unclear how intellectuals can communicate with and stimulate changes in enclosed spaces such as the Extreme Metal scene. Intellectual work, particularly intellectual work that takes place within the paradigms of contemporary forms of textual analysis, all too often seems to sabotage political efficacy. Yet difficult intellectual work remains the only alternative to the brute force and brute thoughtlessness that censorship represents.

Censorship should therefore be opposed in most cases, and not just to preserve freedom of musical expression, although this is clearly important. Censorship does not simply threaten musical freedom; it also ultimately threatens intellectual inquiry as a basis for social progress. If scenes such as the Extreme Metal scene are to develop more egalitarian practices, the most likely route is through carefully thought out, progressive, internal criticism. Censoring individual texts or entire genres does nothing to assist this process. It is not enough to oppose censorship with calls for freedom of expression. Rather, censorship should be opposed through the promotion of critical and intellectual vigor. Intellectual criticism may be rejected as a form of policing by scenes such as the Extreme Metal scene and rejected as a threat by those who advocate censorship. However, it remains the only way of policing popular music that promotes social justice without negating the value of potentially dangerous aesthetics.

Notes

1. The last three albums, made after original lyricist/vocalist Chris Barnes left the band, contain fewer lyrics with male–female violence and contain some lyrics with male victims.

2. Reynolds and Press's analysis (although they do not say so) applies only to the band's first three albums—after this, Carcass began writing more conventional Death Metal lyrics.

3. The only clue to the victim's gender in the example given is the phrase "brittle testes." This is mentioned in passing and is entirely incidental to the lyrical theme.

4. Much of the information in this section comes from an interview with Michael Trengert, European press officer for Metal Blade Records, 4 February 1998.

5. The interview of which this extract is a part is discussed more fully in Harris 1997a.

Discography

Cannibal Corpse. 1990. "Eaten Back to Life," Metal Blade Records, 3984-14024-2.
———. 1991. "Butchered at Birth," Metal Blade Records, 3984-14172-2.
———. 1992. "Tomb of the Mutilated," Metal Blade Records, 3984-14010-2.
———. 1994. "The Bleeding," Metal Blade Records, CDZORRO 67.
———. 1996. "Vile," Metal Blade Records, 3984-14104-2.
———. 1998. "Gallery of Suicide," Metal Blade Records, 3984-14151-2.
———. 1999. "Bloodthirst," Metal Blade Records, 3984-14277-2.
Carcass. 1988. "Reek of Putrefaction," Earache Records, Mosh 6.
———. 1989. "Symphonies of Sickness," Earache Records, Mosh 18.
———. 1991. "Necroticism: Descanting the Insalubrious," Earache Records, Mosh 42.

Bibliography

Badley, L. 1995. *Film, Horror and the Body Fantastic.* London: Greenwood Press.
Bakhtin, M. 1984. *Rabelais and His World.* Bloomington: Indiana University Press.
Bataille, G. 1985. *Literature and Evil.* London: Marion Boyars.

Bayton, M. 1989. "How Women Become Musicians," in S. Frith and A. Goodwin (eds.), *On Record*. London: Routledge, pp. 238–257.

———. 1997. "Women and the Electric Guitar," in S. Whiteley (ed.), *Sexing the Groove*. London: Routledge, pp. 37–49.

Berger, H. M. 1999. *Metal, Rock and Jazz: Perception and the Phenomenology of Musical Experience*. Hanover, N.H.: Wesleyan University Press.

Butler, J. 1997. *Excitable Speech: A Politics of the Performative*. New York: Routledge.

Carter, A. 1998. "Cannibal Corpse: Still Hungry for Death," *Terrorizer*, 54, May, pp. 34–36.

Clawson, M. A. 1999. "Masculinity and Skill Acquisition in the Adolescent Rock Band," *Popular Music*, 18, pp. 99–114.

Cloonan, M. 1996. *Banned! Censorship of Popular Music in Britain: 1967–92*. Aldershot, U.K.: Arena.

Clover, C. 1992. *Men, Women and Chainsaws: Gender in the Modern Horror Film*. London: British Film Institute.

Cohen, S. 1987. *Folk Devils and Moral Panics: The Creation of Mods and Rockers*. Oxford: Basil Blackwell.

Cohen, S. 1991. *Rock Culture in Liverpool*. Oxford: Clarendon Press.

———. 1997. "Men Making a Scene: Rock Music and the Production of Gender," in S. Whiteley (ed.), *Sexing the Groove*. London: Routledge, pp. 17–36.

Fornäs, J. 1997. "Text and Music Revisited," *Theory, Culture and Society*, 14, pp. 109–123.

———. 1998. "Limits of Musical Freedom," in T. Mitsui (ed.), *Popular Music: Intercultural Interpretations*. Kanazawa, Japan: Graduate Programme in Music, Kanazawa University, pp. 185–190.

Frith, S. 1983. *Sound Effects: Youth, Leisure and the Politics of Rock 'n' Roll*. London: Constable.

———. 1996. *Performing Rites*. Oxford: Oxford University Press.

Harris, K. 1999. "'Darkthrone Is Absolutely Not a Political Band': Difference and Reflexivity in the Global Extreme Metal Scene," paper presented to the 1999 conference of the International Association for the Study of Popular Music, Sydney, Aust.

Harris, K. D. 1997a. "'Music Is My Life?': Discourse Analysis and the Interview Talk of Members of a Music-Based Subculture." Working Paper no. 4, Department of Sociology, Goldsmiths College, London.

———. 1997b. "Six Feet Under: Killed, Stoned, Dead," *Terrorizer*, 46, September, pp. 28–29.

Hebdige, D. 1979. *Subculture: The Meaning of Style*. London: Methuen.

Jenks, C. 1998. *Cultures of Excess*. London: Goldsmiths College, University of London.

Jenks, C., and Lorentzen, J. J. 1997. "The Kray Fascination," *Theory, Culture and Society*, 14, pp. 87–107.

Kristeva, J. 1982. *The Powers of Horror: An Essay on Abjection*. New York: Columbia University Press.

Maffesoli, M. 1996. *The Time of the Tribes: The Decline of Individualism in Mass Society*. London: Sage Publications.

McRobbie, A., and Thornton, S. 1995. "Rethinking 'Moral Panic' for Multi-Mediated Social Worlds," *British Journal of Sociology*, 46, pp. 559–574.

Middleton, R. 1990. *Studying Popular Music*. Buckingham, U.K.: Open University Press.

Miller, D. S. 1988. *Youth, Popular Music and Cultural Controversy: The Case of Heavy Metal.* Austin: University of Texas.

Moynihan, M., and Søderlind, D. 1998. *Lords of Chaos: The Bloody Rise of the Satanic Metal Underground.* Venice, Calif.: Feral House.

Reynolds, S., and Press, J. 1995. *The Sex Revolts: Gender, Rebellion and Rock 'n' Roll.* London: Serpent's Tail.

Shank, B. 1994. *Dissonant Identities: The Rock 'n' Roll Scene in Austin, Texas.* Hanover: Wesleyan University Press.

Shepherd, J. 1991. *Music as Social Text.* Cambridge: Polity Press.

Stallybrass, P., and White, A. 1986. *The Politics and Poetics of Transgression.* London: Methuen.

Straw, W. 1991. "Systems of Articulation, Logics of Change: Communities and Scenes in Popular Music," *Cultural Studies,* 5, pp. 368–388.

Theweleit, K. 1987. *Male Fantasies, Volume 1: Women, Floods, Bodies, History.* Minneapolis: University of Minnesota Press.

Thompson, K. 1998. *Moral Panics.* London: Routledge.

Thornton, S. 1995. *Club Cultures: Music, Media and Subcultural Capital.* Cambridge: Polity Press.

Turner, V. 1974. *Dramas, Fields and Metaphors: Symbolic Action in Human Society.* London: Cornell University Press.

van Zoonen, L. 1994. *Feminist Media Studies.* London: Sage Publications.

Walser, R. 1993. *Running with the Devil: Power, Gender and Madness in Heavy Metal Music.* Hanover: Wesleyan University Press.

Weinstein, D. 1991. *Heavy Metal: A Cultural Sociology.* New York: Lexington Books.

Willis, P. 1978. *Profane Culture.* London: Routledge and Kegan Paul.

Appendix A: Fucked with a Knife

Rather than simply reproduce the complete lyrics to "Fucked with a Knife" in this Appendix, in consultation with the editors, I have decided to provide readers with access to the lyrics as part of a complete Cannibal Corpse website. Because the website includes a history of the band, interviews with band members, and a complete discography, I feel it provides the reader with more information about the band than can be included in this chapter and an appropriate context within which to assess the song. Furthermore, not printing the lyrics in this book gives those readers who feel they might be unduly upset by the lyrics the opportunity to avoid looking at them.

The reader can access the song by navigating the Cannibal Corpse website as per the following instructions or by going directly to the link included below.

To access the Cannibal Corpse website, go to

<http://www.geocities.com/SunsetStrip/Palladium/8280/>

Select the "Discography and Lyrics" link, which will take you to a complete listing of album jackets and song lyrics at

<http://www.geocities.com/SunsetStrip/Palladium/8280/disc.html>

To access the lyrics to "Fucked with a Knife," select the song title from the pull-down menu labelled "The Bleeding" and select the album cover hotlink to the right of the song title. This will take you to

<http://www.geocities.com/SunsetStrip/Palladium/8280/bleeding.htm>

This page contains the lyrics to all the songs on the album. Scroll down to find the lyrics to "Fucked with a Knife."

Appendix B: Cadveric Incubator Of Endo-Parasites

The inset of rigor mortis, ulcerous corruption and decay
Saponified fats lather as soap as you slowly eat yourself away . . .
Organs savaged by rotten enzymes, rennin and rancorous cysts
A festering abcess immersed in ravenous autolysis . . .

Breaking down of dead tissue fuels methane gases
A smouldering human compost-heap of self-digesting haemor-
       rhage . . .
Emulsifying carnage, your purpulent torso is mummified
A mortified, marbled feast for drooling parasites . . .

Your lungs consumed in gore, slime and worm encrusted
Brittle testes eroded in hot, corrosive succus
Adhering to the bone, tissue necrosis a maggot feast
A cadaveric crematorium, gaseous spumescence leaks . . .

(Solo: parasitic flesh resection)
(Solo: matted fungus, spawn, eggs, bacteria, germs, mould and
       meat)

Your rump sustaining hostile organisms
—Mould, eggs and larvae
Peptonized spleen, liver and kidneys
—A wasting, degenerate slime
Septicemic mutation
—Of rancid meat and writhing life
Psychedelic, pustular platter of gunge
—Come and take a bite . . .

Dormant fungoid growths
On the smarting human host
Come bathe, cleanse and wash
With livor mortis and dry rot . . .

. . . Lice and ticks . . .

Flesh matted with hatching spawn
Endo-parasites incubate in the warmth
Mortician's implements to tap and bleed
The swarming insects feed . . .

. . . Lice and ticks . . . expel bloody sick . . .

Leathery skin bubbles as blue-bottles hatch
Maggot infestation turns the rotting corpse black . . .
Slushy bowels move as our friends squirm
Flatulent belches—dry, festered and warm . . .

Mike Jones

6 Marxists in the Marketplace

Readers will have to forgive me in advance for this public examination of the experience of making "political" pop music in Britain. Thankfully I was never threatened with death or torture for attempting to express (left-wing) political views through the vehicle of popular music. Further, however "communist" my background and intentions were in the 1980s, the work I collaborated on through 10 years of making records never even threatened to qualify for a "Parental Guidance" sticker. So why would such a seemingly innocuous experience be included in a book about popular music and censorship? I think the answer lies in the versatility of the act of "policing pop."

The Danish Music and Censorship Project cites "fear, xenophobia, intolerance and cultural suppression" (<www.freemuse.org/03libra/speeches/speole04.html>) as the root causes of musical censorship. I would add several more—none of them as physically threatening to the musicians concerned, but each of them pervasive, pernicious, and effective in compromising the expression of pop musicians of a certain variety. I would identify these as censorship by *process,* by *stealth,* and by the *self-as-creator.* None of these conditions is the outcome of direct political oppression, but each is connected with the experience of attempting to remain true to an ideology and an associated political practice (or, more properly, *praxis*) while simultaneously attempting to make records that sell in mass quantities by orthodox routes. Whether I would be so keenly aware of these conditions if the recordings of the songs I wrote had sold in the millions is a moot point. Certainly I do not attribute the failure to be more popular *solely* to these conditions—whether alone or in combination. All I can do is to report them as real and offer them as a perhaps unanticipated dimension of "interference" with "the artistic expression of popular musicians," to quote Martin Cloonan (1996:23).

Latin Quarter

Latin Quarter was formed in late 1983, the culmination of a two-year period of song-writing and home recording I undertook with Steve Skaith. Our relationship was rooted in our membership of the political organization Big Flame, as was, to a certain extent, our songwriting. Superficially, Latin Quarter was a marginally successful British band of the 1980s, with one hit single in Britain ("Radio Africa," February 1986), taken in turn from an album ("Modern Times") that failed to chart in Britain but was a top-20 hit in Germany and Sweden and sold so well throughout western and northern Europe that the act went on to make five subsequent albums.

Despite this track record Latin Quarter is not even a footnote in mainstream "pop history." This lack of impact may be traceable as much to the confusions and complexities surrounding "political pop" as it is to the obscurity of our catalog. Again, direct political censorship is not the hidden hand here; rather, Latin Quarter's attempt to make a politically informed pop music fell foul of the pop commodification process at crucial junctures. Our lack of recognition of, and response to, key dimensions of this process derived from a combination of ignorance and gullibility, the latter stemming directly from "political" expectations and practices that had no place in pop music. Ironically, our lack of success when compared with that of (say) Billy Bragg—a U.K. contemporary of ours and arguably a political ally—was a product of our being more political and less pop than he was! Left-wing activists attempting to make popular music face an obstacle course of contradictions whose difficulty is censorial in its own right.

The Political Roots of Latin Quarter

Big Flame was a neo-libertarian British Marxist group influenced heavily by the Italian Marxist organization Lotta Continua, itself a product of the student uprisings of the late 1960s. Put briefly, what differentiated Big Flame from older left-wing currents and their associated political organizations who shared our conviction that revolution in Britain was imminent was that Big Flame argued that only a remodeled Marxism developed out of a critique of Marxism's own past could meet the demands of that revolution. It called for a reinvestigation of how power was exercised under capitalism, finding the identification of the state as the repository and point of orchestration of ruling class power insufficient and misleading. Instead, Marxists needed to be aware of how oppressive power relations were reproduced within the working class, within the organizations of the working class (the trade unions, political campaigns and movements, community groups, and Labour Party branches), and also within the revolutionary organization itself. These oppressive power relations expressed themselves in and through the reproduction of hierarchies that drew their authority from (and helped maintain) ethnocentric, patriarchal values. Big Flame anticipated some aspects of the postmodernist break with Marxism (especially by asserting the inability of programmatic politics to deal with subjectivity) and also the rise of political correctness, that debilitating and spurious attempt to compensate, through language, for millennia of oppression. Living and practicing these political perspectives was another matter entirely.

Whatever their complexities, it is less onerous to précis Big Flame's politics for a contemporary readership than it is to convey how socially and intellectually saturating membership of a tiny far-left organization is. In short, revolutionary socialism was not forced on me or on Steve Skaith by a reactionary political regime determined to stifle opposition; rather, the "student generation" politics of the 1970s was, truly, little more than a lifestyle choice—one continuous in many vital ways with the embrace of the myths of "rock radicalism" sown (notably but not exclusively) around Bob Dylan and John Lennon and fuelled by the excitement of student demonstrations, feminist uprisings, and the thrilling rhetoric of situationism. Once inside an organization, a kind of cult logic prevailed. In many subsequent Latin Quarter interviews, I described (student) Marxism as a "God pill"—once you swallowed it, the world and the whole of human history became clear, explicable, and open to change. Nonbelievers should not doubt the seductiveness of the notion of the vanguard organization—to be a Marxist was to be, simultaneously, at the center and at the forefront of "history." Taking this kind of (differently derived) self-importance into a cultural industry that thrives on hyperbole was asking for trouble.

Latin Quarter's Music—Where Is "Politics"?

If Big Flame was opaque, in many ways the music of Latin Quarter was transparent— a seventies rock singer-songwriter project, reconfigured for the 1980s, with the acoustic guitar accompaniment to narrative songwriting replaced by (then) contemporary instrumentation—synthesizers supplementing a conventional rock lineup of guitars, bass, and drums. Musically, Latin Quarter was diverse and catholic—rock, reggae, dance, and ballads—but only within the broad parameters of musical forms that support narrative lyrics. This, in turn, raises the question of where "politics" is to be found in popular music. If it was solely in the lyrical content of songs, then Latin Quarter's first album was a veritable manifesto. Side one of the vinyl release covered McCarthyism, football violence, imperialism in Africa, racism in France, and the social ills of the United States. But pop music is more than lyrics, more even than music: Pop is a commodity, and what is sold is a combination of the sound an act makes, the way the act looks and behaves, and the stories that can be told about why the performers sound, look, behave, and perform as they do. Arguably, successful pop careers (as opposed to one-off hit records) are built on the coherent mobilization of all of these dimensions (consider U2 in this light). Where Latin Quarter was concerned, this coherence and its mobilization could not be achieved. No one contrived this. What we experienced was not censorship as the direct prohibition of the expression of a political, moral, or spiritual belief; rather, we were forced to learn that, in a system of commodity production for profit, any aspect of a "proto-product" that is deemed to reduce the chances of profitability will be shorn off or compromised in some way by mechanisms that are concerned only with the maximization of profit, not with the intentions of composers. In a sense this is "blind" censorship, almost a fail-safe device that neutralizes "political" content simply because such content does not complement the demands of the profit system. How this works in practice is what concerns me.

Censorship by Process

One can argue that the pop commodification process begins long before an act signs a deal with a record company. The desire to make popular music implies a willingness, a desire even, to contract with a major record company. Unsigned, aspirant pop acts may well hold contradictory views of record companies and of the music industry while writing their songs and making their self-financed recordings. The idea that record companies rip off pop acts continues to sit effortlessly alongside the idea that their employees are highly discriminating individuals able to recognize "potential" when they stumble across it. To recognize that making pop is a contradictory business is not to argue that its contradictions are themselves evidence of censorship, but, once signed, a record contract needs to be fulfilled. Record contracts tend to be just that—contracts to make records, not to release and market records (although clauses committing companies to release and market are becoming more widespread). For two left-wing songwriters, signing a major deal was a goal from the outset. In attempting to reconstruct why we felt no tension between getting into bed with capitalists and our years of sworn opposition to capitalism, I can only recall the certainty of our conviction that the socialist millennium was at hand.

Many indices in the early 1980s led British left-wing activists to believe that a major and unprecedented shift toward socialism was extremely close. Socialists generally clung to the belief that the experience of a far-right (at least by British standards) government would radicalize the masses. This was reinforced by the renewal of the Campaign for Nuclear Disarmament (CND), which regularly brought tens of thousands onto the streets. In turn, the antinuclear movement and the apocalyptic tensions this kind of movement draws from encouraged the further demonization of both Margaret Thatcher and Ronald Reagan. Meanwhile, internationally, the Nicaraguan Sandinista government seemed to be demonstrating a compassionate Third World model for radical social change that was not reliant on Soviet support, while Nelson Mandela's continuing imprisonment galvanized a generalized repugnance toward the South African apartheid regime. In London, the very heartland of classical capitalist imperialism, the left-wing Greater London Council was pioneering what can only be described as "radical reformism"—instead of piecemeal amelioration, policies were being developed that would demonstrate a linked program of strategic, collective solutions to social issues (transport, education) and social problems (racism, unemployment).

In all of the radical campaigns—for Mandela's freedom and the survival of the Sandinistas, against "nukes" and racism—pop music seemed to have found a place somewhere near the center. The Jam (then Britain's biggest pop group) played from the back of a low-loader truck to CND marchers on the Thames embankment. Earlier the Specials had reached number one in the hit parade with "Ghost Town," a song that helped sustain the agenda, if not the existence, of the Rock Against Racism campaign. Its Two-Tone label continued to act as a point of reference for the ability to sustain a culturally aware (rather than necessarily politically conscious) left-leaning record label (much as Rough Trade also did). Within a wider political context that seemed to presage Socialism, these comparatively isolated, if prominent, exemplars of pop's ability to connect with left-wing campaigns and, more important, to express (in our terms) "progressive" political views was enough to encourage Latin Quarter to ignore the contradictions of attempting to make records both aimed at mass sales and informed with Marxist perspectives. Instead, we headed toward mass sales as if the processes that propelled pop groups toward the charts were somehow politically neutral. They are not: They represent and are articulated by systems of power—the power to decide how and why record company resources should be allocated in the pursuit of profit, rather than for any wider political or social ends.

How the "Pop Process" Produces Its Own Results

If we accept that the pop commodity is the marketed sum of the sound, look, and story of a pop act (and that record company employees and practices will therefore be active in combining these dimensions of the pop-act-as-commodity), then the weakness of a political project in which the "politics" of the act resided primarily in song lyrics should become readily apparent. Before they are heard as words, lyrics are heard as sounds, and as sounds they must find their place within the multivariant, nonverbal symbolic systems we recognize as "music." So skilled are we as music listeners (because so skilled are we as socially and culturally rooted communicators) that we hear certain combinations of sonic sign systems not just as "music," or even more specifically as "popular music," but as music of a certain style. Further, styles will themselves signify meaning. That major record companies wanted to offer Latin Quarter a contract to make recordings of its songs means that record company employees established the meaning of the act through its music. This in turn involved their assessing the likely sales potential of that recorded music—which, at base, involves anticipating the meaning that potential listeners would make of the music. In all of this, no one discussed "politics" with us because that was simply not an issue. The only "meaning" made from our music was that it was potentially commercial.

The reason why record company resources were allocated to Latin Quarter was that mass sales of its recordings were anticipated. In one sense, we could not have wished for more—but, crucially, we entered the "mainstream" *on the terms and conditions of the mainstream.* We did this unwittingly, and not simply because we were naïve souls, but because we were behaving like political activists rather than as individuals now employed in the business of making not politics but music. The cloistering effect of the tiny organization tends not just to reinforce an agenda that almost no one else subscribes to, but to fit external events to that agenda. The foregoing rehearsal of "progressive" political developments that seemed to establish a complementary context for politically "progressive" music is simply a confection. Joining together a selective inventory of (poorly understood) social and political conflicts and adding to them an extremely selective soundtrack is no basis for making either political or musical headway. The early 1980s could be (and were) read in entirely different ways—for example, as a conjuncture in which a popular basis for a radical right-wing politics was established in Britain while the ("left") "radicalism" of rock withered in favor of the emerging underground of a dance music club culture—where "politics" existed in and through new expressions of individual and collective identity not allowed for in Marxist prescriptions.

Latin Quarter wanted commercial success because we wanted people to find our music as thrilling and as meaningful as "Bohemian Rhapsody." An unstated but defining mainstay of our existence was the idea that if people could sing along ecstatically to "Scaramouche, Scaramouche, can you do the Fandango," then how much better would it be if they were inspired by Marx's theory of class conflict set in an equally compelling three verses, a bridge, and a chorus?[1] At this level of our practice as a pop group, there was clearly no need to censor Latin Quarter. "Rock" had established that some acts might write songs with "socially conscious" lyrics: They might even help sales. This was enough of a story to be going on with, and the "look" of Latin Quarter was equally pop and orthodox—three lead singers with an "AOR" (adult-oriented rock) repertoire, apparently a mainstream act in the mold of Fleetwood Mac. It was in attempting to mobilize this mismatched set of conditions that Latin Quarter experienced a comparatively "passive," but still effective, censorship.

Roles and Jobs in Record Making

Record making is much discussed but, I would argue, little understood. Again, people hold contradictory ideas about record companies. For example, record companies rarely draw attention to their own activities; it is not in their interest to do so. In this way, when records are hits, pop acts, journalists, and fans alike will blithely refer to the record as if it were the work of the act alone. Conversely, when records are not hits, the same three constituencies will often cite "interference" from the record company as a primary factor in that "artistic" (for which read "commercial") failure. But, hit or miss, an enormous amount of work goes on behind the scenes in record making—as it must do. Songs do not become records overnight, and pop acts and their material similarly take time to commodify. Latin Quarter offered enough that was commodifiable for (several) A&R departments to sign it, but too little coherence for their associated marketing departments to complete the commodification process by marketing its sound, look, and story and promoting this unified and interesting whole through the mass media to a potential market.

In the case of each of Latin Quarter's record deals, the marketing departments in successive companies actively decided *not* to sell Latin Quarter records. If we consider the activity of the marketing department more closely, the marketer's role is to create a market for a commodity—by converting a perceived need for music into a specific want—but it is not the marketer's job to bring coherence where, from their perspective, coherence cannot be found. Equally, it was not Latin Quarter's job to make itself any more coherent in a pop music sense than it already was. Essentially, the Latin Quarter story is defined by years of stalemate, with each successive record added to a series of "false starts." The commodification process could not make full sense of the act, and the act was unwilling to become more of a commodity. It was the songwriters' political aims that proved the stumbling block: The terms in which Latin Quarter needed to be articulated were not in the vocabulary of major record companies.

If we had been more of a "conscience rock" act—like Simple Minds or Phil Collins or U2—then our occasional political gestures or forays could have been "handled" and situated within the schedules and protocols of business as usual, thereby allowing everyone involved to feel good about being associated with the occasional "thoughtful" single or high-profile live endorsement of causes it is difficult to remain credibly distanced from, such as Live Aid or an Amnesty International tour. But *every* Latin Quarter song was "thoughtful," and the act *did* distance itself from Amnesty and even from the Labour Party–supporting Red Wedge—because we felt that those organizations addressed effects rather than causes. In their inability to understand what kind of act Latin Quarter was, people on the record company side simply switched their attention away from the act and toward some more readily comprehensible signing (all record companies sign more acts than they can meaningfully support in the marketplace). Throughout this time Billy Bragg remained popular—but arguably at the expense of a main-stream impact. Instead, in sound, look, and story, Bragg signaled that the political troubadour was alive and well—an early-Bob-Dylan-as-Woody-Guthrie read through punk rock in sound and style. This does not mean that Billy could not or did not have hits, but they came at the expense of conceding that political pop (at least of the white, articulate, English variety) could be represented only in this limited—and limiting—way. Bragg's career is a visible acknowledgment that the pop process produces its own results. Latin Quarter's career is the invisible obverse of his.

Censorship by Stealth

If Latin Quarter suffered censorship *within* the commodification process through the indifference, bemusement, and hostility of individual members of various marketing departments, it was still the case that records were made and released and that members of the promotions departments of those record companies were charged (usually half-heartedly, always in almost total isolation from the act) with the job of promoting those releases to the mass media. The way those companies allocated resources to making Latin Quarter a pop success was also implicated in the "censorship" of the act. At major record companies, the promotions department is more usually referred to as "Press and Promotions"—and "working" the press has been seen historically as a job demanding different skills from those required to persuade radio and television producers that a record is worth supporting through frequent plays and that an act is worth getting behind through guest appearances on appropriate TV and radio shows.

Over two hundred pop singles are released every week in the United Kingdom. There simply are not enough magazine front covers and column inches to go around—and the same rule applies to the other media. Essentially, editors and producers need compelling reasons to favor one release over another. When no compelling reasons can be furnished by a record company, it is not the job of an editor or a producer to examine a case on its merits. Further, even though it is one of the major markets for pop music, the United Kingdom is a small country when compared, for example, with the United States. Consequently, the pop media community is small and close-knit. If one editor or producer cannot be persuaded to support a release, then none can. Worse still, the individuals who make up the interface between record companies and media firms tend to be of similar ages and tastes, and all at roughly the same point on the career ladder. As media careers tend to be governed by how skillfully an individual can ally himself or herself with an emerging trend, or claim intimacy with an existing act that is retaining "credibility," the like-lihood is that people will distance themselves from an act that has no demonstra-ble cultural capital in these terms.

On the cultural stock market of British pop music, Latin Quarter was in deficit almost from the outset. Our centrality in the world of Marxist ideas simply did not carry over into other, more socially central arenas. Not even advertising (self-financed promotion) went smoothly! Very simply, because no one could come up with a marketable identity for the act, press advertisements and music videos tended, at best, to reflect the "project's" lack of coherence. Worse still, to the punk sensi-bilities then prevalent among the music press, an act like Latin Quarter was anath-ema. Our reviews were some of the most bitter in music press history.[2] Radio plays were less difficult to come by, but, again, while the sound we made (and the sen-timents of our songs) tended not to be suitable for periods of peak listening, our culturally rootless pre-punk aura cut us off from more esoteric shows. Ultimately, we tended to be wheeled out whenever a daytime radio producer wanted to leaven the bright flow of the mainstream with something more "substantial." Where radio was concerned, plays of Latin Quarter were restricted not because we were too "political," but because we were too "serious."

What was censoring about Latin Quarter's experience of press promotion was its corrosive effect on morale and its demonstrably negative effect on sales. In the first instance, I doubt whether later "political" acts such as the Levellers or Chum-bawamba have been so easily deterred, but, lacking a cohesive identity as it did, Latin Quarter simply became more upset, angry, and withdrawn as time went on. Further, nothing in the experience of the far left could have prepared Skaith and myself for this kind of reception. One of the major drawbacks of membership of a tiny Marxist organization is how secure and superior it encourages its members to feel: You are on the "right side," as the whole of human history can be shown to demonstrate, and you bask in the knowledge of your insight. To come out of this kind of cloister into venality is transition enough; to do it and then be told that you and your music are 14 kinds of excrement is, at the least, psychologically demanding. So hostile did the music press become to Latin Quarter that RCA's press office could find no journalist on any of the music weeklies even to review our third album ("They hate you out there," as our then manager Marcus Russell put it). Not surprisingly, RCA then refused to allocate further funds to the pro-motional campaign. British sales of that album were derisory, and, to this day, not one of the three subsequent Latin Quarter albums has been released in Britain. The iconoclasm of punk may well have been historically "necessary," but when journalists draw on iconoclastic zeal to demoralize songwriters to the point where they consider abandoning their music, and to intimidate record companies to the point where they abandon their acts, then a quite decisive act of censorship has taken place.

Self-Censorship

The legacy of Big Flame conditioned a further and surprising form of censorship—perhaps the most disturbing and pernicious of all. In May 1985 Liverpool Football Club played the Italian team Juventus in the European Cup Final. The match was played at the Heysel Stadium in Brussels. Before the match began, skirmishes between supporters turned into a massacre, a stadium wall collapsed, and 38 people were crushed or suffocated to death—38 innocent Belgians and Italians murdered by some of Britain's most extreme football hooligans. In a century that will be remembered more for its atrocities than for any other factor, this particular atrocity demands attention because it pretended to no ideological "justification" and the "grievance" that had provoked it (Roma attacks on Liverpool fans a year earlier) was not the responsibility of those on whom revenge was taken. I had watched Liverpool play for 12 years and had attended earlier rounds of that year's European Cup. Racism in the Liverpool crowd had become more prevalent during the eighties, and the affable image of the "Scouser" (a U.K. nickname for a native Liverpudlian) had always masked a core of violence that had to be experienced to be appreciated. A Liverpudlian friend argued in the aftermath of the massacre that "it was the wall that killed those people," but in fact it could only have been the hundreds of Liverpool fans who charged, again and again, into the mass of bodies.

As I explained to someone at the time, the image of Liverpool's fans as the "best in Britain" was destroyed "in one fell swoop." The phrase gave me an idea for a song about the incidents, and when I discovered that "fell" is an Old English word meaning both "terrifying" and "ruthless," my decision was sealed. As I wrote the lyric, however, I found that my political perspectives, formed as they had been in the Liverpool branch of Big Flame, demanded that I contextualize the actions of the Liverpool crowd—and so, rather than an uncompromising statement of disgust, I delivered almost a paean to a decaying city. There is not enough space here to discuss the entire lyric, but two extracts should suffice:

> VERSE ONE:
> I'm standing hands in pockets
> In a place that's damp and grey and famous
> The air is sharp with accents
> All announcing that "they shouldn't blame us"
> But a place that has its problems
> Just took on another group
> Thirty-eight in the Heysel, in one fell swoop.

From here, I elaborate on the connection between general desperation and a desperate act, and I transfer responsibility for the crowd's actions to those who continue to promote English imperialism through sport.

BRIDGE:

Meanwhile back home in the studio
Are the clutch of bleeding hearts
Who, season after season,
Wave the flag in foreign parts
But who scream for law and order
When their waving comes unstuck
With the message to the "patriots"
That they could not give a fuck.

VERSE THREE:

For the people of a city
Who have lost most in the turn to Europe [etc.].

So my "analysis" was, ultimately, "poor old Liverpool fans misrepresented by nasty bourgeois ideologues in the media"—pretty dreadful, yet explicable in the context of years of political activism, football supporting, and pop music making. But what this pulling of punches really amounted to was *self-censorship*, evidence of a determination, in the language of the far left, to "draw the lesson" from an incident of social conflict, or, in the Italian way, to identify the "mass line" in a "struggle." I am not seeking here to use this platform as a *mea culpa* or announce some shift to the right, but Latin Quarter played some small role in the "politicization" of popular music, and an examination of its history opens to discussion the issue of how and why songwriters and musicians approach, and articulate, political events. Making judgments about popular music (a complex cultural, industrial, and aesthetic product) through the analysis of song lyrics is a piece of "bad practice" left over from the 1960s, but in this instance it is justified because I can report the considerations that made up the act of writing. To condemn the Heysel events without considering their context would be a knee-jerk reaction, but so is an approach that always interprets the actions of working-class people in their favor because they are history's "innocents."

In a 15-year history, Latin Quarter experienced only three acts of overt political censorship of which we were aware: A television station in Spain would not allow us to perform "Sandinista"; in East Germany (where we were the only western pop act ever to release a contemporary pop album), the state record label made us change the album's cover art—again because it supported the Sandinistas; finally, from personal correspondence, it seems that our first album was banned in South Africa because two songs were antiapartheid (in any case, we had demanded that our albums *not* be released there). These are the kinds of actions that we are all familiar with as censorship.

During the years when Latin Quarter was most active, I can recollect a strong, multifaceted sense of frustration. Perhaps "frustration" is too mild a term to take its place in a work on censorship, yet clearly I cannot claim that we were physically prevented from expressing ourselves. Rather, I have tried to show how completely inappropriate were the far left's instincts for progress in the world of pop music. The experience of making records demands a new sense of time. Suddenly, events in the political world seem to take place somewhere on the outside, and when events are perceived, there is no chance to react quickly. In place of the practices and sensibilities of direct political organization came a new and alien work discipline in an equally alien working environment—one that ultimately frustrated our aims more effectively than active state censorship might ever have done.

Much of "political pop" depends on conjunctural factors. In my experience, the most "political" pop can be is in its contribution to raising awareness (mainly) around single-issue campaigns in orthodox pressure-group politics. For example, in late 1970s Britain, Rock Against Racism was successful not so much because it vanquished racism but because it helped to label the British National Front (NF) as a fascist organization at a time of growing electoral purchase for the NF, which, in turn, arguably helped to restrict voting support for that organization. Viewed in this light, "political pop" is not a stylistic choice on offer to pop composers; it can be undertaken only when the time seems ripe for such an intervention. This means that what I tried to achieve through Latin Quarter was misconceived. Even worse than my own dreadful naiveté about how pop works—both as music and as commodity—was my failure to recognize that I was trying to unite two distinct selves. By the early 1980s I was a quintessential member of the last flowering of the "student generation." I was also, still, a rock fan. I was motivated to write pop songs because I desired political change—but the ability I possessed to write such songs was not connected to my willingness to endorse political perspectives, implement political programs, or chase Marxist rainbows.

"Issues" never go away, and anyone is free to sing about them, but pop music is a product. In order to be a viable product, it needs a means of production, distribution, and exchange. Capital doesn't censor—it doesn't need to. What censors is the market: If there are judged to be insufficient buyers for a product, that product will not be offered for sale. Too few people were willing to buy the Latin Quarter product—we were too pop for the "lefties" and too left for the "poppies"—so we dropped out of sight. If I could do it again, I'd examine my own motives more thoroughly and try to decide whether what I wanted most was a revolution or a career as a pop songwriter. The fact that I'd have to think so long and hard is all the evidence anyone would need that I should stick to the revolution!

Notes

1. It is worth recording here that, at least in the case of "Bohemian Rhapsody," the idea that pop music should be "fun" entirely escaped me. I believe this to be the very worst *popular* record in the history of popular music. But, then, so much more passed me by where

Queen was concerned—I didn't realize that Freddie was gay, and that the name was play-ful. My loathing for Queen's *sound* closed the rest of my senses to their "look" and "story"!

2. Consider this sample from a *New Music Express (NME)* review of Latin Quarter's sec-ond album, "Mick and Caroline": "LQ's music is pretty dull stuff. . . . They don't expect a few pop songs to change the world; more modestly, they hope a few pop songs might *help*. . . . While the songs are marked by that sense of restraint and acknowledgement of their lim-itations, they're also paradoxically naïve—it's as if after all LQ *do* believe that a few pop songs can change the world, that their opinions are self-evident truths which only need to be heard to put the world to rights"—and so on (*NME*, 27 June 1987).

Bibliography

Cloonan, M. 1996. *Banned! Censorship of Popular Music in Britain: 1967–1992.* Aldershot, U.K.: Arena.

Rob Bowman

---

7 Argh Fuck Kill—Canadian Hardcore Goes on Trial: The Case of the Dayglo Abortions

In the spring of 1988 in the tiny Ottawa suburb of Nepean, a 14-year-old girl was engaged in activity typical of teenagers throughout the western world. This particular young woman was preoccupied with identity work, using popular music in the form of hardcore punk as one of her primary tools. In her quest to develop into a happy, healthy, fulfilled human being, she had borrowed from a friend an album by a Canadian group called the Dayglo Abortions. Desiring to flagrantly contravene Canadian copyright law, she asked her father, Jim Fitzgibbons, to help her make a tape recording of the record. Typical of such scenarios, Ms. Fitzgibbons' father did not think highly of the music, the cover art, or the lyrics to many of the Dayglo Abortions' songs.

So far, who cares? What separates this story from a thousand analogous tropes was the fact that her father was a police sergeant who decided to take what for most would have been a family matter (e.g., on the positive tip, "Let's talk about what is being expressed in these songs," or, on the negative tip, "I forbid you to listen to such music!") and turn it into a public matter. This resulted in action against several parties—against Fringe Product,[1] the company issuing the recording; against 497906 Ontario Limited, the parent company of a distributor and retail outlet called the Record Peddler; and against Ben Hoffman, the owner of both companies—on charges of possession, and possession for the purpose of distribution, of obscene material as defined in section 159 (subsequently section 163) of the Criminal Code of Canada.

What is remarkable about all this is that a "public complaint," as such, was never filed. The Dayglo Abortions and Fringe Product were simply unlucky in that

(1) one of their fans happened to be the teenaged daughter of a police detective and (2) this particular fan was unable to, or did not want to, buy a copy of the record herself, did not know how to work the family's stereo system, and consequently needed her father to help her make an illegal recording of a friend's copy of the album. Paradoxically, although there was never a public complaint and two-and-a-half years later the two records in question were found in a court of law not to be obscene, the ramifications of the charges were potentially severe. At the time of this writing, 10 years after the trial, neither the record company nor the band has fully recovered.

Like the activities and behavior of the teenage fan in Nepean, the story of the Dayglo Abortions is, in general terms, typical of the experiences of a thousand other rock bands in the western world. Writer/guitarist Cretin (Murray Acton), drummer Jesus Bonehead (Brian Whitehead), and bass player Spud a.k.a. Couch Potato (Trevor Hagen) first came together in 1977 in a Victoria, British Columbia, band known as Airborne. Acton and Whitehead had been friends since the sixth grade, and all three musicians were big fans of Black Sabbath, Rush, the Mahavishnu Orchestra, and King Crimson. A year later the three would-be Dayglos reconvened as the Sick Fucks (a.k.a. Sikphuxz, a.k.a. Sickfucks), fronted by what Acton describes as a "wild, screeching, out-of-tune female vocalist" (MacMinn 1989). After the Sick Fucks broke up, Acton, Whitehead, and Hagen started a three-piece band that they named the Dayglo Abortions, inspired by a raft of headlines in the *Victoria Times* about attacks on abortion clinics.[2]

"It was kinda scary being called that," Whitehead told *Vancouver Magazine* in 1986. "On our first gig, we played five songs and then got into a fight with the audience. The paper said that we were the most disgusting band the writer had ever seen. We thought, 'Wow, we're onto something here'" (Wiseman 1986).

Gigs for the first few years were relatively infrequent, and largely restricted to the Victoria and Vancouver punk scenes. In 1981 the Dayglo Abortions, financed by a friend's lottery winnings, recorded an independent 12-inch release entitled "Out of the Womb" (Sharpe Records). Consisting of 10 original songs sporting such titles as "Stupid Songs," "Argh Fuck Kill—Die Sinner Die," "Dogfarts," "Stupid World," and "Ronald McRaygun," the record was lyrically and musically situated squarely within the post-punk genre of hardcore. Much of the recording, including "Wake Up America" and "Proud to Be a Canadian," was highly political in nature. All of it, including the cover art, was designed to shock. The latter was especially offensive. Playing off both the group's name and the EP's title, it portrayed a topless, gut-slashed woman in a bondage shot.

Getting the Record Contract

Over the next few years, the Dayglo Abortions gradually attained notoriety and expanded their fan base, embarking on short tours of the Pacific Northwest and eventually gigging their way across Canada. While in Toronto to play one of their first eastern Canada dates, the group dropped by the offices of the Record Peddler, a retail store and record distributor that for many years had been Toronto's leading alternative independent record store specializing in punk, post-punk, and new wave recordings.

The same year that "Out of the Womb" was released, Ben Hoffman, owner of the Record Peddler, launched a record label he aptly named Fringe Product. The company's first release came about when Hoffman licensed the domestic pressing rights for the Dead Kennedys' "Too Drunk to Fuck." He subsequently licensed rights to Husker Du's "New Day Rising" and by 1983 had started signing Canadian alternative bands such as Breeding Ground as well as putting out a compilation of unissued songs by the Toronto punk legends the Diodes.

Hoffman was well aware of the Dayglos. In fact, he had sold a number of copies of "Out of the Womb" and found himself in the odd position of being unable to pay for them, since the owner of Sharpe Records had changed his phone number and address without bothering to leave forwarding information. When the Dayglos dropped by the Record Peddler, their primary mission was to collect the outstanding money owed on "Out of the Womb."

The group's reputation revolved around hilarious, edgy, high-energy, confrontational live performances of bone-crushing, buzz-saw hardcore. Drummer Jesus Bonehead often performed nude, and legend has it that he once consummated the love act onstage with a particularly enthusiastic female fan. Hoffman happily paid the band what was owed and told them about his label. Shortly thereafter the two parties agreed that Fringe should handle the group's follow-up recording. In late 1985 Fringe released "Feed U.S. A. Fetus," complete with a cover shot of Ronald and Nancy Reagan sitting down to a dinner consisting of a fetus covered in sauce (catsup in the United States) and garnished with jelly beans. Behind the presidential couple was an American crest consisting of a bald eagle and banners that proclaimed "Flesh + Blood + Splattered Guts," "Dripping Brains and Radiation," "Everybody's Mutilated," "Screaming Missiles," and "Burning Babies." Ronald proudly sported a McDonald's tie clip.

The album contained the 10 songs previously released on "Out of the Womb" plus 11 newly recorded ditties including "Kill the Hosers," "Religious Bumfucks," "I Killed Mommy," "Suicide," "Scared of People—Black Sabbath," and "I Want to Be East Indian." "Feed U.S. A. Fetus" was packaged with a satirical warning sticker alluding to the recent capitulation of the Record Industry Association of America

(RIAA) in the United States to the Parents Music Resource Center (PMRC), which proudly proclaimed that this recording contains "poisonous ideas and corrosive concepts." For the new songs the band had added second guitarist Wayne Gretsky, a.k.a. Chris Prom.

A Fringe catalog issued shortly after the Dayglos' album was released proudly described the group as

> a hardcore band reviled by millions, loved by dozens. Ex members of Sick Fucks/X Men/ Red Tide/Kill City, their music has been described as: Ultrafast, raw, painful, disgusting, poisonous, corrosive, rancid and hyper-stupid. With titles like "Argh Fuck Kill," "Kill the Hosers," and "Religious Bumfucks," they have carved their own little niche in the hearts of the PMRC, and their paen [sic] to Black Sabbath is truly one of the finest recordings—anywhere, any time.

Fringe was clearly aware of the shock value inherent in the group's reputation and song titles and was more than happy to exploit this aspect of the band in its marketing efforts. In the United States the record was distributed by Toxic Shock Records, while Armageddon Records handled sales and distribution in Germany.

Reviews of "Feed U. S. A. Fetus" were extremely positive. Tellingly, most commentators immediately picked up on the quality of humor that ran rampant through the Dayglos' material. In the United States, *Music Connection Magazine* (1986) noted that the group was "hard, fast 'n' heavy, and—a must with this sort of thing—they have a sharp sense of *humor.*"[3] In Canada a reviewer commented: "From their early days in Sickfucks/X-men, the Dayglows [sic] have remained steadfastly crude/crass/ disgusting . . . sometimes *hilarious*, sometimes disturbing." Several years earlier another reviewer had written about the "Out of the Womb" EP: "Some folks consider the Dead Kennedys the ultimate punk *parody*, but the Day Glows [sic] slam the warp-drive into hyper-stupid and leave the DKs eating angel dust. These guys are so far out in their moronic glorification of all things negative, black and sick, that they cause even the most jaded cynic to double over with laughter."[4]

Nor did articles about the band miss the humor incorporated into its material and performances. When the Dayglos were booked to play Winnipeg on one of their earliest cross-country tours, the city's entertainment weekly proclaimed that the local "alternative scene takes a quantum leap in *stupidity* and excitement this week. . . . The D.A.'s bury themselves in raw, metalish energy and absolutely the most extreme/*hilarious* and explicit lyrics ever penned in reaction to Ronald Reagan, Tipper Gore, Washington Wives and boredom-at-large."

The most extensive article on the band was a feature in *Vancouver Magazine* from June 1986. The piece was headed *"Parody* Rules Okay," the subheading reading: "How an ensemble of Victorian gentlemen is *humorously* extending punk's boundaries." The author, Les Wiseman (1986:90), called the Dayglos "one of the *funniest* groups of young men I have ever heard," referring to them as musically "more potent than the Dead Kennedys, plus side-splitting—though unprintable—lyrics."

The band members themselves were more than cognizant of the humor involved in their material. The article quoted bass player Stupid as saying: "You won't hear stuff like this from other bands. This album is for people who want to cut out the world for 45 minutes and *laugh.*" Drummer Bonehead mentioned the "corrosive lyrics" warning sticker and commented: "We thought why hint around that these lyrics might offend somebody, we might as well say right off that they *will* [italics in original] offend everybody. We're sending copies to Jerry Falwell and Oral Roberts, and hopefully they will buy 10,000 at a time for their burnings."

Most tellingly, Bonehead informed the interviewer: "We don't consider ourselves to be a real punk band. We're more a punk *parody.* A lot of other punk bands don't understand us. They're very negative. We go for the morbid stuff, too, but it always has the edge of *humor.* If you take us seriously *you are out of your mind.* It *is* [italics in the original] gross, but it is saying something."

Finally, writer/guitarist/singer Cretin insisted: "People who do not see the *humor* in what we do are either really narrow in their point of view, or else they are a little screwed up in the head. It is blatantly tongue-in-cheek. But we do have a problem with people misinterpreting us. I mean, I have been physically assaulted" (ibid.).

Coincident with the signing of the Dayglo Abortions, Fringe Product began to experience a significant upturn in its fortunes and consequent rate of activity. Whereas the company had issued just over 20 records in its first five years, Fringe put out 16 releases in 1986 alone. The following year it issued another 16 or so albums. The label had clearly entered a growth period and was without question the leading independent alternative record company in Canada at the time.

In early 1988 Fringe issued the Dayglo Abortions' second LP, "Here Today Guano Tomorrow." Although Fringe had a policy of giving artists total creative freedom, viewing its own role as simply manufacturing, promoting, and marketing, according to the band Hoffman had suggested that they make the follow-up album "juicy."[5] If so, the band did not let him down. The cover sported a photo of a hamster with a gun pointed at his head, hovering over a heart-shaped box of chocolates nested innocently on a pink bedspread. The back cover contained a photo of the same scene ostensibly taken several seconds later, only now the gun has been fired and the hamster's blood, guts, and fur are strewn all over the chocolates and pink bedspread. Sample song titles included "Fuck My Shit Stinks," "Fuck Satan to Death," "Drugged and Driving," "Kill Johnny Stiff," and "Hide the Hamster." The latter detailed the practice of shaving, de-fanging, and de-clawing the little critters before inserting them up one's anus for a sexual rush that was quelled only when the hamster suffocated to death. Inside the record was a recipe for "Hamster in Cream Sauce Flambé."

The band's sound on "Here Today Guano Tomorrow" was a little less hardcore, veering more toward heavy metal. Its timing was prescient, since, thanks largely to Metallica, the hardcore and metal audiences had begun to cross-pollinate. By this point Wayne Gretsky had left the group to join D.O.A. Cretin remained the group's songwriter and lead singer in the studio, but having recently become a father (and being employed in a cushy government job), he decided to stop touring. Consequently, two new guitarists came on board: Nev (the Impaler) and Mike Anus.

A Fringe new release bulletin dated 6 May 1988 listed the album, proclaiming: "Hooray! The long awaited 2nd Fringe Product LP release by these sons of Victoria. Known by many, reviled by just as many and calculated to offend. Thrashing, slashing, pulsating rock with savage guitars—hits like F*ck My Sh*t Stinks, Hide the Hamster, Drugged and Driving. A truly great album with a controversial cover." Once again, Fringe was happy to center its marketing efforts on aspects of the group's material that were designed to shock.

Reviews were plentiful, extremely positive, and rarely failed to note the band's pervasive sense of humor. *Sold Out* magazine led off its review with the comment: "These hardcore jokers are back" (*TC* 1988:n.p.). Joe Sary (1988:n.p.) mentioned in *Imprint* that "everything on this album was designed to disgust. But, if you can get over the Dayglows' *[sic]* demented humor, the band's approach to hardcore is actually quite a refreshing change from the more pretentious preachings of most other bands." Another reviewer noted the band's "hard hitting, clever, witty, and downright hilarious" lyrics (Balbier 1988:n.p.).

In *Studying Popular Music,* Richard Middleton (1990) discusses the variation in the level of competence of different listeners/audiences, noting that this variation can, and most likely will, greatly affect which units/parameters become meaningful in a given popular music performance and which meaning(s) will ultimately be conveyed. As should be clear from the reviews cited above, most writers, presumably possessing a basic level of competence with regard to hardcore music, immediately grasped the humor in the Dayglos' work. Back in Nepean, Ontario, Sergeant Fitzgibbons did not possess this level of competence and consequently missed the tongue-in-cheek humor

Charges Are Laid

According to testimony from Sergeant Fitzgibbons at the preliminary hearing, he was disturbed and upset by his daughter's interest in the Dayglos and discussed the contents of the "Feed U.S. A. Fetus" album with his partner and peers. On 17 May 1988 he went to a local Sam the Record Man store at the Bayshore Shopping Center and bought both "Feed U.S. A. Fetus" and "Here Today Guano Tomorrow." After listening to them, he consulted with Sergeant Briar, who headed "Project P," a joint force pornography project of the Ontario Provincial Police and the Metropolitan Toronto Police Force, and with Curt Flanagan of the Crown Attorney's office in Ottawa.

On 13 June 1988 Fitzgibbons applied for a search warrant for Fringe Product's Toronto warehouse. In appendix 4 of the search warrant application, he stated: "After carefully examining the two phonograph records our findings may be summarized as follows: a) Feed U.S.A. Fetus, 1986 Fringe Products [sic]—contents include lyrics outlining explicit violence, oral sex, sexual intercourse and incest. b) Here Today Guano Tomorrow, 1988 Fringe Products—contents include lyrics outlining explicit violence, anal intercourse, rape and bestiality." Copies of the lyric inserts for both LPs were included as addenda to the search warrant application.

On 13 July 1988 police executed the search warrant and seized copies of the two albums, the company's incorporation papers, bank statements, and all paperwork related to the two recordings (communications with the recording studio, pressing orders, royalty statements, invoices, receipts, etc.). On 24 August 1988, after a four-month investigation, charges were laid against Fringe Product and 497906 Ontario Limited of possession and possession for the purpose of distribution of obscene material.[6]

A month later Hoffman hired Toronto attorney Marlys Edwardh of the firm Ruby and Edwardh. On 4 October, in a memo to File, Edwardh noted that she had told Hoffman that the cost of litigation would be between $15,000 and $20,000. Her hourly rate would be $250. That same day Edwardh wrote to the Crown Attorney in Ottawa indicating that she had been retained by Hoffman. She then went on to write:

> The question of whether his possession and distribution of the above-mentioned material involves a criminal offense is of course one, as you will appreciate, that is difficult. It has struck me that we might be able to save both a great deal of time and energy by approaching this case in a different basis. Perhaps in conjunction with your police officers you as the Crown Attorney might review the material in question and if there are some number of deletions that would be appropriate maintaining the integrity of the albums and tapes in question (there are only two for which charges were laid) my client would be prepared to live with these deletions and the record could go forth. For us it is of course difficult to know what precisely is the difficulty, i.e. whether it is the actual words of the songs, or the jacket of the album.

The idea that Fringe might have been willing to acquiesce to being censored is interesting. For a moment or two Hoffman had considered simply editing out the "offending" words so that the album would actually have dead spots. In effect, the censored album would be making an ongoing statement about the fact of censorship itself.[7] Ultimately, though, this game plan was never seriously considered. The real purpose of Edwardh's letter was to get the Crown to reveal what specifically it was alleging to be obscene. The Crown, apparently wanting to get a precedent on the books (no sound recording in Canada had ever been previously deemed obscene), responded negatively, insisting on proceeding by indictment. A preliminary hearing was scheduled for 17 January 1989.

In the meantime, the charges had already begun to affect the regular business of Fringe Product. Roblans, the parent company of Canada's largest record chain, Sam the Record Man, refused to stock Fringe recordings. A handful of smaller retailers followed suit. While these decisions obviously affected sales, a more serious problem loomed on the horizon.

By late 1988, the record industry was in the final stages of switching from the vinyl LP format to compact discs. Only one pressing plant in Ontario—Cinram—was still manufacturing vinyl LPs. On 24 October Hoffman wrote to Edwardh indicating that Cinram had advised him orally that it did not want to fulfill orders that Fringe had recently placed for the Dayglo Abortions' "Here Today Guano Tomorrow" and for an album by the Dead Kennedys. Hoffman wanted to know if the company that manufactured an "obscene" item (as opposed to the company that owns and distributes it) was at risk of being charged. He also wanted Edwardh to tell him if any action could be taken against a company that refused to handle orders for other non-"obscene" product under such circumstances.[8]

In April 1989 Hoffman told Wes Hegg of *Vox* magazine:

> We have two main concerns, the forefront of which is the financial cost of fighting the case. If we can survive that, and presumably we can, our new concerns are dealing with our manufacturers. We have already had manufacturers refuse many of our products. We have submitted a number of things to them recently and they have refused to manufacture them for us.
>
> Essentially what we have now are private individuals censoring. . . . I don't have any objection to industry self regulation but, I think it is a little dangerous when that regulation doesn't come on a voluntary basis [but] comes as a fear of prosecution.
>
> That is one problem, the other which hasn't [happened yet], but that I expect will in the future, is how will this case affect the rest of our releases and how they are treated by the retailers. I'm concerned that stores may have a blatant negative attitude and say, "oh Fringe product thats [sic] that label and oh yeah we don't want any of their stuff" that would be a sad situation for our label and the artists on it. (Hegg 1989:n.p.)

At the time Fringe issued a press release that stated:

> Fringe Product considers these charges to be groundless and a serious breach of the Canadian charter of rights. These charges will convey a substantial financial burden upon those charged, but Fringe is committed to preventing the establishment of any precedent restricting the freedom of expression of Canadian musicians, composers and artists. (Jones 1989:n.p.)

The Preliminary Hearing

At the preliminary hearing on 17 January 1989, Edwardh agreed that the defense would not argue the jurisdiction, lawfulness of the search, or details of the offense as they relate to distribution and production, in return for the Crown's dropping charges against Hoffman personally. The court then discharged Hoffman and heard brief testimony from Vincent Chisholm, an employee at the Sam the Record Man store where Sergeant Fitzgibbons had purchased copies of the two albums, and from Fitzgibbons himself. When cross-examined by Edwardh, Fitzgibbons was asked whether, prior to laying charges, he had spoken with anyone in the music industry to establish "where this kind of music fits, or whether this kind of music and its language was unusual in the genre of music that it represented." He admitted that he had not done this. He also admitted that he had not spoken with any distributors to see if they had received any complaints about this kind of music nor with any psychologists or psychiatrists to see if there was professional or community concern about this type of music. Under cross-examination he also stated that, since the filing of charges against Fringe, he had received a number of letters offering support in condemning this type of music, but that none of these letters indicated that their authors had ever actually listened to the albums. Nonetheless, the judge concluded that there was sufficient evidence to order both of Hoffman's companies to stand trial.

Over the next many months, Edwardh's office began putting together the pieces for the impending trial. Numerous earlier cases were consulted, but the vast majority of these concerned the sale of pornographic videos. Never before in Canada had a record company or distributor been charged with the distribution of obscene material under the provisions adopted in the Criminal Code in 1959.[9] In fact, this was the first case in Canada where the spoken or sung word had been the subject matter of an obscenity charge. There was, though, one interesting Canadian precedent: In 1979 a popular Toronto music and comedy duo named MacLean and MacLean were charged with "unlawfully appear[ing] in an immoral performance by utterances, language, tone, demeanor, singing and otherwise in a theatre" after an appearance at the Water Tower Inn in the small northern Ontario mining town of Sudbury. The pair were originally acquitted on the technicality that the Water Tower Inn was not a "theatre." The Crown appealed the decision, and at a new trial in late October 1981 they were found guilty. Ultimately they were discharged.

In addition to rifling through past court cases, Edwardh's office began to look into potential "expert" witnesses. The kinds of experts they contemplated fell into two general categories: (1) academics and (2) members of the music industry. The latter group included executives at the major record labels, radio station owners and program directors, music journalists, musicians, and Sam Sniderman, the owner of Canada's largest retail record chain. Early on the defense settled on Daniel Richler, a high-profile freelance journalist and broadcaster who came with the added cachet of being related to the famed Canadian novelist Mordecai Richler. On 25 January 1989 Edwardh wrote Hoffman with one more idea for an expert witness from the music industry: "I have done some further work in preparing your case and during one of my conversations with Mel Greene he suggested to me that there was no reason that we should not call upon Frank Zapa [sic] as he has often spearheaded this issue in the United States. Mel thought he might be sufficiently interested to come for as little as his costs." The letter went on to ask Hoffman if he knew how to contact Zappa, and suggested that if he didn't, maybe Daniel Richler did. Nothing was to come of this idea.

A number of academics were approached and offered a small fee to submit written opinions regarding the material on the two Dayglo albums and/or to come down to Edwardh's office to speak with her about the material. Most of the academics consulted called the material juvenile, tasteless, and verging on being offensive, but none interpreted the songs of the Dayglo Abortions as ultimately obscene.

Section 163 of the Criminal Code of Canada defines a publication as obscene when "a dominant characteristic of which is the undue exploitation of sex." To a person, the academics Edwardh consulted found that the Dayglos' recordings were not primarily about sex at all. Verda Berstein stressed that the two defining characteristics of pornography—erotic sex and sexism—were not dominant themes in the songs. She felt that the primary theme was the violence—physical, economic, psychological—that is done daily to numerous people in our society, and further noted that the performances were devoid of eroticism. In its place she heard tremendous distress in the "vocalization," arguing that the Cretin sounded like an "animal in a cage." Berstein went on to say that she very much liked the group's sense of social criticism.[10]

Self-described "feminist sociologist" Mariana Valverde, a professor of sociology and women's studies at Trent University and an active researcher on pornography, told Edwardh that there was no attempt at eroticism in the recordings. She astutely noted that in order to interpret the meaning of popular music performances, one had to take into account performance practice as well as the actual words. To her ears, the Cretin's singing style made no attempt at being seductive. She also stated that violence was not the primary element in the songs, that the aggression that was there was not directed at women, and that "many of the descriptions of gruesome violence are clearly fantastical and meant at least partially as parodies of what right-thinking people imagine punk culture to be." Further, Valverde argued, the aggression that was evident on the recordings was aimed at the "establishment," the performances being deliberately constructed so that they "aimed at offending our good taste." She concluded that this was intrinsic to the group's message and was typical of much expression within adolescent culture (memo from Valverde to Edwardh, 16 October 1988).

Wayne Sumner, then chair of the department of philosophy at the University of Toronto and an expert on moral philosophy, pointed out that the records do not degrade a social group or class, such as a particular race or gender. There was no generic target; rather, the songs targeted individuals. Much of the material, he observed, including the Nancy and Ronald Reagan cover, was designed to shock and might be disgusting by some standards, but it was not degrading. He saw such material as an obvious statement about hypocrisy and noted that under section 163 of the Criminal Code, a "publication cannot exploit sex unless it is about sex. However, most of the material in these albums has little or no sexual content." He saw the Dayglos' material as being about anger, hostility, and an aggression whose principal targets are Americans, religious groups, political authority, and so on, articulated with roughly equal measures of despair, self-hatred, self-destruction, and fantasies of power. He concluded with the salient point (also offered by other academics) that the violence and sexual material in the Dayglos' songs was not designed to titillate or arouse:

> Instead, their purpose seems both personal and political. They are personal in that they are expressions of outrage or anger; they are political in that these feelings are located both in a specific class and in a specific gender. The targets of outrage are the institutions experienced as oppressive by a male underclass of social losers (in their own eyes as well as the eyes of others). That underclass has its own language, and much of it is not very pretty. . . . Given their powerlessness, their only available weapon was shock. But it is not offence for the mere sake of offence; it has a larger political agenda. (Letter to Edwardh, 11 November 1988)

For the trial Edwardh decided to call as a witness a Toronto psychiatrist, Dr. Richard Mean, then head of the Syl Apps Youth Center. Dr. Mean thought that the two albums had a number of positive attributes: (1) they were pro-Canadian; (2) they contained clever political statements; and (3) they were not about self-destruction. Further, he felt that "the theme was not one of dominant sexuality, criminality or aggression but instead is a political theme of despondency and desperation and disappointment in a society that has produced impotent family units and ineffective governments" (letter to Edwardh, 27 March 1989). He concluded by asserting that these recordings were potentially healthy vehicles, since adolescents take comfort in knowing that others have similar feelings. According to Dr. Mean, overprotection of adolescents ultimately produces greater vulnerability.

In April 1989, while the defense awaited a trial date, further complications ensued. Both the Ontario Provincial Police (OPP) and the police force of London, Ontario, received complaints about the Dayglo Abortions, and both were considering laying charges.[11] The Ottawa trial had originally been scheduled for May but was moved to June when Dr. Mean underwent an emergency operation. The new trial date of 12 June was then moved because the Crown attorney had to be at a murder trial in Belleville, Ontario. Upon being informed of the possible charges by the OPP and the London police force, Edwardh immediately put pressure on the Crown to get both police forces to delay pressing charges until a decision had been made by the Ottawa court. If the Crown did not do this, she indicated, she would withdraw her consent to the adjournment of the June court date. After much to-ing and fro-ing, both police forces agreed to not lay charges at the present time. Edwardh subsequently pointed out to Hoffman that if he was convicted in Ottawa, the Crown might take the position that his continued distribution of the records after the charge would "aggravate the question of disposition, in other words, the fine may be greater in light of the continued distribution of the records while facing an obscenity charge" (letter, 9 May 1989).

The Constitutional Challenge

While Edwardh and her staff were busy collecting the opinions of potential experts, they were also preparing a constitutional challenge to the provisions of section 163 of the Criminal Code of Canada governing obscenity. Notice of the constitutional challenge was filed on 20 October 1989, while the particulars of the challenge were filed on 27 October. In essence Edwardh's challenge argued that the provisions were unconstitutional because (1) they represented an unjustifiable restriction on freedom of expression and (2) the provisions contained an unconstitutional reverse onus that violated an accused person's presumption of innocence. The latter claim referred specifically to section 163 (3), which states: "No person shall be convicted of an offence under this section if he establishes that the public good was served by the acts that are alleged to constitute the offence and that the acts alleged did not extend beyond what served the public good." Edwardh argued that the defense should not have to prove that the Dayglos' recordings served "the public good." Rather, the Crown should have to prove "beyond a reasonable doubt" that the group's recordings do *not* serve the public good.

The challenge was heard in court over a period of several weeks (31 October–2 November, 21–23 November, and 28 November 1989) and proved to be quite a circus. The Crown's argument during the constitutional challenge hearings centered on a "notwithstanding" clause in the charter, which, in effect, stated that a law which violates the charter may be held to be constitutional if the intent of said law is to prevent harm. Consequently, the Crown spent most of the hearing attempting to prove that pornography was indeed harmful. If it was successful, the judge would have to conclude that the law was valid even if it did violate the charter.

The Crown relied exclusively on the testimony of one expert witness, Professor James Check of the psychology department at York University. Professor Check had been active for quite some time both as a researcher into the effects of pornography and as an expert witness at a number of trials involving pornographic material. His only work with music had involved a brief study of rock videos. Professor Check stated in the witness box that he divided sexually explicit material into three categories: (1) sexually violent pornography; (2) nonviolent dehumanizing or degrading pornography, in which human beings are objectified to the point where their only value "depends on the quality of their genitals and breasts"; and (3) nonpornographic erotica. In his research he had come to the conclusion that videos with material fitting categories 1 and 2 would increase the likelihood of viewers' committing rape or forced sexual acts. This likelihood increases with repeated exposure, argued Check, and prolonged exposure leads people to not want to have children and to feel reduced sexual satisfaction with a single partner. Finally, Check claimed that such material leads immediately after exposure to feelings of anxiety, depression, and hostility. He felt that this type of material would have an even greater effect on 12- to 15-year-olds, who would typically have relatively little sexual experience. When asked if he could draw any inferences from his research on the possible effect of such material in recorded song form, Professor Check stated that it was his opinion that material in the form of a rock recording that fitted into the first two categories would probably have an even greater effect than similar material in a video, given the fact that rock groups were imaged as something to be looked up to.

For the constitutional challenge Edwardh relied on a different set of expert witnesses than the ones she would use at the trial itself. She called, in order, Professor Edward Donnerstein from the University of California in Santa Barbara, an expert on the effects of pornography; Vivienne Monty, past president of the Canadian Library Association and a librarian at York University; Professor H. Taylor Buckner from the sociology and anthropology department of Concordia University in Montreal, an expert in statistics and survey research; and Professor Daniel Sansfacon from the department of sexology at the University of Quebec in Montreal.

Monty was called simply to state that from the point of view of the Canadian Library Association, recordings such as those of the Dayglo Abortions would be considered valid items of cultural expression and would be worth collecting and preserving. Donnerstein argued that R-rated films have more violence against women than X-rated films, and that social problems arising from film and video were ultimately related to violence, not material that was sexually explicit. Buckner discredited Check's survey and statistical methodology. Even more damning was Sansfacon's testimony. In 1984–85, during the Fraser Commission on pornography, Sansfacon had been head of research for the Department of Justice. The commission had hired Check to conduct a research program but found both his research and his subsequent report to be highly problematic. Two external reviewers for the commission, in fact, found that Check's report did not meet basic scientific research standards, and that his methodology was particularly problematic. It was specifically noted that (1) improper instructions were given to his informants; (2) his surveys were not professionally tested; and (3) his conclusions were much too affirmative, given the constraints and limitations of the methodology.

On 26 January 1990, Ontario District Court Judge Louise Charron ruled on the reverse onus clause of section 163 (3), whereby the defense had to prove that the material served the public good. It was indeed unconstitutional, she ruled, but she disagreed with Edwardh's challenge that section 163 represented an unjustifiable restriction on freedom of expression. Although the judge admitted that sections 163 (1) (a) and 163 (8) limited the freedom of expression of certain individuals to a certain extent, she found that

> these effects are proportional to the objective pursued. The restrictive effect on the individual's freedom of expression does not outweigh the importance of the objective. The matter is too important to be left to the free choice of individuals or to the market. The market does not take into account possible harm to others or to the consumers. It does not take into account affronts to values fundamental to our Canadian society.

Consequently, Fringe Product Inc. and 497906 Ontario Ltd. were still required to stand trial for the possession and possession for the purpose of distribution of obscene material. Hugh Hefner's Playboy Foundation paid the expenses related to Donnerstein's testimony. It had been Edwardh's idea to see whether *Playboy* would lend support for the defense. She similarly sought support from *Hustler*, but none was forthcoming. Not so surprisingly, there was no support from the Canadian record industry at large.

"That played a big part in me becoming disenchanted with the record business," Hoffman told me in the fall of 2000. "For a brief period I was really shocked that I got no support from the industry. . . . There were a couple of people who expressed 'not for publication' support. I thought that was kind of weak kneed." These unnamed individuals, in fact, told Hoffman outright that if he mentioned their support in public, they would simply deny it. After the trial he complained to writer Paul Kelly that "nobody from the majors or the trade media spoke out on our behalf. This is a problem which could very well affect themselves. Everyone is vulnerable but nobody high up wanted to stick their neck out" (Kelly n.d.). Clearly, everyone in the industry was running scared.

Particulars of the Charges

Both prior to the constitutional challenge and subsequent to it, Edwardh hounded Crown Attorney Curt Flanagan and his successor, Celynne Dorval, to provide the defense with "particulars by way of identifying whether [the Crown] would be relying on one or both covers of the albums or whether or not [the Crown] would be identifying any particular song or songs that [it] alleges to be obscene. As the matter now stands, I have no ideas which songs or whether the covers themselves are alleged to be obscene" (letter from Edwardh to Flanagan, 19 October 1989).

On 13 February 1990 Assistant Crown Attorney Celynne Dorval finally provided the particulars, informing Edwardh that the Crown was alleging that the following 11 songs (out of the 31 contained on the two albums) were obscene: "Argh Fuck Kill," "Inside My Head," "Proud to Be Canadian," "Kill the Hosers," "Religious Bumfucks," "1967," "I Killed Mommy," and "Suicide" from "Feed U.S. A. Fetus" and "Fuck Satan to Death," "Hide the Hamsters," and "Kill Johnny Stiff" from "Here Today Guano Tomorrow."

Edwardh asked Hoffman to get the Dayglos' songwriter, Cretin (Murray Acton), to put on paper what the songs were about. His responses were quite revealing:

"Argh Fuck Kill": This song is basically a retaliation to a review we recieved [sic] in which the reviewer accused us of being another stupid punk rock band with nothing to say but "bla bla bla arg fuck kill lyrics."

"Kill the Hosers": This is a song that portrays the bad attitude and single minded desire for sex and violence in many of todays [sic] youth. The story is told from the participants [sic] view point, using language common to the character.

"I Killed Mommy": This song is the ultimate paridy [sic] of the cliche punk rocker. It is about a kid who hates his entire family, and feels repressed by their guidance. He exaggerates little flaws of character he feels his parents have, and rebels in the ultimate fashion when his mother tries to deal with him.

"1967": This is a song about the arrogance displayed by the children of the rich. It is told from their point of view because it made it easy to portray a feeling of self superiority.

"Hide the Hamster": I suppose this song could prove to be highly offensive to some listeners and I can't dissagree [sic] with them on that. I will say however that it is completely based on reality. The idea came from a newspaper clip I saw in SanFrancisco [sic] about a man who was given 5 years in jail on an animal cruelty charge for, you can guess. I know this is a repulsive story but I felt it had to be covered.

"Religious Bumfucks": This is a pretty harsh song about evangelical religius [sic] fanatics told from the point of view of a person who is completely fed up with the scare tactics they use to recruit followers. Strong language is used to enforce the feeling of anger felt by the person on whom the song focuses.

"Suicide": Yet another parody of a punk rocker but this one is alot [sic] blacker. The star of the story talks about the hideous acts of rebellion he has already committed and about his desire to commit the ultimate act of rebellion by taking his own life.

"Fuck Satan to Death": This is another Dayglo paridy [sic]. It is a spin off on the standard Satin [sic] worshipping Heavy Metal mongrels that so many people are trying to protect us from.

"Kill Johnny Stiff": This song stirred up a real hornets [sic] nest. It is our generic hate
song, and has been performed with many other people as the focal point. No Names
have been changed to protect the guilty so I guess it could be hard to justify, even
though it is an obvious exaggeration. (Fax from Acton to Fringe, January 1989)

Clearly the majority of the Dayglos' songs were written from the point of view
of a recognizable, real-life protagonist. Acton recognized and deliberately used the
literary devices of parody and exaggeration, writing in a fictional voice to get the
essence of these characters across. "The way I write songs," he explained to Bruce
Skeaff (1988) of the *Victoria Times-Colonist,* "is seeing things I think are naive or
stupid, like a mindless television commercial, then twisting it around to make
something satirical about it. Strong language has to be part of the message when
writing from the perspective of some characters in the music." Acton concluded that
calling his lyrics obscene was analogous to labeling a novel involving a murder as
obscene because society considers murder an obscenity.

While trying to get the particulars of the charge from the Crown, Edwardh also
suggested to the Crown that the case be tried before a judge alone. On 19 February 1990 Dorval replied by letter, registering surprise at such a suggestion:

In view of the nature of the community standard of tolerance test and the novelty of
the subject matter alleged to be obscene, I strongly believe that the case should be tried
before a judge and jury. In my view, the jury representing a cross-section of the population can more easily assess the "pulse of the nation" on this issue.

The "community standard of tolerance test" proved to be an important part of the
trial. In the United States the community standards test is a test of majority approval
of the ideas represented. It is a test of taste (what the majority likes or believes). In
Canada the community standards test is a test of tolerance—what the average Canadian will tolerate other Canadians' seeing or hearing, not what the average Canadian will watch or listen to himself or herself. Under Canadian law, the community standards test is ultimately a test for obscenity, not merit *per se.*

Dorval was to hold sway, and the case was ultimately heard before a jury in
November 1990. One of the interesting ramifications of this outcome was that
since the decision in this case was rendered by a jury and not by a judge, it is not
considered a binding precedent. Consequently, how the obscenity provisions in
Canada's Criminal Code should be interpreted with regard to popular songs is still
very much up in the air.

Money Blues

As the case dragged on, Edwardh's original estimate to Hoffman that the trial would
cost between $15,000 and $20,000 was proving to be unrealistic. In fact, the trial
would ultimately cost nearly $90,000. By the spring of 1990, Hoffman was well

behind in his payments. With Hoffman's unpaid bill in mind and anticipating that, no matter who ultimately won this round, the case would be appealed to the Ontario Court of Appeal and perhaps the Supreme Court of Canada, Edwardh wrote to Alan Borovoy of the Canadian Civil Liberties Association on 16 April 1990, inquiring whether the association would be willing to handle the appeal. Borovoy indicated that the CCLA would be interested, but when asked later if the CCLA might take on the trial itself, he demurred.

The files in Edwardh's law office pertaining to the case are filled with letters and memos concerning the state of Hoffman's account. On 20 April 1990 Hoffman wrote to Edwardh outlining a payment schedule whereby he would send a check for $1,500 every two weeks. Hoffman ended the letter: "I will of course try to make additional payments from time to time but I don't want to make promises. This of course leaves a substantial amount that will not be forgotten, as you know anything can happen in this business, one hit and everything is taken care of."

The first check was included with the letter. Checks followed through the end of May, and then they appear to have stopped. At some point efforts were made to see if Legal Aid would pay for the case, but since Hoffman was no longer personally charged, this was not an option.

On 16 August 1990 Hoffman wrote to Edwardh saying, "I'm sorry that I have not been in contact over the past couple of months. Basically the financial state of Fringe Product has been none too good as of late and I have not been able to live up to the promises I made in May. I've put together a few dollars ($1,200.00) to send you and I am hopeful that I will be able to send more in the coming weeks. Thank you for your patience and understanding, be assured that I will make every effort to clear up the account prior to the November trial date."

Attached to this letter in Edwardh's file was a sticky note written by her secretary and dated 20 August. It stated that Ruby and Edwardh employee "Dan [Brodsky] has left messages for Ben to call but he hasn't returned Dan's calls. Dan says he will continue to try and fire him unless you state otherwise." Clearly Edwardh and her office were not happy.

On 24 August 1990 Brodsky wrote a memo to Edwardh stating that he had spoken to Hoffman that morning and informed him that Ruby and Edwardh had no alternative but to apply to "withdraw from the record" in the case. On 8 October 1990 Brodsky wrote to Hoffman stating: "We are now formally off the record in your case which is currently scheduled to commence in early November." He went on to request that Hoffman contact him, since Brodsky and Edwardh had ideas to discuss

so that your appeal may be preserved if a conviction is registered. As I am sure you are aware the Canadian Civil Liberties Association has expressed a great deal of interest in carrying on the appeal without cost to you following the trial. In my opinion we have worked far too hard to give up at this stage.

When push came to shove, Hoffman phoned Edwardh a few days before the trial to tell her that he intended to show up in court and simply state that his lawyer would not come because he was behind in paying his bills. Hoffman was gambling that Ruby and Edwardh were too media-conscious to allow this to actually happen. The next day Edwardh phoned him to say that she had her ticket for Ottawa and would see him in court.

While the charges clearly had a negative impact on Hoffman, they also had some adverse effects on the Dayglos' career. When the group began to prepare to record their next album in the summer of 1990, their usual studio, Legacy Productions, refused to book them studio time, having been advised by a Victoria lawyer that the studio, too, could be liable for obscenity charges under the vaguely worded Criminal Code. At least one club refused to honor a previously arranged booking, and another refused to advertise the band's name, resulting in a sparsely attended show and reduced earnings. In 1990 Acton stated that the charges had kept the group from recording for two years and thereby cost them a number of performing opportunities. The net effect was a loss of income from the only two significant revenue streams available to a band.

It should also be noted, though, that at various points the Dayglo Abortions gleefully stated that the charges, ironically, helped them to raise their profile considerably. In the *Ottawa Citizen* they were quoted as saying that the charges were "the biggest lottery ticket possible" (Bindman 1990). Earlier Acton was quoted in the *Victoria Times-Colonist* (21 October 1988) as saying: "Bad publicity is the best publicity. It seems like people never learn." According to Hoffman, sales of Dayglo Abortions records and CDs increased by about 25 percent as a result of the charges.

In the meantime, the increasing costs of the trial were undermining the relationship between Hoffman and the band. As is the case with all record and book contracts, the agreement between the Dayglo Abortions and Fringe included a liability clause giving the record company the right to withhold royalties due the band to pay the costs of any litigation arising as a result of the band's material. When Fringe began to withhold royalties and apply them to the mounting cost of the defense, the band was outraged and retaliated by writing and recording a disparaging song called "Ben Gets Off," included on the subsequent Fringe-distributed album "Two Dogs Fucking." This would be the last Dayglo album to be released by Fringe; the next several Dayglo albums included more songs that maligned Hoffman in every conceivable way.

The Trial

The trial finally got under way on Monday, 5 November 1990. Crown Attorney Celynne Dorval spent the first two hours presenting her case, which included the playing in court of both albums. During the remainder of the day, Edwardh presented the defense's case. On Tuesday Daniel Richler took the stand, followed by Dr. Mean on Wednesday. The Crown presented no witnesses. On Thursday Dorval and Edwardh summarized their respective cases, and Judge Charron spent an hour instructing the jury on the law.

Richler spoke at length during his initial examination and cross-examination about the tradition of punk. He repeatedly stressed that punk in general, and the Dayglos' material in particular, expressed disaffection, cynicism, anger, and mistrust. He pointed out that in punk language tends to be raw and that songs tend to mirror society and are often designed to shock. Both attorneys walked Richler through the allegedly obscene material song by song. He repeatedly pointed out that the songs were written from the point of view of fictionalized characters, that there was actually very little sex in them, and that the sexual content that was there was not designed to titillate. Finally, he took pains to explain that words such as "fuck" in "Argh Fuck Kill" and "bumfucks" in "Religious Bumfucks" had nothing to do with sex and instead were simply widely recognized intensifiers used routinely within the punk/alternative community that would be consuming this material.

Dr. Mean was presented as an expert witness whose regular consultations with parents of troubled adolescents gave him a good grip on the concerns of parents at large. He testified that he approached the two albums as he would a patient. The overall theme that he heard being expressed was a combination of desperation, despondency, and impotence. He interpreted the Dayglo Abortions' material as a statement that they are isolated and crying for help. When asked about the sexual content in several songs, he pointed out that there was no sexual fulfillment in the songs and that there was no titillation. The violent imagery, he felt, was used primarily to get attention. Neither violence nor sex, though, according to Dr. Mean, was a dominant theme in the Dayglos' work. Further, the issues that their material addressed were ones routinely talked about by adolescents. Dr. Mean saw this as extremely important, asserting that the Dayglos' material provided catharsis for its audience. Much of the material might be in bad taste, but it was ultimately healthy for adolescents to hear that they were not alone in their concerns and to see the act of making music as an alternative, in and of itself, to antisocial or self-destructive behavior. He also pointed out that one cannot separate the words from the music, that most adolescents would not take much that was stated in the words concretely, and that they would interpret the material as a complete package, not as isolated images from specific songs.

Edwardh's summation on the last day of the trial was nothing short of brilliant. She pointed out to the jury that the only real issue was whether the two records are obscene and that the Criminal Code of Canada states that "a matter will be obscene if (1) a dominant characteristic of the material is the undue exploitation of sex or sex and violence, crime, harm or cruelty."[12] Therefore, she stressed, if the jury found that sex or sex and violence, crime, harm or cruelty were not dominant themes, they must acquit. She defined dominant themes as those that run through albums as complete entities, not themes that are present in one or another specific song, and she recapitulated Richler's and Mean's testimony to assert that sex was in no way a dominant theme on either record. If the jury was unable to find a theme for each record, she continued, then each of the songs identified by the Crown in its list of particulars must be assessed separately. Reviewing the testimony of both witnesses song by song, she again concluded that sex was not a dominant characteristic of the Dayglo Abortions' material.

In part two of her summation, Edwardh told the jury that if they *did* find that sex or sex and violence, crime or cruelty was a dominant characteristic of the recordings, then they must ask themselves if the exploitation of sex was undue. There is no impropriety in Canadian law regarding the exploitation of sex. Material is only obscene if such exploitation is undue. To be undue, the exploitation of sex must go clearly beyond contemporary Canadian community standards of tolerance. This standard has nothing to do with personal taste, nothing to do with liking or disliking the material, and nothing to do with approving the acts described. Edwardh stressed that this standard had to be reflective of all Canadians coast to coast, south to north, in "our modern society," of those who live in Newfoundland fishing villages, northern Ontario mining towns, and large "sophisticated urban centers," not just of a segment of the community. She also pointed out that this standard relates to what would be acceptable for *adults* to hear. If the jury found that the material was inappropriate for certain age groups, then that would be an issue for governmental or industry regulation, but it had nothing to do with whether the material was obscene.

Edwardh spoke of what Canadians clearly do tolerate in films and the arts in general and pointed out that the only line that Canadians seem willing to draw occurs at the point where seeing or hearing material might cause harm. From what had been heard in court, it was clear that no potential harm would result from hearing these records. Edwardh summarized both Richler's and Mean's testimony that these records fell well within the Canadian community's standard of tolerance and that they would not cause harm. Far from causing harm, in fact, she asserted that Dr. Mean found positive social value in these albums.

Edwardh concluded her summation by pointing out that the Crown did not call any evidence to rebut that put forward by Richler and Mean:

> Our law entitles her to this. Ask yourself Why? Only one answer—none was to be had. I urge you, Ladies and Gentlemen of [the] Jury, on behalf of all Canadians render a verdict of not guilty—and thereby take the side of open expression and communication over silence—of tolerance over the imposition of controls—of contact with and understanding of the turbulence of adolescents.

Crown Attorney Celynne Dorval, summarizing the Crown's case, pointed out various lines in the Dayglos' lyrics that depicted violence, sodomy, and bestiality. She went on to assert that the group's material did not use sexual imagery as thematic expressions of alienation and rage, but to sell records, adding that the sexual imagery in the albums was "brutal, cruel and salacious" and fell outside the boundaries of existing community standards (Harris 1990b). She concluded by urging the jury to rely on its own common sense rather than on the testimony of supposed experts.

The jury of three men and nine women took nearly ten hours to reach a decision. At first they were deadlocked, but the judge refused to declare a hung jury and urged them to continue discussions. At one point they came back in and asked the judge if only one song needed to be judged obscene beyond a reasonable doubt. The judge replied that one song would be enough to render a conviction. Later the jury requested that a stereo system be brought in so that they could hear the records again. Late at night on Thursday, 8 November, they finally returned a unanimous verdict of not guilty, ending two years of hell for Ben Hoffman. Seven days later Edwardh wrote to Hoffman to tell him that the OPP had decided to respect the court's decision and therefor would not lay charges against Fringe. The London Police Force also elected to drop its investigation. The Crown eventually decided not to appeal.

Edwardh told the *Globe and Mail* (Harris 1990b) that the verdict "sends out another message to government"—namely, that they needed to write better legislation if they wanted a statute to deal with these issues. She also suggested that redress in such cases would be better sought through regulation than through prosecution (ibid.). The *Ottawa Citizen* quoted her as saying that the jury's struggle to reach a verdict was evidence that the obscenity laws needed to be changed: "It's a classic example that the governing notion of community standards is one that's awfully hard for [a jury] to actually find and then apply. . . . It's almost a mystical notion" (Payne 1990).

The reaction in the Canadian media was predictably mixed. Church groups railed against the acquittal, as did right-wing columnists. Des Burge, a spokesman for the Roman Catholic archdiocese of Toronto, told the *Globe and Mail* that the church was disappointed with the verdict. "The law is meant to protect decency and public morals. If it's not doing that, then it should be tightened up and improved" (*Globe and Mail*, 10 November 1990). Burge urged the Crown to appeal the acquittal. Ken Campbell of the evangelical Renaissance International Church expressed similar sentiments. Daniel Weller, general secretary of the Anglican Church, said that although the lyrics shocked him, the trial verdict did not. "All kinds of abhorrent things are allowed to go on," he told the *Toronto Star*, "and this appears to be one of them" (Dafoe 1990a).

Conservative newspaper columnist Tom Harpur attacked the jury's decision in his 18 November 1990 column, expressing his concern that "the recording industry in Canada has virtually carte blanche when it comes to the corruption of the taste—and minds—of our youth" (Harpur 1990a). On 7 December 1990 he noted:

> My [earlier] column ended with a call for a ban on records "pushing or celebrating suicide, rape, incest or murder" and an appeal of the DayGlo [sic] acquittal. At the moment of writing, I haven't received one letter agreeing with my stand while there have been half a dozen or so castigating me for allegedly espousing censorship and opposing true freedom of speech. There have been angry letters to the editor as well.

Despite his acknowledgment that his readers were clearly not on his side, he concluded his second column on the subject by labeling the Dayglos' songs as "cruel, racist, misogynist, violent, toxic waste that ought to be dealt with. . . . I don't care if a hundred juries pronounce it innocent; it is sheer, unmitigated filth for filth's sake," and stating, "If more people knew what their kids are listening to, my bet is these groups would soon either have to discipline themselves or face some real consequences" (Harpur 1990b).

Members of the country's music industry, just as predictably, hailed the acquittal as a landmark decision upholding the right of musicians as well as other artists to freedom of expression. Brian Robertson of the Canadian Recording Industry Association (CRIA) was quoted in the *Toronto Star* as stating: "We're very pleased with the result. If (the jury) had found against them, I think you would have had a red alert at all the record companies. Every company would be pouring over lyric sheets and cover graphics" (Dafoe 1990a).

The same article quoted Ben Hoffman as saying that the verdict sends a message to the record industry that some caution must be used, "but it reinforces what the record industry has always believed—that people should be able to express themselves the way they want to." It also quoted Dayglo songwriter Murray Acton as saying that the verdict "reaffirms my faith in the average citizen of Canada." Acton also happily informed the press that the title song of the group's subsequent release, "Two Dogs Fucking," was "about the mayor of this small uptight community who's walking through the park and sees these two dogs . . . uh, fornicating. And he freaks out because this obscene act is happening in a public place and he calls the police and they throw a bucket of water on the dogs. But it turns out that one of the dogs—I get really contrived sometimes—is an alien life form who gets mad and destroys the planet. It's kind of a parable about the trial" (Dafoe 1990b).

Alan Borovoy, general counsel for the Canadian Civil Liberties Association, pointed out that the case, as well as a charge filed a month earlier against a London, Ontario, book retailer for selling copies of 2 Live Crew's "As Nasty As They Wanna Be," helped to challenge Canada's obscenity laws:

> What's most important about these cases . . . is not so much what's on the record or that, but rather the fairness of the law itself. That is what must be challenged. There's something patently unfair about a law that imposes such vague standards as this one does, which talks about "undue exploitation of sex" and says material to be sold must measure up to "community standards." (Harris 1990a)

Borovoy further asserted that the law as it stands makes police forces into "public arbiters of artistic taste (ibid.). Hoffman had pointed out a year earlier that when the charges were laid, he was unable to get a definition of obscenity: "The big problem when you are going to put out a record like this is there is no place to go to get guidance" (Payne 1989):

> The difference between myself and someone who's caught stealing is that a thief usually knows he's breaking the law. . . . I find it a little scary that these things originate from the police and never seem to arise from legitimate complaints or public outrage. The matter seems to be entirely in the hands of the authorities. (Kelly n.d.)

While the acquittal was obviously great news for Hoffman, the matter of an unpaid bill remained. "When you are confronted with this type of charge you are automatically in a no-win situation," he complained. "It's going to cost you in terms of time, energy and money no matter what the verdict is and because this was a test case the fines levied would have been small compared to what we've actually had to pay. Even during the trial it seemed the onus was on us to prove that the records were not obscene which is a bit of a reverse of the 'innocent until proven guilty' dictum" (ibid.).

The Aftermath

A number of benefits were held in both Toronto and Vancouver, the most successful being staged by No Means No and Jello Biafra at Vancouver's Commodore Ballroom on 11 November 1990. That particular gig netted Fringe close to $8,000. In total between $20,000 and $25,000 was raised by benefits and donations mailed in by fans and supporters. Counted among the latter were a number of five- and 10-dollar contributions to the Fringe Defense Fund by punk rock fans scattered across the country. Fringe itself probably paid $25,000 to $30,000 out of pocket (although some of this would have come from royalties due the Dayglo Abortions), leaving Ruby and Edwardh short $35,000 to $45,000.

Judging from outside appearances, Fringe was crippled in the short term and never recovered its position as the country's dominant cutting-edge alternative label. In addition the Record Peddler sharply curtailed its activities as both a distributor and a retailer in the aftermath of the trial. In 1996 Hoffman formally shut Fringe down, and the Record Peddler became a shadow of what it used to be, finally shutting its doors in 2001. Just before the trial, Hoffman was quoted in the *Globe and Mail* as saying that the cost of mounting a defense forced him to scale down operations at both his companies. "It has prevented me from releasing a number of records that I otherwise would have. Also, it's affected how we look at new product coming in—you begin to see potential trouble in everything" (Harris 1990a).

"There's been no growth for three years," he told Paul Kelly (n.d.), "and we were never able to commit money to new projects due to our uncertainty about the future." In an interview with Mitch Potter in mid-1989, Hoffman stated that "Fringe is established enough to survive, but I'd say at least five Canadian acts won't be released on our label this year because of what this fight has cost" (Potter 1989). In late 2000 Hoffman had a somewhat different point of view, claiming that the downturn in his companies' fortunes was only tangentially connected to the trial. The slow demise of Fringe and the downsizing of the Record Peddler he attributes to three factors: (1) the refusal in the same time period as the trial of two of Canada's largest independent distributors, Cargo and Electric, to pay Fringe money owed in excess of $50,000; (2) the drastic change in the retailing of CDs caused by the opening of megastores such as HMV and Tower in the early 1990s; and (3) the Dayglos' trial. These three developments in combination left Hoffman severely disenchanted with both music and the music business.

Although it would be inaccurate to state that the Dayglos' trial destroyed Fringe, Hoffman admits that the label probably would have been forced into bankruptcy had Ruby and Edwardh decided to play hardball in collecting the fees owed them. All this because one parent did not like what his daughter was listening to, and that parent happened to be a police officer. While Sergeant Fitzgibbons was undoubtedly sincere in his actions, it is a cruel fact of the Canadian justice system that when the police decide to lay charges, one is going to be penalized by massive legal fees even when one is found to be innocent. If a private citizen brings a suit against an individual or company that proves to be without merit, the plaintiff must pay court costs. When the state brings an ultimately meritless suit, the targeted citizen or private company bears the cost. This means, of course, that the police and the Crown have nothing to lose in bringing forward such charges, and it also means that members of Canada's record industry undoubtedly have, since the Dayglo Abortions case, become a little more circumspect about what they are willing to release. It has also meant that the liability clauses in record contracts are now much more extensive and complex, attempting to protect the record company from any and all possible costs. All of this will, of course, trickle down to most artists, causing them to pause before deciding to issue musical performances that might raise the ire of someone like Sergeant Fitzgibbons.

No public complaint existed against the Dayglo Abortions before obscenity charges were filed in August 1998. In November 1990 Fringe Product and its holding company, 497906 Ontario Limited, were acquitted of all charges. At no time were "Feed U.S. A. Fetus" and "Here Today Guano Tomorrow" ever taken out of the marketplace, but censorship, at some level, *did* occur. In the short term, some retailers refused to stock the recordings, and one major manufacturer refused to press it (as well as other Fringe releases). Although it is difficult to assess the long-term effects the trial has had on the Canadian record industry, it is hard to believe that

Canadian artists and record companies, large and small, have not engaged, at least subconsciously, in self-censorship. The costs are simply too high to take such risks. At the very least, an artist wishing to push the envelope at this level is most likely forgoing any chance of being signed by a major label.[13]

In a truly free and democratic society, these events should simply never have happened.

> We've always shocked people and grossed them out—that was part of the fun. But it was always intended to be so blown out of proportion that it would have been taken as a black joke. (Acton, quoted in Dafoe 1990c)

Notes

1. While it is commonly referred to as Fringe Records, owner Ben Hoffman has always very specifically insisted that the company is called Fringe Product.

2. The bass player on the band's first EP, "Out of the Womb," is named Stupid. Although he does not appear to be the same person as Spud a.k.a. Trevor Hagen, later Dayglo promotional material refers to Spud as "an original Dayglo."

3. Unless indicated otherwise, italics in this chapter were not in the original articles.

4. These quotations come from undated and unattributed photocopies from the files of Hoffman's former lawyer, Marlys Edwardh.

5. Hoffman does not remember saying this, although he told me it is plausible that he was asked if they should "tone it down," and that he responded, "No, go for it," which could easily have been interpreted as "make it juicy."

6. The band could not be charged, since in Canada it is not a crime to create obscene material, but only to possess or distribute it. The maximum penalty Ben Hoffman faced personally was two years imprisonment and a $50,000 fine. At the outset he told *Vox* magazine that he did not expect to be convicted, and if he was, he thought that at most he would receive "a token modest fine."

7. The band was unaware of Edwardh's offer to the Crown, but obviously would have been consulted before any such tampering with the album occurred.

8. A few weeks later the company that had previously been pressing Fringe LPs reversed its decision to get out of the vinyl business and continued to press all Fringe product, including LPs by the Dayglo Abortions.

9. The federal government had tried to refine the obscenity law in 1987, but the legislation, introduced by the then-in-power Conservative government and enthusiastically supported by Catholic and evangelical Protestant groups, was abandoned after demonstrative protests from the artistic community.

10. Unless otherwise indicated, the sources for the opinions of the potential expert witnesses are Marlys Edwardh's notes from her interviews with them.

11. The complaint to the Ontario police came from a detention center that housed a child who had one of the records and seemed preoccupied with it. In London a rather disturbed young person responsible for a lot of damage had a copy of a Dayglo Abortions tape in his

possession, and a psychiatrist in that city believed that the behavior and the tape might be linked.

12. All quotations are taken from Edwardh's handwritten notes, from which she delivered her summation.

13. In the intervening years there have been no known examples of censorship in Canada by either record labels or the government, but no Canadian CD has even remotely approached the Dayglo Abortions' songs in terms of potential obscenity charges. At least one vice-president of a Canadian major label insists that although record companies in Canada continue to exercise due diligence regarding potentially actionable material, after a few years had passed the Dayglo case had virtually no effect on activities within the industry.

Discography

Dayglo Abortions. 1981. "Out of the Womb," Sharpe Records.
———. 1985. "Feed U.S. A. Fetus," Fringe Product, FLP 3031.
———. 1988. "Here Today Guano Tomorrow," Fringe Product, FLP 3053.
———. 1991. "Two Dogs Fucking," Fringe Product.

Bibliography

Most of the secondary sources consulted for this chapter were accessed in photocopied form from the legal files of Marlys Edwardh. Many of these photocopies lacked such routine bibliographic information as author, page number, date, and, in some cases, the name of the publication. Consequently, such information is also missing from some text citations and some of the references below. Edwardh's files were a gold mine nonetheless, with photocopies of virtually every article on the band or the trial, from the most obscure fanzine to major newspapers in several Canadian cities. Much of this chapter is based on letters, faxes, inter-office memos, handwritten notes from meetings and the trial itself, and court transcripts, all found within Edwardh's voluminous files. Such items are not listed individually below but are referenced in the body of the chapter. All quotations from Ben Hoffman not specifically attributed in the chapter are from interviews conducted by the author in the fall of 2000. I would like to thank both Ben Hoffman and Marlys Edwardh for their support for this project.

Balbier, L. 1988. "Dayglos Latest: Hardcore's Not Dead," unsourced.
Barr, G. 1989. "DayGlo Abortions Ready to Confront the Court," *Ottawa Citizen*, 4 May.
Bindman, S. 1990b. "Rock Trial: Ottawa Court to Hear Charges in Canada's First Rock Obscenity Trial," *Ottawa Citizen*, 4 November.
Blanchfield, M. 1988. "Keep Offensive Records off Shelves, Nepean Police Urge," *Ottawa Citizen*, 21 October.
Dafoe, C. 1990a. "Record Industry Relieved by Ruling on Rock Band Lyrics," *Toronto Star*, 10 November.

———. 1990b. "Whew! Bad Taste Not Against the Law," *Toronto Star*, 12 November.

———. 1990c. "Cretin and His Abortions Look Forward to Creating," *Toronto Star*, unsourced.

Harpur, T. 1990a. "Record Industry Can't Have Free Rein to Corrupt Youth," *Toronto Star*, 18 November.

———. 1990b. "Lyrics Filth for Filth's Sake No Matter What Jury Ruled," *Toronto Star*, 7 December.

Harris, C. 1990a. "Record Company Trial Challenges Canadian Obscenity Laws," *Globe and Mail*, 3 November.

———. 1990b. "Not-Guilty Verdict in Obscenity Trial," *Globe and Mail*, 9 November.

Hegg, W. 1989. "Censorship Wars: The Ben Hoffman Case," *Vox*, April, n.p.

Jones, C. 1989. "Abortions Case Looms in Lawbooks," *Now Magazine*, 11 May, n.p.

Kelly, P. No date. "On the Fringe of the Music Industry," unsourced.

MacMinn, D. 1999. "Murray Cretin Acton," *Offbeat*, May, p. 5.

Middleton, R. 1990. *Studying Popular Music*. Milton Keynes, U.K.: Open University Press.

Payne, E. 1989. "Citizen Convinces Judge to Lift Publication Ban," *Ottawa Citizen*, 31 October.

———. 1990. "Jury Says LPs Not Obscene," *Ottawa Citizen*, 9 November.

Potter, M. 1989. "DayGlos' Only Defense Is . . . ," unsourced.

Sary, J. 1988. Review of "Here Today Guano Tomorrow," *Imprint*, 15 July, n.p.

Skeaff, B. 1988. "Victoria Band's Discs Leave Record Label Facing Obscenity Rap," *Victoria Times-Colonist*, 20 October.

TC. 1988. Review of "Here Today Guano Tomorrow," no. 5, Summer, n.p.

Wiseman, L. 1986. "Parody Rules Okay," *Vancouver Magazine*, June, p. 90.

David Parvo

8 Strelnikoff: Censorship in Contemporary Slovenia

For 46 years Slovenia was a republic in the Socialist Federated Republic of Yugoslavia (SFRY), traditionally considered one of the most liberal and progressive of the Eastern European communist countries (Ramet and Banac 1992:94). After Slovenia's secession from the SFRY in 1991 and the subsequent fall of communism, this liberal atmosphere continued to flourish (ibid.:144). As I write in 2002, more than 10 years after the fall of communism, that tradition is being threatened. The Slovenian Roman Catholic Church, which has been extremely influential throughout the country's history, is beginning to consolidate its power and exert its will on the Slovenian populace. Its close affiliation with the Christian Democratic Party (SKD) and their combined efforts to return the church's nationalized property and prohibit abortion are threatening to violate Article 7 of the Slovenian constitution, which clearly establishes a separation of church and state.

On 7 February 1998 the Slovenian rock band Strelnikoff released "Bitchcraft," a song that asks whether the Slovenian Catholic Church has the right to intervene in politics in order to prohibit abortion. On its inflammatory cover is an icon-like portrait of the Virgin Mary holding a rat. Within days, conservative politicians and church leaders had reacted to this provocation by linking the members of the band with what they say is an organized effort to destroy the church and repress its followers. For them, the single was one element of a systematic, organized attack on Christianity (Rebula 1998). Two of Strelnikoff's members, Vasja Ocvirk and Sergej Steblovnik, are, at the time of writing, in danger of going to prison for three years for violating Article 299 of the Criminal Law of the Republic of Slovenia.

But Strelnikoff is not the only group or individual being threatened. The Slovenian Catholic Church and the SKD are proposing legislation that would prohibit *anything* that they judge to contain anti-Catholic propaganda from being distributed or produced anywhere in the country.[1] If Strelnikoff is prosecuted and this legislation actually promulgated, every citizen of Slovenia will be affected.

The Background

Slovenia has traditionally been a Catholic state. Under the communist regime of Josep Broz Tito (1945–1980), the Slovenian Catholic Church was repressed, as it was throughout the communist world. After Slovenia achieved its independence from the SFRY on 25 June 1991, the church was presented with new opportunities to act without fear of reprisals from the communist authorities (Ramet and Adamovich 1995:3). Today, Catholicism is increasing in popularity as the Slovenian populace searches for a new ideology. In early 1998, roughly 70 percent of Slovenia's two million citizens considered themselves to be believers, up from 46 percent in 1978 and 58 percent in 1988 (CIA 1998). The Slovenian Catholic Church is not only growing in numerical strength, but is becoming influential in politics (as evidenced by the political clout of the SKD) and in the judicial system. As a result, the church and the SKD have prominent voices in establishing the future course of Slovenia, both politically and culturally.

There is increasing danger that church leaders and their political allies will turn the postcommunist Slovenia into a "servant of the Catholic church," warns Zdenko Roter, a Slovenian sociologist of religion. He further asserts that several political parties, the SKD in particular, look on Catholic interests with favor and intend to return Slovenia to the condition that prevailed before the Second World War, when the church flourished and dominated the moral and political spheres (Ramet and Banac 1992:121). Political opponents accuse the SKD of spending more time opening churches than mending the country's economic and social ills (*International Herald Tribune*, 15 July 1992).

The Slovenian Catholic Church's political ambitions were evident at the Bishop's Conference held in the fall of 1992. There church leaders called for the dissolution of parliament, which, they charged, embodies "nondemocratic principles." Instead, "the people should place their trust in those who have a correct stand regarding Christian values and the Catholic Church" (Ramet 1993:203). In 1996 the inauguration of Archbishop Frank Rode instigated a campaign by the church to take a leading role in civil society and once again become the moral, spiritual, and political leader of the Slovenes. Indeed, they promote the idea that only a Catholic can be a "real" Slovene (Ramet 1993:203). Thus, Archbishop Rode has argued that: "Who wants to contribute to Slovenia, who wants to be a real Slovenian, must be a Christian or at least be influenced by Christian culture" (Milheljak 1998).

Despite the power and influence the Slovenian Catholic Church and the SKD acquired in the 1990s, leaders of both groups continue to profess that Catholics are treated as second-class citizens whose religious rights are continually violated. They point to two controversial issues, privatization and abortion, as examples of their mistreatment at the government's hands.

The Christian Democrats and the Slovenian Catholic Church

Large tracts of forest and agricultural land were held by the Slovenian Catholic Church before the communist takeover in 1945. After the fall of communism, the SKD and the country's first postcommunist prime minister, Lojze Peterle, sought to privatize the land expropriated during Tito's nationalization program (ibid.:197–200). Many left-wing parties viewed the proposed plan as too favorable to the church. For example, Parliamentary Deputy Spomenka Hribar of the Democratic Party argued that privatization would cause economic growth to stagnate, resulting in instability. Critics charged that the policy would effectively turn back the clock 50 years to the time when the church controlled much of the country (ibid.:199). In April 1998, two months after Strelnikoff released "Bitchcraft," the Slovenian Catholic Church recovered its nationalized land with little fanfare or controversy. The members of the band believe that they were used to divert attention away from this controversial action (personal interview with Ocvirk and Steblovnik, 10 July 1998).

An even more divisive issue facing the nascent democratic government is abortion. This has created a sharp left–right split within the government, as it has throughout the rest of the world. The right-of-center parties and the church take a moral stance against abortion and continually lobby politicians to ban abortions in Slovenia, except when the pregnant woman's life is at risk (Ramet 1993:201–202). Today, the right to choose is protected by constitutional amendment, but the church has promised to protest until that amendment is repealed. The controversy surrounding the release of "Bitchcraft" has provided increasingly influential church leaders with an opportunity to air their grievances and further their political agenda.

The Strelnikoff Affair

The alternative rock band Strelnikoff was founded in 1988 in Celje, Slovenia, named after a character from the classic book and film *Dr. Zhivago*. Ivan Antipovic Strelnikoff is a Bolshevik who tours the Russian countryside by train, exterminating every enemy of the revolution that he encounters. The band does not, however, identify with him; they simply use the character as a reference for their chosen form of expression, the inverse perspective, the villain's point of view. Their music is a unique blend of punk, heavy metal, and electronica dance music, and their lyrics are spiked with dark, satirical humor. The band has been described by right-wing

FIGURE 8-1.   Cover of "Bitchcraft." Reproduced by permission of Vasja Ocvirk, Strelnikoff.

Slovenian groups as everything from fascistic to communistic, but it is neither, Ocvirk and Steblovnik told me (interview, 1998).

Although the band's music is oriented toward international audiences, it has a strong following among Slovenian youth and is considered to be one of the country's most exciting concert attractions. Strelnikoff has released five compact discs and contributed songs to several international compilations. The members are clearly aware of the political realities of Slovenia and seek, through their art, to resist any suppression or restriction of freedom of expression by totalitarian political systems. When asked if they intended to be a political band, band member Vasja Ocvirk responded: "We just ask questions [that we feel] need to be answered . . . that is what we think politics is—giving answers to questions" (ibid.).

"Bitchcraft" ignited a storm of political controversy. Even the cover, with its portrait of the Virgin Mary holding a rat, makes a strong political statement (Fig. 8-1, reproduced here by kind permission of the band). The lyrics are as follows:

> Why did you kill your unborn baby? Why did you flush the foetus
>   down the drain?
> Where did you hide the knitting needle? You are the poison in our
>   nation's veins!
> Bitchcraft! Bitchcraft! Bitchcraft! Someone's gotta stop it!
> Don't you know that life is sacred? Can't you see there are other
>   ways?
> Love is the biggest deal life has got to offer! Don't you love God
>   and the human race?
> Bitchcraft! Bitchcraft! Bitchcraft! Someone's gotta stop it right
>   now!
> You were blind but we'll open your eyes. We'll make your love true
>   and strong.
> You live to breed and not to question! We will teach you right
>   from wrong!
> We will teach you right from wrong! You live to breed and not to
>   question!
> You live to serve and obey the Lord! We will stop your fucking
>   Bitchcraft!
> We will teach you right from wrong![2]

As noted above, Strelnikoff's lyrics are written from the "villain's" point of view. In this instance, the villains are right-wing extremists, and the lyrics reflect their views about abortion.

The band firmly believes that eliminating abortion will reduce the role of women in Slovenian society and effectively relegate them to the function of breeder. The song asks whether the Slovenian Catholic Church should be crossing the line separating church and state by challenging the constitutionality of abortion. The lyrics also suggest that the church's ultimate goal, as represented by Archbishop Rode, whose sermons are sampled by the band, is to use democracy in order to institute a dictatorial, "user-friendly" totalitarian government (Ocvirk and Steblovnik interview, 1998), which can then be used to promulgate Catholic values in the political sphere. "Bitchcraft" should not be considered an attempt to provoke religious hatred. Rather, it is a form of political expression intended to make the Slovenian populace aware of the profound political realities that they face on a day-to-day basis.

The church strenuously objected to both the lyrics and the depiction of the Virgin Mary on the cover, which they believe denigrated their beliefs and ideology. In the Catholic weekly newspaper *Druzina* ("Family"), Archbishop Rode asked: "Mother, what did they do to you?" Slovenian Catholics were deeply and profoundly wounded, he wrote (Mursic 1999). A Catholic youth organization called the Young Christian Democrats and General Prosecutor Anton Drobnic, a leading member of the SKD, demanded that the government prosecute the members of

Strelnikoff for this "offense against religious sensibilities." Initially they tried to use Article 300 of the Criminal Law of the Republic of Slovenia, which reads as follows:

> Anyone who provokes or arouses national, religious, racial, or religious [sic] hatred, dissension or intolerance, or spawns ideas about superiority of one race over another . . . if the deed was done with force, with insult to national and religious symbols . . . is punished with up to five (5) years in prison. (Superintendent of Documents 1991)

This law is intended to prosecute fascists and racists for their actions, not to stifle political discourse.[3]

The SKD, the church, and many Catholics demanded that the single be banned and confiscated and that members of the band be incarcerated, threatening mass demonstrations and boycotts if this did not occur. Band members were issued with summonses and interrogated by the police. Archbishop Rode then organized a special mass on 7 March 1998, ostensibly to ask for forgiveness for the "blasphemers." At the mass, which drew over seven thousand people, Rode preached that "believers continually suffer under an enormous burden of insults" and needed to organize themselves to fight this threat (Hocevar 1998).

At the peak of the controversy, Janez Markes, a writer for the political magazine *Mag*, stated on national television that if the members of Strelnikoff could create such an offensive CD, they "should not seek the protection of the police even if someone throws a Molotov cocktail at them during their concert" (TV Slovenia 1998). An article entitled "Is There an Organization Behind This?" by Alojz Rebula (*Druzina*, 7 June 1998) suggested that Strelnikoff was affiliated with an organization (with, it is implied, Satan as the ringleader) that intends to destroy the church and everything it stands for. Strelnikoff strongly denied this accusation (Ocvirk and Steblovnik interview, 1998).

The Slovenian Catholic Church sponsored the circulation of two petitions demanding that the group be prosecuted to the fullest extent of the law. Meanwhile, the church and the SKD used this opportunity to discuss proposing legislation that would prohibit the distribution or production of what they deem anti-Catholic propaganda anywhere in the country (Mursic 1999).

Druzina, at Archbishop Rode's urging, opened a website to permit young Catholics to voice their anger at Strelnikoff and their so-called blasphemous expression. The website had to be closed, however, overwhelmed by the volume of pro-Strelnikoff statements and messages condemning the repressive tactics of the Slovenian Catholic Church. A majority of intellectuals in Slovenia supported Strelnikoff, including then-President Milan Kucan. Kucan, according to an Associated Press report (1998), said: "We should react with acts and words of tolerance and cooperation . . . we should not react with suppression and censorship."

The first district attorney in charge of this case, Milan Brisa of Celje, refused to press charges because of lack of formal evidence. Dissatisfied with this decision, on

23 June General Prosecutor Drobnic reassigned the case to an SKD-affiliated district attorney, Elizabeta Gyorkos, who is more sympathetic to both his politics and the Catholic faith. This is not a common practice in Slovenia, and if this tactic works, it could be used more often in the SKD's effort to further insinuate the church into Slovenian politics (Mursic 1999).

On 17 June 1999 District Attorney Gyorkos pressed formal charges against Ocvirk and Steblovnik, contending that "Bitchcraft" is a violent, offensive act and basing her argument on Article 299 of the Slovenian Criminal Law.[4] She had apparently decided that an accusation based on Article 300 would most likely fail in the court of law. At the time of writing, Strelnikoff has been indicted but not formally prosecuted in court.

Fighting the Censors in Slovenia

The Strelnikoff affair is the first instance of artistic censorship in postcommunist Slovenia, and the church's first attempt to interfere with artistic expression since the beginning of the century. If the church is successful against Strelnikoff, it is likely to become much more involved in Slovenia's political and cultural affairs. Moreover, if it makes a habit of dealing with "offensive" material as it has dealt with Strelnikoff, freedom of expression in Slovenia will be threatened to a greater degree than it ever was under communist rule. The members of Strelnikoff have been put into a situation where they must fight for their own freedom—and the freedom of all others in Slovenia—to voice their opinions.

One of the goals of repression is to make the offending party feel guilty. Once this happens, then the repressor has, to some extent, already succeeded, because its act of repression is seen as justified. The members of Strelnikoff liken their situation to a witch-hunt. They believe that they are being harassed simply for expressing themselves and asking questions that need to be answered. But they refuse to feel guilty for raising important questions about the future of Slovenia (Ocvirk and Steblovnik interview, 1998).

Initially, the public outcry against the album was intense, and band members were deluged with requests for statements and appearances. After consulting with a lawyer, they issued several public statements in which they maintained the validity of their beliefs and said that, if presented with the opportunity to go back in time, they would still release the single (ibid.). Although they did not attempt to antagonize the church or Catholics, the members of Strelnikoff were threatened with physical abuse and death. They refused to respond to provocation, threats, or accusations because engaging in the opponents' tactics might seem to justify their attack. Like the band, I believe that the accused should never stoop to the censor's level.

From the outset, public opinion was strongly against Strelnikoff, and the members felt that they needed to tell their side of the story. Ocvirk and Steblovnik appeared on a respected political and cultural program on national television, where they read their public statement and refused to rescind their opinions or admit guilt. *Mladina*, a left-wing cultural journal that heavily promoted the band, published an article giving Strelnikoff's side of the story.[5] Up to this point, most newspaper and magazine coverage was extremely one-sided, representing only the views of General Prosecutor Drobnic and Archbishop Rode. The band's effort to get its point of view across has swayed public opinion, and sentiment is now more evenly divided between Strelnikoff and the church.

Sympathetic organizations are prepared to help the band, particularly by petitioning the populace of Slovenia. In Slovenia, petitioning is an extremely important tactic, used by the authorities to gauge public opinion. For example, the church used petitions to drum up support in its fight against the band, and these petitions were then used by General Prosecutor Drobnic to justify his continued attempts to prosecute it.

Strelnikoff and its supporters believe that they are fighting not only on their own behalf but also for the free speech rights of all of the citizens of Slovenia. Freedom of expression exists to protect unpopular speech and activities; it is not necessary to protect popular opinion. The band is prepared to go to jail to honor its commitment to this principle. As a result of their antagonists' threats, they fear for their personal safety, but they are not afraid of the tactics used by the censors.

Strelnikoff members adhere to what they call the "Three Fs Lesson"—Fear, Friends, and Fight. Fear, along with guilt, results from repression. No matter how unreasonable the complaints are, no matter how much organizations like the Slovenian Catholic Church and the Christian Democrats distort the issues, Strelnikoff believes that one should neither panic nor be afraid to stand up for what is right. One must make careful and reasoned responses to all allegations and attempt to keep the focus on the issue of freedom of expression. In a 1998 interview, Ocvirk and Steblovnik told me: "If you panic or are afraid of your enemies and their tactics or if you feel guilty for your actions, you have already allowed the repressors to win. You must remember that it is you who are the victim, not the individual or group who seeks to repress you."

Freedom of expression, a legal right recognized by the Slovenian constitution, is not a luxury; it is widely considered a universal right, even though it is continually challenged by religions or ideologies. I would argue that any attempt to stifle expression is undemocratic, regardless of the censors' rationale.

Friends—like-minded individuals and organizations that are also concerned about censorial activities and preserving freedom of expression—are one of the most important resources in the fight against censorship. The importance of rallying friends must not be overlooked because of its simplicity. No matter how vehement the attack, the would-be censor tends to be in the minority. Friends will realize that cutting off one person's voice endangers everyone.

Starting an anticensorship campaign is an excellent way to proclaim the need of individuals to express themselves freely in an open, democratic society. It also sends a message to politicians and community leaders. Without the support of sympathetic individuals and organizations, the fight against censorship is compromised.

Silence is a form of self-censorship. It is unconscionable to sit back and let the repression progress; when the right to speak one's mind is questioned, speaking out becomes an obligation as well as a way of fighting back. Speaking out and fighting back effectively require information—not only about censorship, but about civil rights in general; not only about the current situation, but about the historical context. The members of Strelnikoff say that "you should never regret the action that created the controversy. . . . Stand by your words, art or any other form of expression" (interview with Ocvirk and Stebvolnik, 1998).

Knowledge about the pro-censorship forces is integral to the fight, as John Stuart Mill asserted long ago (1955, 1958). The censors' own words can expose them to public scrutiny, so it is important to study their literature. See the enemy for who they are, not only as they present themselves in public forums. The censors may be hypocrites. Censorship is designed to distract public attention away from an issue the censors want obscured, as in Slovenia, where the church may be violating the constitution in its attempts to make abortion illegal. By focusing public attention on a supposed violation of Catholics' human rights, the church is deflecting it from its own questionable activities in relation to the constitution.

The historical context opens up another dimension in the fight against censorship and repression. This aspect is particularly poignant in Slovenia, where the church itself was repressed under communist rule. Knowledge of both censorship and the censor allows besieged individuals and groups to formulate clear and concise responses, the better to defend their rights.

The Choice

Slovenia is at a crossroads, and its government is faced with a choice: Will it build upon the success of the past few years and establish a vibrant democracy? Or will the government turn back the clock 50 years to a time when the church dominated the country's cultural and political affairs?

By attacking the alleged "blasphemy" of Strelnikoff in a political forum, the church and the SKD are seeking to flex their new-found political muscles and consolidate their power. If they successfully prosecute Strelnikoff, they may be encouraged to attempt more ambitious repressive projects in the future.

The members of Strelnikoff exercised their constitutional rights to free speech and artistic expression when they asked whether the church has the right to intervene in Slovenian politics. In the absence of a clear answer, General Prosecutor Drobnic's liberal use of criminal law to prosecute the band indicates that the Slovenian government's commitment to allowing a true democracy to take root is beginning to waver.

If Strelnikoff is successfully prosecuted, Slovenia will have taken the first step toward a repressive democratic theocracy, and freedom of expression would be threatened to a greater degree than it ever was under the communist regime of Tito.

Notes

1. In my opinion, the decision on whether to pursue this legislation will depend on the outcome of Strelnikoff's trial.

2. Lyrics reprinted by kind permission of Vasja Ocvirk and Sergej Steblovnik.

3. On 4 June 1998, the State Council of Slovenia demanded the resignation of General Prosecutor Drobnic, mainly because of his participation in the Homeguard, a Slovenian military force sympathetic to the Nazis. Drobnic has made negative comments about the Slovene Liberation Front in several interviews, saying that the holiday honoring the SLF's founding is meaningless—that it merely celebrates a day of communist terror. He concluded by calling the partisans common criminals. These comments offended the League of Veterans, whose members charged Drobnic with violating Article 300. Ironically, church leaders and right-wing politicians then protested that his right to free expression had been violated. At the time of writing, the matter remains unresolved.

4. Article 299 reads as follows: (i) Anyone who offends someone, treats him/her badly, is violent against him/her or threatens his/her safety and, with such an act, provokes revolt or fear in the general population, will be punished with a sentence of up to two years. (ii) If the act described above is done by two or more persons, without bodily injury, said act will be punished by a maximum of three years in prison.

5. See *Mladina*, 3 March 1998, for further insight.

Bibliography

Hocevar, B. 1998. "Special Mass in Brezje," *Delo*, 9 March.

Kucan, M. 1998. Public speech, reported by the Associated Press, 1 March.

Milheljak, V. 1998. "Erotica," *Dnevnik*, 3 March.

Mill, J. S. 1955. *On Liberty*. Chicago: Henry Regnery Co.

———. 1958. *Considerations on Representative Government*. Indianapolis: Bobbs-Merrill.

Mursic, R. 1999. "Provocation and Repression after Socialism: The Strelnikoff Case," paper presented to the International Association of Sociologists and Psychologists, Sydney, Australia.

Ramet, S. P. 1993. "Slovenia's Road to Democracy," *Europe-Asia Studies*, September, pp. 189–210.

Ramet, S. P., and Adamovich, L. S., eds. 1995. *Beyond Yugoslavia: Politics, Economics and Culture in a Shattered Community.* Boulder: Westview Press.

Ramet, S. P., and Banac, I., eds. 1992. *Balkan Babel: The Disintegration of Yugoslavia from the Death of Tito to Ethnic War.* Boulder: Westview Press.

Rebula, A. 1998. "Is There an Organization Behind This?" *Druzina*, 7 June.

Superintendent of Documents. 1991. *The Slovenian Constitution.* Ljubljana.

TV Slovenia. 1998. "Odmevi," 25 February.

U.S. Central Intelligence Agency. 1998. *The Agency Factbook, Slovenia.* <www.odci.gov/cia/publications/factbook/geos/si.html>.

Websites

Delo: <www.delo.si>.

Mladina: <yellow.eunet.si/yellowpage/0/mediji1/mladina/mladina.html>.

Slovenian Christian Democrats (SKD): <www.skd.si/english>; accessed 2001.

Slovenian Roman Catholic Church: <www.rkc.si>; accessed 2001.

Strelnikoff: <www.ljudmila.org/strelnikoff>.

Virtual Slovenia: <www.matkurja.com/slo>.

Part III

Up Against the State

Michael Drewett

---

9 Music in the Struggle to End Apartheid: South Africa

The South African elections of 1994 installed a democratic and liberal system of government in a country previously ruled by the National Party. When the Nationalists assumed power in 1948, they instituted the repressive apartheid system of severe racial inequality and enforced racial separateness. Many musicians opposed this system through their music and support of antiapartheid political cause. In response, the Nationalist government attempted to minimize the impact of musicians by preventing controversial music from being heard and by repressing the musicians themselves. Notwithstanding the government's attempt to maintain its hegemony, musicians fought back in a multitude of ways.

In this chapter I focus particularly on the censorship of music in the 1980s—the decade immediately preceding the political transition that started in the early 1990s. I begin with the mechanisms of censorship and then consider strategies of resistance. Not all instances of censorship were overtly political, but they were always framed by, and took place within, an extreme legal-political system. No matter what their message was, censored musicians developed strategies to reach as wide an audience as possible. In doing so, they articulated and transformed culture, opening spaces in which particular forms of artistic expression emerged (Eyerman and Jamison 1998:160–165). I conclude with a brief overview of the changes that have taken place since 1994. Not only did cultural struggle play a part in local changes, but musicians attempting to overcome censorship in other parts of the world can learn important lessons from the South African experience.

The Mechanisms of Music Censorship

Legislation

The Publications Act of 1974 was the central mechanism for direct censorship of publications (including sound recordings) in South Africa. The act provided for the establishment of the Directorate of Publications, which responded to complaints from the police, customs and excise officers, and members of the general public. The directorate decided whether or not to ban material submitted to it. Objections were referred to the Publications Appeal Board (PAB), a government-appointed committee designed to set aside or confirm the directorate's decisions. The government also made use of several security laws (such as the Internal Security and Protection of Information Acts of 1982) to ban publications. Organizations such as the African National Congress (ANC) were banned under the 1982 Internal Security Act, and as such their publications were automatically banned without having to be reviewed by the directorate. During the 1980s the relatively liberal directorate and PAB were the sites of contests between board members and the police and government. When the director of the Appeal Board, Kobus van Rooyen, decided not to ban the film *Cry Freedom*, it was banned under the Internal Security Act. Van Rooyen received death threats, his house was set on fire, and he was the victim of a variety of other "dirty tricks" (personal interview with van Rooyen, 11 September 1998).

With the declaration of consecutive states of emergency in the mid-1980s, the state was further empowered to ban material. The 1986 emergency regulations "made it an offence for any person to make, write, record, disseminate, display, utter or even possess a 'subversive statement'" (Marcus 1987:9). According to Director of Publications Braam Coetzee, the government used these regulations as a "parallel system" to ban material independently of the directorate (personal interview with Coetzee, 14 July 1998).

Despite all the mechanisms in place, music was, in fact, rarely banned by the Directorate of Publications: Fewer than one hundred music records were actually banned at this level during the 1980s. The main reason was that the directorate itself did not go in search of material to ban: It only responded to complaints received. The board received very few complaints about music—not only because most music was listened to by youths who were unlikely to complain anyway, Coetzee believes, but also because lyrics were generally unclear or inaudible (ibid.). Some complaints came from parents who overheard or read the lyrics, but most came from the police. The case of Roger Lucey is representative. The police targeted Lucey in the early 1980s, when his overtly antiapartheid lyrics began to receive widespread coverage in the press. But the directorate was unwilling to ban music that was not likely to be an immediate threat to state security. In general, political music rarely sold more than one or two thousand copies. "One of the key reasons that the state un-banned my fourth LP 'Beachbomb' was the fact that I never sold more than one thousand copies of any of my records," musician Warrick Sony argued. "If the system works on its own there is no need to ban records or anything" (1991:115).

Broadcasters: SABC and Independent Radio Stations

The system to which Sony referred is a combination of radio play and record company support that is almost always crucial for success, especially in a limited market such as South Africa. The state-owned South African Broadcasting Corporation (SABC) had a virtual monopoly over the South African airwaves and rigorously vetted the music played on its stations. Like the Directorate of Publications, it was concerned with political and rebellious messages, blasphemy, and overtly sexual lyrics but went even further by actively supporting the government's ideology of separate tribes, independent homelands, and cultural purity. Thus, no slang or mixing of languages was permitted, and groups like Sankomota—whose members sang in a variety of languages—suffered as a result. The SABC committee regularly held "record meetings" to scrutinize the lyrics of all music submitted to it for airplay (lyric sheets had to be submitted with music). This committee prohibited thousands of songs: Sometimes the entire repertoire of a group would be restricted, as was the case with the Beatles in the late 1960s, following John Lennon's claim in an interview that the band was "more popular than Jesus Christ"; Stevie Wonder was banned after he dedicated his Oscar award to Nelson Mandela in 1985. Once a song was denied airplay on SABC, "Avoid" was marked alongside the song title on the album sleeve. On occasion a sharp object was used to scratch the vinyl, making it physically impossible for a DJ to play a particular song. Although very little was directly banned by the directorate, the SABC's relentless attack on musicians' freedom obscured the degree to which the government was censoring music, since the general public was unaware of the extent to which radio play was controlled. The SABC's attitude is aptly captured in a *Sunday Times* article (11 June 1989): "An SABC records committee member, Mr Roelf Jacobs, denied that the SABC 'banned' songs. 'We just don't play them,' he said" (quoted in Maclennan 1990:152). SABC Television followed a similar line in terms of censoring its very sparse music coverage.

Apart from the SABC radio stations, two independent stations operated within South Africa. Capital Radio (launched in 1979) and Radio 702 (1980) were the official commercial music stations of two of South Africa's "independent homelands,"[1] Transkei and Bophutatswana respectively. Although not strictly bound by South African legislation (given that the government had granted the homelands "independence"), these radio stations generally adhered to the decisions of the Directorate of Publications. They did not, however, carry out the sort of internal censorship practiced by the SABC. Consequently, in the early eighties in particular,

Juluka, Via Afrika, and other groups who were not played on SABC were played on Capital—the more liberal of the two independents. But the Artists United Against Apartheid's antiapartheid song "(Ain't Gonna Play) Sun City," released in 1985, was not played on either of the stations because both were partly owned by Southern Sun, proprietors of the Sun City Holiday Resort.

Record Companies

The SABC's stance put pressure on record companies, and they in turn put pressure on musicians, to practice self-censorship in order to receive airplay. As a result, record companies often made changes to songs. In 1987, for example, the EMI International Label Manager wrote to the supervisor of the SABC record library about a song that had not been passed by the committee:

> Due to problems arising from certain sections of the lyric content of this song, we have received a re-mixed and edited version of which I enclose a cassette dubbing plus revised lyrics. This is to confirm that no further copies of the original version are available or will be pressed and distributed by this Company, and that this will be the only version available for Radio play and Retail Sale in South Africa.[2]

In a similar dismissal of artistic integrity, when the directorate banned Peter Tosh's "Equal Rights" album because of the song "Apartheid," CBS re-released the album without the banned track. "Offensive" songs were regularly left off albums. Rob Allingham, archivist for Gallo Records, described the companies' motives: "The record companies in no way took it upon themselves to reinforce whatever machinations the state had in mind as far as directing culture, but the bottom line for them was, and always is, and always probably will be, that they want to make money" (personal interview with Allingham, 17 April 1998). Most record companies (particularly the majors) made use of racial inequality to exploit black musicians by paying them extremely low royalties.

Independent record companies like Shifty Records and Third Ear Music were progressive in their antiapartheid stance, but still occasionally practiced self-censorship. In 1983 Shifty toned down the lyrics of Bernoldus Niemand's satirical "Hou my vas Korporaal" ("Hold me tight, corporal") in an unsuccessful attempt to get the song played on the radio (Sony 1991:113–114). In 1979 the director of Third Ear Music, Dave Marks, toned down Roger Lucey's "The Road Is Much Longer" album because his lawyers had warned him that certain lyrics could lead to severe prison sentences for those involved. These lyrics were left out, and some superficial songs such as "Pay Me the Dues on My Bottles" were included. The album nevertheless contained four hard-hitting songs, and the Directorate banned it and made its possession a criminal offence. From the outset Lucey was opposed to the compromise, believing that Third Ear should have disregarded the warnings and released the album in its original form (personal interview with Lucey, 17 July 1998). Had they done so, he acknowledged, there was a good chance that Dave Marks would have been prosecuted and Third Ear Music closed down.

Self-Censorship

Musicians often avoided political messages altogether in order to receive airplay. "We keep the radio in mind when we compose," Joseph Shabalala, leader of Ladysmith Black Mambazo, explained: "If something is contentious they don't play it, and then it wouldn't be known anyway" (Andersson 1981:87). Timothy Taylor (1997:78–82) defended Shabalala, arguing that to divide musicians in terms of resistance versus complicity is to accept "the very grounds of the oppressor/oppressed paradigm that European colonialism imposed." Apartheid presented many obstacles to would-be black musicians, and to succeed despite lack of education, poverty, urban squalor, and other difficulties was certainly a triumph. To celebrate all aspects of human life despite apartheid was part of the struggle to live the kind of life to which all people have a right. Nevertheless, Shabalala's statement pointed to a deliberate decision to silence his own political voice in the face of SABC censorship.

Other musicians wrote figuratively about the South African situation, expressing their convictions through symbols and innuendo. An example is Steve Kekana's song "The Bushman," released in 1982, about a Bushman who taught himself to shoot with a bow and arrow. This fitted in well with apartheid notions of blacks as primitives and was consequently played on SABC. However, Kekana's lyrics were open to radical interpretation. "In my mind," he explained, "I didn't really think of a real Bushman, I was thinking of the guerrillas" (personal interview with Kekana, 16 September 1998). Symbolism had to be very vague in order to receive airplay on SABC. Roger Lucey opposed this approach:

> What's the point of having an antifascist message with lyrics like "I'll take the high road and you take the low road and we'll go and smell the daisies." This is bullshit. It meant nothing. I didn't believe in that approach. I believed in an in-your-face, tell-it-like-it-is approach. The cops are out there. They're fucking throwing people out of windows. And that is what it's all about. And that's what the song says. Simple. (Personal interview, 17 July 1998)

The South African Police

If other means were not sufficient to prevent musicians from recording or performing political music, then the police were prepared to intervene. The Security Branch targeted Lucey in the early 1980s. His music was banned, his record company and venue owners were threatened, live shows were disrupted. The police bugged his phone, thus finding out about future gigs and putting an end to them (*Mail and Guardian*, 1995). Mzwakhe Mbuli, who put his poetry to music, was the victim of even more serious attacks in the mid- to late 1980s. A hand-grenade was thrown at his house, he was shot at, and his passport applications were turned down. His first album, "Change Is Pain," released in 1986, was banned by the Directorate of Publications, and he was arrested, detained, and tortured.[3]

The police often broke up concerts by overtly political groups such as Juluka, and they used the full range of apartheid laws to victimize and harass musicians—arresting them under the pass laws (this applied to black musicians in white areas without a permit), taking hours to search their vehicles at roadblocks, and closing down concerts that did not have a valid permit by declaring them illegal gatherings. Steve Gordon (1997:5) illustrated a common form of harassment whereby black musicians were told to play for the police to prove their musicianship. In one instance in the early 1960s, jazz musician Kippie Moeketsi was arrested for being in a venue where illegal alcohol was being sold. At the police station he was asked to play something and played "Don't Fence Me In." They responded: "Jy speel lekker man. Hardloop" ("You play well man, push off!").

Musicians in a Counterhegemonic Struggle: Strategies of Resistance

Overt Lyrics, Camouflaged Messages, and Disguised Tunes

Despite police harassment, many musicians refused to bow down to state repression. Their most obvious form of resistance was through their music, most of which was never played on radio and some of which was not even recorded. Mzwakhe Mbuli and the Cherry Faced Lurchers, for example, confronted the state directly through the lyrics of "Behind the Bars" and "Shot Down" respectively. The Directorate of Publications banned some of this music, and none of it was played on the radio. Many musicians nevertheless attempted to get potentially "subversive" music played on the SABC. Singing about issues in a roundabout way rather than making outright statements (when that is what the artist really wants to do) is self-censorship. Yet for many musicians faced with severe state censorship, this seemed to be the only option, better than saying nothing at all or having music banned so that very few ever got to hear it.

Many musicians tried to sneak controversial ideas onto radio using innovative methods. Keith Berelowitz of Carte Blanche revealed that they submitted counterfeit lyric sheets with albums sent to the SABC, replacing controversial words with ones that had a similar sound. In one instance they changed "policeman" to "please man" (personal interview with Berelowitz, 15 April 1998). In 1985 Shifty Records released a compilation album of rebel rhythms called "A Naartjie in Our Sosatie" ("A tangerine in our kebab"), a play on "Anarchy in our society." The Directorate of Publications file on the album (which it deemed "not undesirable") included no discussion whatsoever of the contentious album title.

One of the most astute (and successful) attempts at getting through the SABC's controls was represented by the 1987 release of Bright Blue's "Weeping." The group used symbolic lyrics to sing about a man living in fear within a heavily repressive society. These lyrics were sung against the backdrop of a haunting version of "Nkosi Sikeleli," the ANC national anthem. The song became a major hit on SABC's Radio 5. Strains of freedom songs were often used with new lyrics or performed as instrumentals (especially by jazz musicians). Ian Kerkhof (1989:12) discussed how "(Abdullah) Ibrahim has for many years now utilized the melodies of various freedom songs in his piano improvisations. . . . In this way instrumental music, charged with the melodies of freedom songs, gains a level of political meaning for the South African audiences who hear the unstated lyrics in their hearts." Ibrahim was one of many jazz musicians who gave political titles to instrumental pieces, such as his "Anthem for the New Nation," released in 1979. Similarly, some bands' names made their stance absolutely clear and told the audience how to read their music: Illegal Gathering, Gramsci Beat, Amandla (meaning "power" and used as a call of defiance at political rallies and meetings).

Antiapartheid Censorship: The Cultural Boycott

Beginning with Trevor Huddleston's call in 1954 for a cultural boycott of apartheid South Africa (Nixon 1994:157), pressure was brought to bear on cultural performers to refuse to play there. In December 1968 the United Nations General Assembly accepted Resolution 2396, according to which all member states and organizations were asked to cut "cultural, educational, and sporting ties with the racist regime" (Willemse 1991:24). By December 1980 the call had been stepped up (in terms of UN General Assembly Resolution 35/206E) through the establishment of a Register of Artists, Actors and Others who have performed in South Africa. The cultural boycott prohibited musicians from outside South Africa from playing there and prevented South African musicians from performing, recording, or releasing their music elsewhere, unless they no longer performed in South Africa or went into exile.

Support for the boycott grew with the release of the "Sun City" album by a collective of musicians calling themselves Artists United Against Apartheid. The album was an attempt to create awareness about apartheid and in particular to call for an artists' boycott of the Sun City hotel complex in the "phoney homeland" of Bophutatswana. The boycott strategy deprived apartheid's supporters of live performances by overseas musicians and kept them from having their message heard outside South Africa. Yet it censored all musicians within the country, whatever their stance—including many antiapartheid musicians who were thus silenced not only internally through censorship but also externally through the boycott. For example, in 1988 Johnny Clegg and Savuka were barred by the British Musicians' Union from playing at the Nelson Mandela Seventieth Birthday tribute concert at Wembley, even though they had been given the go ahead by the United Democratic Front (UDF), the internal wing of the ANC. The ban was instigated because Clegg lived and worked in South Africa (Bell 1988:12).

By 1987 the ANC already felt that the political credentials of each South African group or performer should be taken into account when deciding whether or not they should be allowed to perform outside the country. However, the interpretation of this policy and other aspects of the boycott were always shrouded in disagreement. Many South African musicians supported the boycott insofar as they refused to perform at Sun City, although few agreed with banning South African groups from performing and releasing their music overseas. They disagreed either because they were not sufficiently politically involved or because they were, and wanted their message to be heard. Furthermore, the cultural boycott made it very difficult for South African bands to make a living from their music. Although several overseas artists broke the cultural boycott by performing in South Africa or, as in Paul Simon's case, by recording there, there were those who supported the struggle against apartheid through boycotts, campaigns, and their music. South African musicians in exile also supported the struggle in this way.

The mid-eighties saw a trend of releasing songs collectively performed by a multitude of musicians in aid of a humanitarian cause (for example USA for Africa's "We Are the World," aimed at raising money for, and awareness of, famine relief in Africa). In 1986 the South African government decided to exploit this trend. A propaganda song entitled "Together We'll Build a Brighter Future" involved a cross-section of South African musicians promoting peace and multiracial harmony in South Africa, despite ongoing police brutality and the erosion of freedom which came with the state of emergency. The government offered musicians large sums of money to participate, but, in an instance of left-wing censorship, most top musicians refused. The severity of the cultural struggle was emphasized when arsonists burned down the house of Steve Kekana, who participated in the recording. A friend who was staying there was burned to death.

Live Performances, Festivals, and Compilation Albums

At music festivals and concerts in support of various causes, including the End Conscription Campaign (ECC) and campaigns for detainees or striking workers, bands could make political statements that might not have been allowed on their albums. As musician Jennifer Ferguson commented: "You had a sense of the importance of live work because there was so much repression on many other levels that the theaters and cabaret venues were often the only place where any kind of truth could be uttered" (personal interview with Ferguson, 8 April 1999). Shifty Records was also pivotal in focusing much resistance music that might otherwise have remained isolated. It produced two compilation albums of resistance music in the mid-

1980s—a time when major companies were hesitant to record a single political song on any of their albums. In addition, in 1989 Shifty organized a tour of alternative antiapartheid Afrikaans performers known as the "Voëlvry" tour (meaning "free as a bird," sounding like "feel free") and released a corresponding compilation album. The tour went to small and large urban areas alike, often taking its political message into the heartland of conservative Afrikanerdom. Not surprisingly there was a strong backlash in the form of death threats, cancelled venues, slashed car tires, and teargas sprayed into venues. Many of the musicians used pseudonyms to maintain a degree of anonymity (personal interview with Ralf Rabie, 10 September 1998).

Foreign Funding

Deprived of the radio play that generates broadcasting royalties and sales, Shifty Records sought overseas sponsors to pay for recording costs. Although the company attempted (mostly unsuccessfully) to get songs played on SABC, the production costs were in most instances paid for through financial aid. This freed Shifty to record many marginal artists and musicians with a political message, such as the Kalahari Surfers, Jennifer Ferguson, and Mzwakhe Mbuli. The drawback of this approach was that Shifty tended to be less innovative in its marketing strategy than many of its musicians would have liked. As a result Shifty Records has made a major and crucial contribution to archiving resistance and other alternative music, but most of its music was not heard by a wide audience.

Mobile Studio and Self-Production

Shifty's most innovative strategy was the use of a mobile studio. Lloyd Ross of the label explained how it worked:

> We put a little studio together in a caravan. The idea was of mobility and hence the name Shifty—it could shift from here to there. . . . We recorded in quite a few locations in Southern Africa, the first one of course being in Lesotho [a small mountain kingdom completely landlocked by South Africa] because Sankomota wasn't allowed to come into this country. They were banned from being here because of a tour they'd done in seventy-nine, and they had a message which wasn't exactly acceptable to the powers that be. (Personal interview with Ross, 14 April 1998)

Warrick Sony (1991), who worked with Shifty, bypassed the major pressing plants by releasing his first album on cassettes that he produced at home and distributed personally. This strategy was adopted by a number of people, sometimes for commercial reasons, but often for political ones. Barry Gilder (1983:19) released an album of his songs in this manner, and it was banned after police found copies of it during a raid on the University of Cape Town student union offices. Scott Marshall (1995:212) emphasized the importance of cassettes as a small, cheap, and easy-to-use format, providing an important opportunity for tiny production companies. The advent of digital recording, computer technology, and home compact disc production also offers an important opportunity to political musicians wanting to release their music. As musician and studio owner Willem Möller said:

> I know a lot of bands who just form their own record companies. They don't bother with anybody else. They've got a computer. They master the thing. They make their own cover. They print the minimum order of a few hundred. They sell it at gigs, easily make their money back on the recording, and then finance a slightly bigger album the next time. And do it themselves. . . . They control it. They own it. They do it on their own terms. (Personal interview with Möller, 15 April 1998)

This approach bypasses large record companies with commercial interests and can allow for the small-scale release of albums that might otherwise be banned by repressive governments. The option of pirate radio stations was never seriously undertaken in South Africa during the apartheid era because of the heavy political repression. This strategy has, however, been successful in other parts of the world. An alternative is provided by community radio stations, which are an increasingly popular airplay route in contemporary South Africa.

Challenging the Directorate of Publications

Record companies often challenged Directorate decisions and sometimes got them reversed. For example, in 1989 Shifty challenged the banning of the Kalahari Surfers "Bigger Than Jesus" album, which was eventually unbanned on condition that the title of the album be changed (even though the song with that title was allowed to remain). This strategy demonstrated a reluctance to accept the Directorate's decisions passively while also forcing it to provide reasons for its decisions and thus expose "not just the enemy within, but a whole set of cultural power relations and antagonisms" (Hill 1992:42). Justifications for banning songs were generally insubstantial, thus illustrating the undemocratic process that censorship is: a practice indulged in by the few to the disadvantage of the many. Roger Lucey was informed that his album song "Thabane" was "undesirable" simply because it "contains a reference to Steve Biko and his death as one of many."[4]

Formal Links with Political Organizations

Finally, musicians made good use of formal political organizations to strengthen their position. In the early 1980s it was difficult for musicians to align themselves with political organizations because of a lack of internal structures. The launch of the UDF in 1983 provided the beginnings of a clearer structure through which musicians could operate. As discussed above, musicians were able to perform on UDF platforms and show their commitment to the antiapartheid cause in different formats. The UDF encouraged musicians to adopt principles in line with a "people's culture" position, involving a general commitment to the antiapartheid movement, especially through lyrics/music, performance, and principled stands on a variety of issues. The role of musicians within the antiapartheid struggle became formalized only with the formation of the South African Musicians' Alliance (SAMA) in September 1988. Musicians finally had their own political union through which they could channel their efforts and receive guidance. While SAMA did not affiliate with the UDF, it supported a lot of its work. In particular SAMA focused on three basic freedoms central to the work of any musician: freedom of association, freedom of expression, and freedom of movement. An important consequence of the formation of SAMA—which supported a selective boycott—was that it (in conjunction with the UDF) was able to give clearance to performers wanting to perform overseas (personal interview with Johnny Clegg, 20 April 1998).

Beyond Apartheid Censorship

Throughout the struggle to end apartheid, musicians voiced the protest of many South Africans, and sometimes challenged apartheid laws and beliefs. Musicians of different races played together—at the risk of being arrested—when it was still illegal to do so. Thus white musician Johnny Clegg and black musician Sipho Mchunu together explored Zulu culture on stage in front of South African audiences who had been taught that intercultural and interracial mixing was wrong. Despite government attempts to stop them, many South African musicians remained committed to the fight against apartheid and censorship, often at the expense of commercial success. Musicians were able to play a role in the counterhegemonic struggle that ultimately saw the demise of apartheid in the early 1990s. Through developing ways of overcoming censorship as discussed in this chapter, musicians became political as well as cultural agents and helped shape an emergent cultural formation. Indeed, the postapartheid South African constitution places strong emphasis on freedom of expression, a right for which many musicians fought furiously during the previous era.

Policies regarding censorship in present-day South Africa reflect the new freedom that has been secured. The new government's Film and Publication Board has not banned any music, and under the new constitution the Board is extremely unlikely to do so in the future. SABC policy is also far more relaxed. According to Cecile Pracher, manager of the SABC Record Library:

> There is virtually no formal censorship practiced by the SABC regarding lyrics of songs on CD. Record Librarians indicate on CDs when unacceptable words or content appear as part of the lyrics, and it is up to the announcer or DJ, to decide whether the song is to be played, or not.[5]

This is in stark contrast to the apartheid era. Through all the efforts of those who resisted the apartheid system, musicians in South Africa are finally at a stage where they are able to concentrate on the more "normal" problems confronting bands in peripheral societies. They have secured a quota system (of 25 percent local music content) on South African radio stations. An increasing number of performers have recorded music independently and released their albums over the internet or through other alternative distribution networks. This alone does not secure them sufficient income to survive as musicians, and breaking into a larger (particularly international) market remains the central problem for most. But they can embark on this new challenge without the threat of prosecution or seeing their music banned: a significant advance for those musicians who suffered under the widespread censorship of the apartheid regime.

Notes

Acknowledgments: The Rhodes University Joint Research Committee, the National Arts Council, and the Arts and Culture Trust are acknowledged for their financial assistance in funding the research trips that made my research possible, while Shifty Records and Third Ear Music are thanked for supplying albums used in this research. Much appreciation goes to all those interviewed, who gave generously of their time.

1. Attempting to give credence to its policy of separate development, the South African government established separate homelands for each of South Africa's ethnic groups. The plan was for these to be granted independence so that blacks could gain full citizenship in these "independent states" only. Just four of the nine homelands were ever granted such independence: Transkei, Bophutatswana, Ciskei, and Venda. The Sun City holiday resort in Bophutatswana exploited its "independence" to attract a host of international musicians to perform in South Africa despite the cultural boycott.

2. Letter from the EMI International Manager to Cecile Pracher, supervisor of the SABC record library, 3 April 1987. The letter is part of the SABC radio archives.

3. Personal correspondence, Pretoria, October 1998 (an in-depth, open-ended, written response questionnaire).

4. Letter from the Directorate of Publications to Roger Lucey, October 1982.

5. Personal correspondence with Cecile Pracher, 17 March 2000.

Bibliography

Andersson, M. 1981. *Music in the Mix: The Story of South African Popular Music.* Johannesburg: Ravan Press.

Bell, A. 1988. "Musical Discord," *Time Out* (London ed.), 29 June–6 July, p. 12.

Eyerman, R., and Jamison, A. 1998. *Music and Social Movements.* Cambridge: Cambridge University Press.

Gilder, B. 1983. "Finding New Ways to Bypass Censorship," *Index on Censorship*, 1, pp. 8–22.

Gordon, S. 1997. "Basil Breakey—A Brief Biography," in B. Breakey and S. Gordon, *Beyond the Blues: Township Jazz in the '60s and '70's.* Cape Town, S.A.: David Phillips, pp. 5–7.

Hill, T. 1992. "The Enemy Within: Censorship in Rock Music in the 1950s," in A. De Curtis (ed.), *Present Tense: Rock & Roll Culture.* Durham, N.C.: Duke University Press, pp. 39–71.

Kerkhof, I. 1989. "Music in the Revolution," *Journal of Black Musical Traditions,* 2, pp. 10–21.

Maclennan, B. 1990. *Apartheid: The Lighter Side.* Plumstead, U.K.: Chameleon Press.

Mail and Guardian. 1995. "Music to Security Branch Fears," 7–13 July, p. 8.

Marcus, G. 1987. "The Gagging Writs," *Reality,* 19:3, pp. 8–10.

Marshall, S. 1995. "Long Live the Humble Audio Cassette—A Eulogy," in R. Sakolsky and F. Ho (eds.), *Sounding Off!: Music As Subversion/Resistance/Revolution.* New York: Autonomedia, pp. 211–214.

Nixon, R. 1994. *Homelands, Harlem and Hollywood.* London: Routledge.

Sony, W. 1991. "Strange Business: The Independent Music Culture in South Africa," *Staffrider,* 9:4, pp. 113–119.

Taylor, T. 1997. *Global Pop: World Music, World Markets.* New York: Routledge.

Willemse, H. 1991. "Censorship or Strategy?" in D. Smuts and S. Westcott (eds.), *The Purple Shall Govern.* Cape Town, S.A.: Oxford University Press, pp. 24–25.

Jeroen de Kloet

10   Confusing Confucius: Rock in Contemporary China

Silencing Culture

According to the ancient Chinese philosopher Confucius, two kinds of music are dangerous. The first is the loud and jarring kind that stimulates chaos. The second is the pleasing but lewd kind. Both disturb the harmony that Confucius considered crucial for society (Tuan 1993:89). If Confucius were to enter a music store in Beijing today, he would most likely classify rock (*yaogun yinyue*), predominantly produced in Beijing, as the loud music, and pop (*liuxing yinyue*), mostly produced in Hong Kong and Taiwan, as the pleasing but lewd kind. Since the 1980s pop and, to a lesser extent, rock have rapidly conquered the Chinese market. However, this process has not gone unchallenged. Confucius might be pleased to know that the current authorities in China share his view of music's dangerous potential and do their best to censor popular music, especially rock.

In this chapter I discuss the censorship strategies of the Chinese government with regard to popular music. My comments are largely based on field work conducted in Beijing between July and December 1997, in August 1999, and in April 2000. My intention here is not to write a genealogy of censorship in China, but rather to map out the impact of censorship on the production of music there.[1]

Generalizations that depict the artistic circle in China as either completely suppressed by or completely compliant with the communist state are inadequate. As I will show, the artist is neither fully a victim nor fully an accomplice.

Modern China studies describes a model of censorship called the "velvet prison." I begin with this model and then compare it with models of censorship in other (post-)communist societies. I then discuss the structure of the Chinese music industry and point out the crucial, yet ambiguous, role that the state plays within it. Rock directly confronts state regulations in three domains: (1) production and distribution, (2) broadcasting, and (3) live performances.[2] I outline the means of negotiating the restrictions in each case, focusing on lyrical content, since lyrics appear to be the authorities' main concern: I have not heard of a case where a song was banned because of its melody.[3]

I wish to move beyond a top-down, hegemonic view in which (state) power is interpreted as suppressing music cultures in China. Instead, I argue for a more dialectical view of power by presenting the tactics used by both musicians and the industry to negotiate their way through the regulations. We also need to move beyond interpreting censorship as solely a political concern. Censorship is more a playground than a political battlefield. It can even contribute to the promotion of rock, as I will show.

Rock and Pop in China

However crude the distinction might seem to westerners, Chinese audiences classify rock as different from pop. This becomes clear when one enters a record shop in Beijing, where the rock tapes are usually grouped together but separate from pop. "Rock" is louder, and both music and lyrics are written by the bands themselves. "Pop" is more melodic, and pop singers are usually not involved in the writing of either the music or the lyrics. Rock lyrics tend to touch upon personal struggles that often signify the political; pop lyrics more often elaborate on issues related to love. Western bands like Nirvana and U2 would be considered rock by Chinese audiences, while singers like Celine Dion and Ricky Martin would be seen as pop. Specific record labels, such as Magic Stone, Red Star, Modern Sky, and New Bees, are involved in the production of Chinese rock. Given its arguably more conspicuous political and sexual content, rock faces stronger censorship than pop does.

Chinese rock culture emerged after 1986 when Cui Jian—the most famous rock singer that China has produced thus far—released his hit single "Nothing to My Name." The Chinese audience was shocked by his hoarse voice. His eclectic music merges rap, reggae, and other forms with Chinese traditional sounds. In his wake other bands started to experiment with rock music.

Cui Jian's relationship with the authorities over the last 15 years has been contentious. In 1987 he was forbidden to perform after he played his rock version of the revolutionary classic "Southern Muddy Bay" (Nanniwan) before an audience that included government officials (Jones 1992:94). When he toured in China in 1990 to raise money for the Asian Games, his performances stirred up the audiences so much that the tour was cut short (ibid.:2). Yet Cui Jian manages to release his often controversial songs, albeit with both delays in production and various tricks by the artist. His political stance is clear in the following fragment from his song "Eggs Under the Red Flag":

> The red flag is still flying
> Without any fixed direction
> The revolution is still continuing
> The old men have more reasons
> Money is floating in the air
> We don't have any ideals.

In a personal interview (26 August 1997), Cui Jian expressed his annoyance at 15 years of struggle with the authorities: "I think the Chinese government plays a child's game that I cannot play. Maybe you can treat them as kids. Or maybe worse. Maybe you should lie. Or be patient. Only then you can win."

This "child's game" is the focal point of this chapter, and its complexity is shown by Cui Jian's previously cited 1990 tour, in which he started out working with the authorities and ended up being banned again.

Velvet Passions

How should we interpret Cui Jian's experience and censorship policies under a communist system in general? In order to answer this question, Geremie Barmé (1999) has adopted the idea of the velvet prison from Miklós Haraszti (1987), who analyzed the relationship between artists and the communist Hungarian authorities during the post-Stalinist period. In postrevolutionary China, argues Barmé, the Party cannot scrutinize and control artists as it did during the Cultural Revolution (1966–1976). Instead, by co-opting artists into its bureaucratic system, it has replaced a system of top-down control with self-imposed compliance from the artist: "Technocrats reformulate the social contract, one in which . . . consensus replaces coercion, and complicity subverts criticism. Censorship is no longer the job of a ham-fisted *apparatchik*, but a partnership involving artists, audiences, and commissars alike" (Barmé 1999:7). Via the co-opting of artists by the state, Barmé believes that self-censorship has become the major form of ideological control. Only a few artists, the naive heroes, dare to speak out against self-censorship. More maverick artists work independently, and in China they are sometimes generously funded by regional and global capital (ibid.:12–13). Interestingly, neither of these authors draws the obvious link to Gramsci, who was already arguing in the 1930s that hegemony by the state had moved from coercive control, manifested through direct force or its threat, to consensual control, in which individuals "voluntarily" assimilate the state's view (Gramsci 1971; Femia 1988:23–60).

The idea of a velvet prison positions artists vis-à-vis the state. Such politicization of art and popular culture is not restricted to China; it can also be found in writings on other (post-)communist societies. Commentators differ in their interpretations of the role of rock music in such societies, some seeing a potential for rock to be involved in political change. Peter Wicke, for example, argues that "rock music contributed to the erosion of totalitarian regimes throughout Eastern Europe long before the cracks in the system became apparent and resulted in its unexpected demise" (Wicke 1992:81). In his discussion of rock in Czechoslovakia, Mitchell (1992:187) makes a similar statement: "Rock music has represented probably the most widespread vehicle of youth rebellion, resistance and independence behind the Iron Curtain."

Sabina Ramet draws less on a fixed hegemonic model in her writing on Russian rock in the 1980s. Rather than seeing the music itself as intrinsically political, she points out that it was the authorities who politicized rock. In the USSR rock was just one part of the cultural scene that blossomed along with other realms of art when a new political climate dawned. Rock's complicated dependency on the state can be shown by analyzing USSR rock in the early 1990s. The erosion of the Soviet political order badly affected the rock scene, which, she says, lost energy once the fight with communism disappeared (Ramet 1994:10). Ramet's study shows that, in contrast to what Wicke and Mitchell suggest, there is little evidence that rock and socialism are natural enemies: On the contrary, the state in East Germany used rock as one of its propaganda tools (Rauhut 1998:343). (I am unaware of any similar direct use of rock by the Chinese authorities.) In her critique of the often assumed political role of rock in socialist societies, Pekacz (1994:48) concludes, in line with the velvet prison model as sketched above, that "relationships between the social-ist state and rock were more often symbiotic than contradictory, hence many rock musicians were more interested in 'adapting' to the *status quo*, rather than destroy-ing it." Rock can come into conflict with the authorities in socialist countries, but there is no inevitability about this.

Although the Gramscian idea of a velvet prison offers an appealing analogy, it unfortunately carries with it the danger of easy generalizations that miss the pecu-liarities of different systems. As I will show, it is sometimes an accurate way to describe how musicians deal with the authorities, but it can result in a rather vio-lent, paternalistic, and overpoliticized narrative: violent because it imprisons artists in a position of compliance with the authorities; paternalistic because the model's subtext suggests that true artists ought to resist any cooperation with state institu-tions; overpoliticized because it reduces complex cultural realities into a stereo-typical dichotomy of the artist against the state, a reduction emblematic of the west-ern gaze on China.[4]

As in other socialist societies, the relationship between the state and rock in China involves neither full compliance nor plain opposition. We have to release Chinese artists from the discursive construct of the velvet prison and search for understandings that interrogate the political by highlighting the tactics used by bands, companies, and publishers within the system in their attempts to circumvent it. I explored such themes in the interviews that form the basis of this chapter. All the parties are involved in a continuous negotiation of the rules set by the state. As I will show, such negotiations do not necessarily signify a desire to challenge the political; rather, the parties involved may simply want to release a commercially profitable album.

The Record Industry in China

In order to understand the particularities of the Chinese record industry, it is useful to elaborate briefly on the industry in the west.[5] An important distinction in the western music business is that between publisher and producer. A publisher signs a contract with the "authors" of a song (the composer and lyricist), and sells the song to a record company. The record company signs a contract with an artist who sings the song. Although some independent publishers still exist, most major record companies have both a publishing unit and a production unit. The production unit records the master tape, takes care of the production of the units (cassette, compact disc, LP, etc.), markets the product, and arranges the distribution to the retailers. A band that writes its own songs signs contracts with both the publisher (for the authorship rights) and the record company (for the mechanical rights), and receives royalties from both. Often one publisher, such as Universal, will sell a song to another company, such as Sony.

The role of publishers in China is significantly different from the western model and can best be compared to that of a book publisher. In China, the publisher actually decides to release a music product, often arranges the duplication of the master tape, and is responsible for its distribution throughout the country. A music publisher in China thus performs the roles that are performed by record companies in the west. What, then, is left for the record companies to do? A record company signs a contract with the artist, records the master tape, takes care of the design, and is responsible for the marketing, sometimes together with the publisher.

Under present regulations, foreign record companies are not allowed to set up independent offices in China; only joint ventures are legal. Nor are record companies allowed to release music independently. All music in China appears on the market through a publishing house, and all the publishers are state-owned. This is a crucial point, since it strongly influences the possibility of releasing products that might be considered sensitive. The publishing houses are affiliated to either the National Broadcasting, Film and Television Bureau (*guojia guangbo dianying dianshi zongju*)[6] or to the Ministry of Culture (*Wenhuabu*). Through the publishing houses, the government has a firm hold on the entire music market of China. Apart from the obvious financial advantages, this also provides the government with optimal opportunities to censor music.

It should also be noted, however, that most releases that appear on the Chinese market are pirated copies. A thriving unofficial music industry operates parallel to the official one, and piracy constitutes a market outside the domain of official regulations. It is, moreover, driven by the rules of supply and demand. But it takes an original to make a copy, and only those releases that appear on the official market—inside or outside China—are pirated. The existence of this market does suggest that regulations can be overcome, and it is to regulations that I now turn.

Regulations

The Product

According to Article 102 of the Chinese criminal law, it is an offence for any person "to confuse right and wrong, to poison people's minds, to incite the masses and create chaos, to undermine socialist revolution and construction, and to achieve the final goal of overthrowing the people's democratic dictatorship and socialist system" (Fu and Cullen 1996:145). This statement offers insight into one of the key features of Chinese law: ambiguity. What is meant by "right and wrong"? What is poisonous in popular music? In a personal interview (24 October 1997), Song Zufen from CMSP, one of China's biggest publishers, concisely summarized its policy: "There should not be any sexual content, or anti-China, antigovernment content. We just cut these inappropriate parts out."

With regard to the content of popular music, the issues that are deemed the most sensitive or—to retain the jargon of the law—most poisonous to the minds of the people are politics and sex. However, this simple dichotomy masks a more complex picture. Fu and Cullen (1996:162) correctly note that "in China the dividing line between what is unacceptable because it is obscene or indecent and what is politically unacceptable is less clear than in most Western jurisdictions." It is however possible to distinguish between laws directed against cultural expressions that might incite sedition, subversion, and defamation (and are thus focused on the political) and those directed against obscene and indecent expressions (thus focusing on the moral). In the political sphere a text issued by the Party's Political and Legal Commission in 1981 states that the political offence of counterrevolutionary incitement would be committed:

> Where counter-revolutionary elements, anti-party, and anti-socialist elements, and leading members of reactionary societies attack and defame the party leaders as the representatives of the proletarian dictatorship and the socialist system, in order to achieve the purpose of confusing the masses and subverting the proletarian dictatorship. (Quoted Fu and Cullen 1996:151)

Article 2 of the 1988 law on pornographic publications helps clarify the meaning of "obscene" and "indecent." Under these rules "obscene" includes:

- obscene and explicit portrayals of sexual behavior, sexual intercourse and their psychological effects;
- open publicity of pornographic and lewd images;
- obscene portrayals and teaching of sexual skills;
- explicit portraits of incest, rape, or the means or details of other sexual offenses sufficient to induce the commission of crimes;
- explicit portrayals of child sexual behavior;
- obscene and explicit portrayals of homosexual or other abnormal sexual behavior, or explicit portrayal of violent, abusive and insulting behavior related to abnormal sexuality; and
- any other obscene portrayals of sexual behavior that cannot be tolerated by ordinary people.

An ordinary person is defined as an adult who is physically and mentally normal (quoted ibid.:171).

Indecent publications are defined in Article 3 as those which:

- contain materials of the kind mentioned in Article 2;
- may poison the mind and health of ordinary people and especially minors; and
- lack artistic or scientific value. (Ibid.)

Although most stipulations on obscenity and indecency, such as those against child pornography, can also be found in western law, the rules focusing on the political are more alien to western juridical systems. It is sufficient here to note that in China a wide array of regulations and laws have been developed on which officials can fall back when they want to censor cultural expressions. During the 1990s these laws became increasingly detailed, but the ambiguity continued.

The rules cover both domestic and foreign-made products, but that latter are subjected to greater scrutiny. One reason for this is the economically informed desire to "preserve" national culture. Again this is not unique to China: For example, Canadian radio has specific quotas for Canadian content and French-language content (Grenier 1993). Fear of "spiritual pollution" from foreign cultures is reflected in the import regulations. Not only does China limit imports to 250 titles a year (Laing 1998:341), but foreign albums face stronger scrutiny, since they have to pass the Copyright Bureau as well as other control mechanisms. Publishers intending to release the works of foreign bands have to translate the lyrics into Chinese for the censors, whereas locally produced music only needs approval from the publishers. In the case of domestic music, only in those rare cases deemed to be sensitive will the Ministry of Culture check the product further. For a foreign product, the official approval of one of the ministries is obligatory. This is arranged by the local publisher. Song Zufen explained the impact of this practice:

The difference is that if we work with a domestic record company, we just reach an agreement and they send the master tape. But a foreign record company has to get official permission. They have to get the right from the Copyright Bureau. Then we go to the National Broadcasting, Film and Television Bureau to get the permission. (Personal interview, 24 October 1997)

Hong Kong and Taiwan are both considered foreign; the return of Hong Kong from British to Chinese rule in 1997 did not change its status in this respect. Thus, regional record companies that produce Chinese rock, such as Magic Stone from Taiwan, face stronger scrutiny than their competitors on the mainland, such as Modern Sky. Red Star, a Hong Kong–based company, cited this scrutiny as one of the reasons it set up a local company in Beijing.

Broadcasting

The regulations outlined above are applicable to broadcasts. Given its rebellious reputation, and at times content, rock is considered inappropriate for Chinese television. According to Li, a producer for a Beijing Television (BTV) pop show:

Rock 'n' roll is out, but even softer music finds itself in trouble if the performer doesn't look right. Certain areas of the body are more forbidden than others and nudity is not allowed. We can't show bands with men with long hair or women who have very short hair, earrings and strange make up. The decision-makers think it conveys a bizarre image that is not good for our young people. (Reitov 1998:139)

The limited broadcasting of rock on either television or radio is often cited by record companies as a factor that severely affects their opportunities to market rock music. It also indicates the inconsistency of official policies, which permit the release of rock, but not its promotion on television. In this respect, the music has not become "normalized." In some cases the imagery associated with rock can also serve as a barrier to a career in the media. For example, radio disk jockey Zhang Youdai started his career as a producer for a Beijing radio station. Because of his long hair, the radio officials did not trust him to present a program: "I asked them to let me try to host the program. 'Don't even think about it,' they said, 'because the radio station is the voice of the government; you should not be doing this'" (personal interview with Zhang, 16 July 1997). This statement underlines the general rule that the authorities consider rock unsuitable for airplay on national radio or television.

Live Performance

On 1 October 1997 a new set of regulations concerning artistic performances came into force, with 55 articles defining what is permissible. The regulations stipulate that organizers of performances need a business license and, furthermore, are required to obtain licenses for each specific performance. Special permission is required in the case of foreign artists. Other items shed a revealing light on what is considered sensitive:

Article 3: Performances should be held in order to serve the people and serve socialism; to put the social benefits in the first place, to improve the excellent culture of our nation and to enrich and improve the people's spiritual life.

Article 16: The government forbids the establishment of cultural performance organizations that are run or partly run by foreign capital.

Article 22: The government bans performances such as the following ones:

- those endangering the nation's security;
- those encouraging ethnic segregation, those infringing on the customs of minorities, and those damaging the unity of our nation;
- those expressing sexual, superstitious, and violent contents;
- those that are cruel and inhumane, doing harm to the performer's health;
- those attracting the audiences with the defects or deformation of the human body;
- other contents prohibited by the law and administrative rules. (*People's Daily* [*Renmin Ribao*], 27 August 1997)

With their focus on the political and the moral, as well as their national protectionism, these regulations resemble those dealing with music production, outlined above. However, the inherent limitations of this official discourse should be noted here. Implementation of regulations like these is far from consistent, and the actual text of the regulations is itself ambiguous. Furthermore, it is apparent that many of those involved in either writing or carrying out the regulations often do not believe in them themselves.[7] Thus, the regulations can be seen as in part a discursive masquerade, meant to legitimize the Party yet not really taken seriously by anyone. In comparison with other countries, Fu and Cullen (1996:274) argue that it is not so much the wording of China's laws that is "problematic," but their enforcement.

Overall, two interpretations of these sets of rules and regulations seem equally plausible. First, despite the disbelief among policy makers and enforcers in the rules, and despite their inherent ambiguity, they allow for selective enforcement. The state has the legal tools to censor anyone, anytime, for just about anything. Such a reading is very much in line with a view of China as an overtly politicized space—a view predominant in the west. However, I wish to move away from the statism of such a view and argue that the ambiguity of the regulations simultaneously confines *and* offers a space for all those involved—including the state-owned publishers—to negotiate their own way through. The negotiation may take the form of self-censorship, circumvention, ignoring the rules, or other tactics as creative as the music itself. Following are some of the ways in which the regulations are negotiated.

Negotiating Regulations

Negotiating the Product

Earlier I illustrated the key role of music publishers in China. Although all publishers in China are state-owned enterprises and operate under the production regulations outlined above, they are far from identical. According to Gene Lau from ZOOM Music, the competence of publishing houses depends largely on their "relationship" (*guanxi*) with the ministries they belong to. If that relationship is good, their products are more likely to be approved. A record company would look for a publishing house that enjoys a good relationship with the ministries in order to reduce the risk of its product's being rejected. Besides establishing and maintaining good *guanxi*, a good publisher also knows how to negotiate the rules. Dickson Dee from the Sound Factory, an independent Hong Kong record label, explains how he succeeded in releasing an album by Wang Lei, a Guangzhou-based rock singer:

> The publisher knew that some of the lyrics might lead to problems, but then they also knew how to play the game. They simply did not send anything to the censorship department, they just released it, and so far there has been no problem. (Personal interview with Dee, 6 July 1997)

Since the publishers are state-owned companies, this is a clear example of the state's direct involvement in circumventing its own rules and of the arbitrariness of the enforcement of the law. Such arbitrariness is in turn traceable among the publishers themselves: Some are more conservative than others. Either the record producer or the music publisher may employ "linguistic camouflage." The release of a Wang Yong album by the record company Magic Stone is a case in point. Wang Yong's 1996 album "Samsara" mixes "traditional" and Buddhist music with rock 'n' roll. Magic Stone's Beijing manager Niu Jiawei explained how they changed the lyrics on the jacket in order to circumvent censorship:

> We never put restrictions on the singers, in order to give them the freedom to perform the best they can. But we have to use some tricks to evade censorship. Usually we coin some words which are similar in pronunciation to replace the prohibited lyrics on the jackets. For example, Wang Yong's lyric *"wo jiu cao ni made"* ("fuck your mother") was changed into *"wo jiu qu ni ma?"* ("shall I marry you soon?"). (Personal interview with Niu, 16 September 1997)

Linguistic camouflage was also applied to the printed lyrics from the punk noise band the Fly's "Gun or Bullet," which appeared on a compilation album in 1994. "Sex" (*xing*) was turned into "heart" (*xin*); "making love" (*zuo ai*) was changed into "loving wrongly" (*cuo ai*).

Through the publishing houses, the state not only exercises control over the market, but also ensures a share in the revenues. The latter function of publishing houses helps explain why linguistic camouflage tactics are at times applied with their direct involvement. The urge to make money often outweighs the urge to censor. While Niu's assertion that they give absolute freedom to their singers corresponds with the romantic myth of the individual artist, Louis Chan from Red Star took a cautious approach: "We give them a warning to avoid any political content in their lyrics. They are pretty clever in this. They usually don't write about politics but more about personal issues" (personal interview, 28 August 1997).

There are more examples of self-censorship. The jacket of the 1997 release of "The Fly" depicts scenes by Beijing artist Song Yonghong that, according to the law texts quoted earlier, would be considered obscene. These images appeared only on the Taiwan and Hong Kong jackets (Figure 10-1). In order to get this album released for the mainland market, the record company Modern Sky removed these "obscene" images and replaced them with pictures of the band. Furthermore, the explicit sexual content of the lyrics was camouflaged.

In 1999 Modern Sky released an album by NO containing a weird mix of noise and new wave on a variety of instruments, some of them self-made. The lyrics of four out of nine songs are missing from the jacket, including those of a song entitled "Injustice," part of which runs:

> You have taken action to feel easy, feeling easy is freedom
> Freedom is human rights
> But human rights is politics!
> Comrade, you have foolishly entered the stage of politics.

Audiences are aware of the industry's tactics. One fan, Zhang Weiyun, complained in a letter to the band that the lyrics on the jacket of "The Fly" were censored: "Was the publisher too careless, or was it because of the strict censorship system? Whatever the reason was, if this album was to be released officially, I believe it should be done in a way that is responsible to rock fans like us" (personal correspondence, 20 April 1999).

Other fans are more understanding and simply ask for the correct version of the lyrics or express their admiration for the band's successful passage through the censorship system. In any case, it appears that at least some members of the audience are aware of the restrictions and are able to read between the sung and the written (or nonwritten) versions.

The band Zi Yue (meaning "It Says" or "The Master Speaks," a reference to Confucius) combines Beijing opera, rap, and traditional Chinese music with a straightforward rock sound. This eclectic mix eventually brought them not only popularity in China but also invitations to perform in Canada in 1999 and in Italy in 2000. Their case illustrates how record companies, in this case Jingwen, can get past the censors simply by biding their time. The album was released almost a year after the recording of the master tape was finished. This tape did not pass scrutiny by the

FIGURE 10-1. Illustrations from "The Fly" (Can Yin I), Taipei: Mud Records, 1997; illustrator: Song Yonghong. The censored version of the album was produced by Modern Sky in Beijing, 1999.

censorship department of the Ministry of Culture, and eventually one song had to be omitted. However, the incident is less political than it seems. The mother of Zi Yue's drummer Zhang Yue is a director of a Beijing television station. She accused the band's lead vocalist, Qiu Ye, of being a counterrevolutionary after she found out that her son was using marijuana. She then forced the Ministry of Culture to pay extra attention to their master tape. This was the only reason for the censors' getting involved at all, since Jingwen is a local company whose releases would normally face only the scrutiny of a publisher, not the closer scrutiny that foreign product undergoes. Eventually the complaints were found to be unsubstantiated, but the release was deliberately delayed by the band in order to avoid further problems. In the words of Jingwen's manager, Song Xiaoming:

> We have changed one song, not because of political content, but because of sexual content. . . . Now that the government is paying more attention to this one, we have to

use all kinds of methods. One of the methods is to wait, to drag out the time. (Personal interview with Song, 31 October 1997)

This case shows how much the censorship procedures can depend upon personal circumstances rather than on state surveillance. Zi Yue's problems were caused by one enraged mother. The lyrics of "Traffic Accident," which was censored because of her anger, run:

> My ass keeps on moving up and down
> Accompanying you into yet another orgasm
> You boast of the unique odor of your body
> Suggesting that I come and laugh like you.

Once again we can see similarities with procedures in the west. This song would undoubtedly have earned a parental warning sticker in the United States; it has never been released in China.

Cobra, an all-women rock band from Beijing, could not get the song "1966" released (the song had the Cultural Revolution, which started in 1966, as its theme). Their record company, Red Star, tried its utmost to get the full CD accepted. The first publisher it approached refused four songs; eventually it found one that wanted to ban "only" one song. Thus the CD was released minus "1966."

As already noted, pop music from Taiwan and Hong Kong is even more thoroughly scrutinized than domestic products, since it is considered foreign and thus has to be licensed. However, given its less controversial content, most pop can enter the Chinese market without too much difficulty. Nevertheless, some artists have still been confronted with censorship. The Taiwanese pop icon Ah Mei performed the Taiwanese national anthem during the inauguration of Taiwanese president Chen Shuibian on 20 May 2000. Following this, all advertisements in which she either featured or sang were banned from the mainland market, as were her CDs (Meijdam 2000:15).

Given the huge piracy market in China, banning CDs by popular artists like Ah Mei has relatively little impact. Censorship of foreign music, which includes regionally produced pop music, is beyond the scope of this chapter, as are the tactics developed by the producers of pop to circumvent censorship. It is sufficient here to note that censorship of music is not restricted to rock. But because of the often more explicit political or sexual content of its lyrics, it can be assumed that rock faces stronger restrictions than other genres. As noted earlier, the role of the unofficial market in circumventing official regulations is also important.

Negotiating Broadcasting

Despite a media landscape that seems not to favor rock, the genre continues to grow, and space for it is slowly opening up. The radio DJ Zhang Youdai, who at first was not allowed airtime because of his rocker image, eventually, in 1993, got his own program on a new station, Beijing Music Radio. He has now presented both Chinese and non-Chinese rock music.

Satellite technology poses another challenge to the authorities: An estimated 20 percent of the population can receive Star TV, which includes Channel V, an Asian equivalent of MTV that frequently shows clips of Chinese rock (Chan 1994:73). Furthermore, many magazines, such as *Music Heaven* and *Modern Sky Magazine*, present Chinese rock to the public and can be bought all over China. They normally include CDs with the latest western music and, in *Modern Sky*'s case, recent Chinese rock. Such new media offer challenges to existing regulations.

Li, the television producer quoted above, relies on her own form of self-censorship by cutting parts out of video clips and replacing them with other, less sensitive, shots. But she also recalled examples of the unpredictability of the system. On one occasion a ballad she considered suitable for airing was rejected by a more senior colleague on the grounds that the contents were "not very healthy." The song was about confusion and asked questions that appeared to have no answers. This was considered to be too sensitive, since official ideology did not sanction feelings of confusion. Questions could be asked, but they had to be resolved. After airing a performance by Chinese folk singer Ai Jing, Li's television show was banned for a month. The reason was Ai Jing's performance style: "She normally sits down quietly and plays gentle songs. This time she just jumped about on stage a bit, very gently, and my bosses said this was rock. It wasn't and we were all depressed" (quoted in Reitov 1998:141).

Li's statement reveals the power of genre distinctions. By reclassifying a folk singer as a rock singer—a reclassification based on the singer's appropriation of a part of the rock idiom by jumping around on stage—the heads of the television station constructed the act as politically sensitive.

Before the folk-rock singer Zheng Jun appeared on television, the police asked him not to say anything between the songs, and he agreed in order to be able to perform (personal interview with Zheng, 21 July 1997). This can be considered as a *moment* of compliance through self-censorship, in the same way that the critiques of modern life contained within his songs create in their live performance potential *moments* of subversion.

He Yong is a singer with a rather schizophrenic oeuvre that includes the punk-rock classic "Rubbish Dump" as well as melancholy folk songs. After he made fun of the model worker Li Xuli on television in late 1996, he was forbidden to perform for three years. However, he simply went to Kunming in southwest China and performed there, demonstrating not only the ambiguity of the system, but also the importance of *locality*. In general, regulations are less rigidly enforced the farther one goes from the political center, Beijing. Once again, this is not unique to China: Martin Cloonan (1996) has shown the importance of locality in pop censorship in the United Kingdom.

Negotiating Live Performance

When I attended a concert by Tang Dynasty in a bar owned by rock musician Wang Yong in July 1997, policemen cut the performance short. One week earlier the same venue had to close for a few days after a "rave party" to celebrate the handing back of Hong Kong to China was designated an illegal gathering. Wang Yong remained vague when I asked him what went wrong with the Tang Dynasty concert. He had not got the official permission, he said. Afterward he had to spend quite some time improving his relationships (*guanxi*) with the local police. Apparently he did that so well that before he closed the bar in 1999 (for personal reasons) it hosted rock concerts every Friday and Saturday night. Tang Dynasty had become one of its regular acts. The case again points to the importance of locality. China is not a monolith where rules and regulations are implemented everywhere in the same way. On the contrary, it is divided into many police districts. Once a bar owner has established good relationships with the local authorities, regulations can rapidly be loosened up.

Thus, club owners and concert promoters can avoid problems by establishing good relationships with the police.[8] Even then one ought to remain careful. Drug use should at all times be avoided in bars. Furthermore, in a move consistent with the model of the velvet prison, owners close their bars during sensitive periods (e.g., around 4 June, the day student protests in Beijing were violently suppressed in 1989). They do not stage any live performances when a Party congress is being held.[9] Former bar owner Fei Fei clearly had not established good relationships with the police:

> The police come unexpectedly to the bar to make sure no one dances and there is not too big an audience. If you have 15 seats in the bar, then you can only have 15 guests. If more than that, you might run into trouble. But you can never tell. Sometimes they do not allow, sometimes they do. (Personal interview with Fei, 21 September 1997)

His last remark is characteristic. The only thing everyone knows is that one never knows. The only thing one is sure of is that no one is sure of anything. The crucial strategy in organizing performances is to establish good relationships with the local authorities; yet even this does not guarantee an untroubled future. Care is needed when trying to explain the reasons for this. One should not overemphasize political reasons when explaining the limited amount of performances in Beijing. Yun Yin, keyboard player from the rock band Cobra, has a different explanation for why there are now fewer concerts than in the early 1990s:

> It is not that the government gets stricter—the government has always controlled rock music. I think there are now fewer organizers. In 1992 and 1993 people were very interested. . . . Later they found out that they really cannot make so much money from this. So fewer people organize rock concerts now. (Personal interview with Yun, 25 November 1997)

Not only government censorship, but also disappointment with rock's commercial potential, has affected the number of performances. Economics can censor as much as the state.

The regulations outlined above are more pertinent to large-scale concerts, for which official licenses are needed, than for semi-underground performances in bars. The authorities see large-scale concerts, especially in Beijing, as particularly problematic because they are scared of large gatherings and especially large gatherings of young people. Once again, this fear is not particularly Chinese or communist; in the west a whole body of literature discusses the "problems" represented by large gatherings of youth (see Cohen 1980; Hebdige 1988).

When I attended a major concert organized by the record company Magic Stone in November 1997, the line of policemen in front of the concert hall made me wonder whether I was going to a concert of five renowned bands or to some secret Party committee meeting. My ticket was checked three times. The record company was not allowed to sell tickets or promote the concert, which was sponsored by a foreign brewery and mainly organized for marketing purposes. Channel V broadcast the concert in Asia. On this occasion, concert organizer Niu Jiawei could not resist the temptation to give away 700 tickets instead of the 500 he was allowed to distribute. Although the place remained half-full, the police noticed the "mistake" and assured him that it would be noted in his personal file. The half-empty space, the ban on alcohol, and the large proportion of policemen in the hall successfully turned the concert into a bore. The regulations allowed the concert, but not the atmosphere that would have made it work.

Shortly after He Yong's appearance on television in 1996 and his subsequent banning, a large-scale concert by pop-rock singer Zang Tianshuo was cancelled. Neither his music nor his lyrics, which reflect upon issues such as friendship and love, are particularly sensitive. The concert was just badly timed: The authorities had been alarmed by He Yong's provocative television appearance. In a personal interview, Zang Tianshuo complained to me that artists like He Yong frustrated the development of Chinese rock. In this instance the idea of the velvet prison is rather accurate, as those, such as He Yong, who transgress the boundaries of the prison and do not comply with the authorities face condemnation by other musicians who opt for compliance. He Yong's rebelliousness in mocking a model worker is not seen as something to be emulated, but rather as responsible for denying others the opportunity to perform. In Zang's words:

> The most important thing is that the bands and the government should cooperate with each other. For example, both I and Cui Jian got cooperation from the government and then we got successful, but many new bands are not famous. With more cooperation, people would get to know them. (Personal interview, 2 December 1997)

In other words, a certain level of compliance is necessary to avoid upsetting the system, and Zang Tianshuo accepts it as crucial for the further development of the rock scene. Half a year after He Yong's action, Zang was able to perform in a fully booked Workers' Stadium. He Yong's act had ruffled the political feathers only for a brief period. However, the success of Zang's performance, in turn, annoyed Niu Jiawei, who had faced many problems while organizing the Magic Stone concert mentioned above:

> Zang Tianshuo applied for one year for this concert. Furthermore, he keeps on saying in public that he is not making rock 'n' roll and that he only wants to do something for the government and the common people. (Personal interview with Niu, 16 September 1997)

Thus, people within the rock scene deal with the velvet prison in different ways. Zang Tianshuo argues in favor of compliance with it, whereas He Yong chooses to transgress its boundaries and Niu Jiawei occupies something of a middle ground. All are involved in exploring the limits of the permissible in China. At times, transgressions of boundaries occur, after which the state becomes stricter for a while. The velvet prison is omnipresent. But it would be wrong to assume its omnipotence.

The Illusion of Confusion

Chinese censorship might best be interpreted as a playground where cats and mice play a game in which the cats do not care to enforce the rules seriously, while the mice want to avoid them as much as possible. Self-censorship—the basis of the velvet prison—proves to be only one of the ways in which artists and producers deal with censorship regulations in China. These regulations are, as I have shown, both ambiguous in content and selectively enforced. I have argued against a top-down, hegemonic model of power in which the state suppresses culture; instead, I have presented the tactics used by both musicians and the industry—such as linguistic camouflage and delaying release dates—to negotiate their way through the regulations. I have also suggested that government regulations are circumvented by a thriving local music industry.

It is more appropriate to think of censorship as a contested domain. Its boundaries are constantly being challenged and negotiated by musicians, producers, state-owned publishers, and audiences, as well as by the music industry. The government's inability to clearly define the boundaries, let alone impose them, produces a creative space for the rock scene to manifest itself in, even in a country in which the state is seen as being in almost absolute control.

Censorship can be considered to be more a playground than a political battlefield. It can even contribute to the promotion of rock. By attempting to censor rock, the Party is part and parcel of rock's production as a distinct musical world because the Party's actions correspond so well with the (marketable) image of rock as a suppressed and therefore rebellious sound. The case of the punk band 69 is illustrative in this respect. Together with three other hard-core punk bands, its members released their first album in 1999. I asked vocalist Peter about censorship problems, and he replied:

> Before we released it we expected problems. We *hoped* we would get problems. You know why? Because if we had problems, we would get famous. Everybody would know it. "Oh this band's got problems." "What's the problem? Let's buy it!" You know what I mean? We hoped, but nothing happened and we were disappointed. (Personal interview, 18 April 2000)

In other words, 69 had hoped that the state would officially legitimate their rebellious image, but the state declined. Nevertheless, the state can be implicated in such legitimations. The importance of government restrictions for the proliferation of the Chinese rock scene cannot be ignored. Censorship of rock in China can be interpreted as both restrictive and productive. It confines rock while at the same time creating a space for it.

I would like to argue for a modification of the concept of censorship. In order to escape from a prevailing political bias, it might be useful to broaden the issue to *strategies of exclusion*. Apart from strategies that are based on either political or social considerations (the protection of the state, the protection of the people), we can also distinguish those based on economic considerations. After all, as other chapters in *Policing Pop* illustrate, most music is excluded from the market not because of censorship, but simply because the music industry is not convinced of its market potential. Following China's inclusion in the World Trade Organization in the near future, such economic forces will increasingly define the sound of popular music there. Thus, economic factors have to be included in debates over censorship or, rather, over exclusion of certain music genres. The music industry must be seen as one of the actors who silence potentially critical voices even before they can be heard. As China becomes increasingly part of the world market, economic forces may prove to be more formidable than the "velvet prison" ever was.

Notes

Acknowledgments: I would like to thank Chow Yiufai for his critical reading of the text and inspiring support and Qin Liwen for her eagerness to explore with me the rock scene in Beijing. I am grateful to both for their help with the translations. I am equally grateful for the financial support provided by the Amsterdam School for Social Science Research (ASSR) and the Dutch Organization for Scientific Research (NWO).

1. It is worth noting that Chinese has no real equivalent for the word "censorship." In Chinese the most commonly used expression is *shencha*, meaning "to inspect" or "to check." The emphasis is thus on the act of inspecting, and the connotation is arguably less strong than that of English "censorship."

2. I confine my analysis here to practices directly related to music and have left out coercion tactics related to musicians' personal lives. Sometimes (rarely) singers are charged under the law against hooligans (*liumang*); more often bands (e.g., Tang Dynasty) or singers (e.g., Luo Qi) are taken into custody under charges of drug use.

3. On the contrary, I have heard of a case where the Ministry of Culture subsidized a compilation tape of revolutionary classics because of its lyrics. They would certainly not have been aware that these were being used in punk songs. Here the government subsidized a musical parody of itself.

4. For example, in 1999 China's internationally acclaimed movie director Zhang Yimou withdrew his entry for the Cannes film festival. He blamed the festival authorities for misreading his movies and reducing them solely to the political. In his words: "I cannot accept that the West politicizes Chinese cinema over all these years. If a movie is not against the authorities, it is immediately considered propaganda" (*De Volkskrant*, 21 April 1999, translation mine). I often find myself trapped in the same bias. Chinese pop-rock star Zang Tianshuo got irritated when I interviewed him in Beijing (2 December 1997). Halfway through the interview, he told my Chinese interpreter: "These westerners always ask questions about politics. So annoying. They never ask me questions about my music!"

5. I would like to thank Olav Vlaar from the Dutch Federation for Producers and Importers of Audio-Visuals (NVPI) for his exposé on the Dutch record industry. Unless otherwise indicated, my information on the western record industry is drawn from my interview with him in March 1999.

6. This is the new department founded in 1998 after the reorganization of China's administrative structure. It replaced the earlier Ministry of Radio, Film, and Television (*Guangdianbu*).

7. Tony Saich, an American sinologist, told me in October 1997 about a talk he had with an internet censor in China. The official agreed that it was senseless to screen the net, since new pages pop up constantly. What was important, said the censor, was that the higher officials *believed* that the net was under control.

8. The police are also directly involved in the entertainment industry. Policemen own Beijing's "Hot Spot" discotheque (*Re Dian*), not only controversial as a cruising place for homosexuals, but also notorious for the gun fights that have taken place there. At the time of writing, however, it remains one of the better places for dancing in Beijing.

9. From mid-August until mid-October 1997, there were hardly any concerts in Beijing because of the Fifteenth Party Congress. After that the scene quickly recovered.

Bibliography

Barmé, G. 1999. *In The Red—On Contemporary Chinese Culture*. New York: Columbia University Press.

Chan, J. M. 1994. "Media Internationalization in China: Processes and Tensions," *Journal of Communication*, 44:3, pp. 70–88.

Cloonan, M. 1996. *Banned! Censorship of Popular Music in Britain: 1967–1992*. Aldershot, U.K.: Arena.

Cohen, S. 1980. *Folk Devils and Moral Panics: The Creation of the Mods and Rockers*. Oxford, U.K.: Martin Robertson.

Femia, J. 1988. *Gramsci's Political Thought: Hegemony, Consciousness and the Revolutionary Process*. Oxford, U.K.: Clarendon Press.

Fu, H. L., and Cullen, R. 1996. *Media Law in the PRC*. Hong Kong: Asia Law & Practice Publishing.

Gramsci, A. 1971. *Selections From the Prison Notebook of Antonio Gramsci* (ed. Quintin Hoare and Jeffrey Nowell Smith). London: Lawrence and Wishart.

Grenier, L. 1993. "Policing French Language Music on Canadian Radio: The Twilight of the Popular Record Era?" in T. Bennett, S. Frith, L. Grossberg, J. Shepherd, and G. Turner (eds.), *Rock and Popular Music: Politics, Policies, Institutions*. London: Routledge, pp. 119–141.

Haraszti, M. 1987. *The Velvet Prison: Artists Under State Socialism*. New York: Basic Books.

Hebdige, D. 1988. *Hiding in the Light*. London: Routledge.

Jones, A. F. 1992. *Like a Knife: Ideology and Genre in Contemporary Chinese Popular Music*. Cornell East Asia Series. Ithaca, N.Y.: Cornell University.

Laing, D. 1998. "Knockin' on China's Door," in T. Mitsui (ed.), *Popular Music: Intercultural Interpretations*. Kanazawa, Japan: Kanazawa University, pp. 337–342.

Meijdam, A. 2000. "Chinese Girl Power," *Trouw*, 2 June, p. 15.

Mitchell, T. 1992. "Mixing Pop and Politics: Rock Music in Czechoslovakia Before and After the Revolution," *Popular Music*, 11:2, pp. 187–204.

Pekacz, J. 1994. "Did Rock Smash the Wall? The Role of Rock in Political Transition," *Popular Music*, 13:1, pp. 41–49.

Ramet, S. 1994. "Rock: The Music of Revolution (and Political Conformity)," in S. Ramet (ed.), *Rocking the State: Rock Music and Politics in Eastern Europe and Russia*. Oxford, U.K.: Westview Press, pp. 1–14.

Rauhut, M. 1998. "Looking East: The Socialist Rock Alternative in the 1970s," in T. Mitsui (ed.), *Popular Music: Intercultural Interpretations*. Kanazawa, Japan: Kanazawa University, pp. 343–348.

Reitov, O. 1998. "Rock a Spiritual Pollution," *Index on Censorship*, 27:6, pp. 139–141.

Tuan, Y. F. 1993. *Passing Strange and Wonderful: Aesthetics, Nature, and Culture*. New York: Kodansha International.

Wicke, P. 1992. "The Times They Are A Changin': Rock Music and Political Change in East Germany," in R. Garofalo (ed.), *Rockin' the Boat: Mass Music and Mass Movements*. Boston: South End Press, pp. 81–92.

Alenka Barber-Kersovan

---

11 German Nazi Bands: Between Provocation and Repression

Introduction: The Role of Ian Stuart and Skrewdriver

The term "Nazi bands" comprises a number of German skinhead groups whose output is connected with an extreme right-wing ideology. Like the skinhead subculture in general, these groups at first emulated British role models. The key personality of the British scene was Ian Stuart Donaldson, an ex-punk and active member of the extreme right-wing National Front. Donaldson's band, Skrewdriver, was among the first Oi! bands to politicize their music in order to articulate rightist sentiments (Nevill 1993:58).

In 1985 Stuart founded the Blood and Honour Movement as a production and distribution network for White Noise music, with branches in Scandinavia, France, and Germany.[1] Stuart also had personal connections with the German label Rock-O-Rama, which issued some of his early records (ibid.:59). Thus, although Stuart and Skrewdriver did not perform in Germany until 1989 (when they appeared along with other British bands such as No Remorse and Brutal Attack), they must be considered one of the main influences on the local skinhead scene (Funk-Hennigs 1994:49).

German Punks Playing Reich 'n' Roll

The origins of the right extremist politicization of a rock music genre can be traced to the late 1970s. At this point West Germany already had a number of local punk groups that were flirting with fascism—quoting slogans of the Nazi regime or adopting names like Blitzkrieg, Hitlers Oberste Heerleitung ("Hitler's Supreme Army Command"), and Proissens Gloria ("the Glory of Prussia"). Such sentiments were not unique to German pop; they were also found in Britain and other places.[2] They were, however, given an added piquancy in Germany because of its Nazi past. Other groups who flirted with fascism included Extrabreit ("Extra broad"), who used a portrait of Hitler as stage decoration, and Deutsch-Amerikanische Freundschaft ("German-American friendship"), who produced the song "Tanz den Mussolini" ("Dance the Mussolini"). This alarmed some commentators because it contained the lines "Dance the Mussolini, dance the Adolf Hitler, lower your knees and shake your bottom" (Stark and Kurzawa 1981:110).

The diffuse flirting with Nazi ideology within the punk subculture was generally considered nonpolitical (Deutscher Werkbund 1986; Seeßlen 1994),[3] until a worried press stumbled on the scene and began writing articles about "a new Hitler Youth on the march." An article in the monthly Der Spiegel ("The Mirror") entitled "Punk—Kultur aus den Slums—Brutal und häßlich" ("Punk—culture from the slums—brutal and ugly") played a key role in the attribution of right extremist overtones to this subculture. The cover of that issue featured a punker wearing a badge with the swastika on it (Lindner 1978:5–6).

It was unclear whether the initial flirtation with fascism was meant to be a provocation, a matter of generational conflict, a breaking of taboos, a fashion, or simply a joke. In most cases neither the political-sounding songs nor the apparently political iconography transmitted any direct political messages. Nevertheless, their ambiguity opened a politically sensitive space for such political messages to be added either by the (far) left or by the (far) right or in some cases by both (Laing 1985; Reynolds and Press 1995:70; Seeßlen 1994). Within the prepolitical punk scene, political groups supporting different—and sometimes incompatible—ideological positions had managed to build support. They would later use this support for real political goals.

The German Skinhead Scene

German Oi! music also lacked political significance at first. Furthermore, the first skinhead generation was characterized by a hatred of any kind of politics. Böhse Onkelz,[4] a punk/heavy metal group that later became known as one of the first "Nazi bands," stated: "When we started . . . there was football, drinking with comrades, having fun" (quoted in Eberwein and Drexler 1987:191). Gradually, however, the scene was politicized and split into two hostile parties.

One impulse came from outside the scene (Drechsler et al. 1993:34–36). According to Böhse Onkelz, "the leftists appropriated the punks" and "the rightists tried to appropriate the skins" (quoted in Eberwein and Drexler 1987:191). The second impulse came from within and was due to the "ideological" division between the punks and the "true" skins at the end of the 1970s. During this process parts of the skinhead scene started to drift in the direction of neo-Nazi political parties as a sign of their "political emancipation." In a process similar to the one that was also taking place in Great Britain, a handful of bands treated Oi! as an overtly political medium. The extreme New Right, discovering this subculture as a new field for political indoctrination, met these bands on common ground.[5] Some key personalities had connections with both the bands and the extreme right. For example, Torsten Lemmer, the executive secretary of an ultra-right political party,[6] was also the manager of the group Störkraft ("Disturbance Force"), one of the most subversive German Nazi bands, who frequently toured with Skrewdriver (Nevill 1993:60).

In East Germany the first skinheads appeared during the early 1980s. Although they listened to the same groups and followed the same stars as their West German peers, their situation was totally different. In the West, being far left and being far right were equally dissident. In the East, where the establishment itself was left, youths had to orient themselves toward the far right in order to rebel politically. Moreover, whereas in the West flirting with far-right ideology can be seen as primarily a subcultural pose, skinhead slogans like "Smash Communism" had a more explicitly political meaning in the East. Although the East German media did not report the scene, the skinhead subculture was under constant observation by the secret police and by the Ministerium für Staatssicherheit (Ministry for State Security). As a result, a number of fans were detained by the authorities—some for up to four years (Funk-Hennigs and Jäger 1995:170; Süß 1993:40).

After the Kids Were United

Following the collapse of communism in the German Democratic Republic (GDR) and the unification of both German states in 1989, initial euphoria turned into a growing social unrest, especially in the Eastern part of the country. This unrest was largely due to the overall deterioration of the economic situation. High unemployment was a particular problem, especially among Eastern youth. After unification, the unemployment rate in some parts of the former GDR reached 20 percent, and most of the unemployed were youngsters. The situation was exacerbated by a lack of lodging and housing; by substantial reductions in the health and social security services; and by large cuts in the culture, science, and education budgets (Fischer and Zinnecker 1992; Förster et al. 1993).

In addition, the unification process itself focused on the administrative, financial, and economic adjustment of the East to the West (hard currency, access to consumer goods, etc.), while neglecting the cultural and psychological aspects of the new situation (Wicke 1992:2). In this process the economic losers of the unification process in particular were left in a state of moral disorientation.

Eastern youths experienced a particularly acute disadvantage because of the dismantling of the existing network of youth organizations and institutions, including clubs and communication centers. The basic function of these infrastructures had, of course, been ideological indoctrination through free-time activities, but in practice they also provided space and facilities for other events, such as dances and rock concerts (Weigel 1994:78ff.). When they ceased to exist, youngsters who had no work and no place to go in their free time found themselves literally on the street.[7]

Under these circumstances, tension and frustration were inevitable. In some cases these feelings acquired a nationalistic dimension, and the main targets of the verbal (and sometimes physical) aggression that resulted were *ausländische Mitbürger* (literally "foreign citizens") living in Germany. For example, a 1992 study by Wolfgang Melzer (1992:117) found that 40 percent of young people in the West and 60 percent of young people in the East said that they were disturbed by the foreigners. In addition, 29 percent of youngsters in the West and 40 percent in the East wanted all foreigners to leave the country. A 1994 study found that 40.3 percent of young males from the Eastern part of the country believed that foreigners were responsible for the high unemployment rates; 51.0 percent believed that foreigners were trying to lead a comfortable life at the expense of the Germans; and 47.7 percent believed that foreigners were to blame for their bad housing situation (Sturzbacher 1994:64–67). Furthermore, in a study conducted by the Forschungsstelle Sozialanalyse in Leipzig, 14 percent of the schoolchildren and 25 percent of the apprentices stated that they had already taken part in violence against foreigners (Förster et al. 1993).

Other statistical data showed that criminal assaults against foreigners were increasing. Between 1987 and 1990 there were on average 250 criminal assaults a year; in 1991 this number climbed to 2,457 assaults, and by 1992 it was 6,336. During 1992–1993 this wave of violence culminated in a series of attacks on the homes of foreign nationals, including arson attacks in which 17 persons were killed. Most of these attacks were carried out by young skinheads, stimulated by alcohol and Oi! music (Willems et al. 1993:7–13).

The Radicalization of the Scene

Originally, the skinhead subculture was a marginal, insider scene. In the early 1980s West Germany had approximately fifty bands with a hard core of some five thousand fans. Skinzines, the print media of this scene, were issued in editions of 50 to 3,000 copies[8] and incorporated concert reports, record reviews, band interviews, football information, and semipolitical articles. No band could make a living purely from their music, and even cult bands would perform for fuel, lodging, and beer. Since bigger clubs and communication centers seldom gave Oi! groups the opportunity to play, most concerts were given on improvised open-air stages. The first Oi! record (by Böhse Onkelz) was not issued until 1984, and the number of tapes available at this point did not exceed a couple of thousand (Farin 1994:141).

Because of the political changes described above, in the late 1980s parts of the scene were radicalized to a previously unknown degree (Baacke et al. 1994:136). According to statistics produced by the Bundesamt für Verfassungsschutz (Federal Office for the Protection of the Constitution), at the beginning of the 1990s some 1,200 skinheads in the West were classified as right extremists, along with some 3,000 skinheads in the East (Funk-Hennigs 1994).[9] In addition, a number of Oi! songs contained statements that can be considered racist or nationalist, as the following examples show:[10]

Werwolf: If I look around me, I am in pain. Foreigners, repatriates, people seeking asylum. One seldom meets a friend. (*In mir drin, da tut es weh, wenn ich heut so um mich seh. Ausländer, Aussiedler und Asylanten, selten trifft man noch einen Bekannten.*)

Radikahl: Foreigners are destroying our country. What do they have against our history? (*Die Fremden machen unser Land zunichte. Was habt ihr gegen unsere Geschichte?*)

Stuka: Soon the people seeking asylum will be our masters. Parasites that they are, they do not want to work. (*Bald sind Asylanten unsere Herrn. Parasiten, das sind sie, arbeiten, das wollen sie nie.*)

Störkraft: We are the German right-wing police. We make the German streets free of Turks. (*Wir sind Deutschlands rechte Polizei. Wir machen Deutschlands Straßen Türken frei.*)

Radikahl: Stop cheating with the asylum. Germany for us Germans. Out with the flood of people seeking asylum. Germany for us Germans. (*Schluß mit dem Asylantenbetrug. Deutschland uns Deutschen. Weg mit der Asylantenflut. Deutschland uns Deutschen.*)

Kraftschlag: Our culture is a thousand years old, the Niggers are still sitting in the dark forest . . . Germany awake. (*Unsere Kultur ist 1000 Jahre alt, doch die Schwarzen sitzen noch im finsterem Urwald . . . Deutschland erwache.*)

Kraftschlag: They came to Germany and all they do here is crap it up. One has to kill them, nothing else makes sense. (*Sie kommen hier nach Deutschland und machen hier nur Dreck. Man muß sie einfach töten, alles andere macht keinen Zweck.*)

Endsieg: If you meet a Turk with a German wife, then that is racial disgrace and you know that perfectly well. So wait for him on a corner and cut off his cock so that he will die. (*Triffst Du mal 'nen Türken mit einer deutschen Frau, dann ist*

das Rassenschande, und daß weißt Du ganz genau. Drum wartest Du auf ihn auf
irgend einer Ecke, schneid ihm seinen Schwanz ab, auf daß er dann verrecke.)

Endsieg: Put them in the jail or put them in a concentration camp or send them
to the desert. I do not really care, just send them finally away. Kill their kids,
rape their wives, exterminate their race. *(Steckt sie in den Kerker, steckt sie ins*
KZ, von mir aus in die Wüste, aber schickt sie endlich weg. Tötet ihre Kinder, schän-
det ihre Frauen, vernichtet ihre Rasse.)

Nazi Bands As a Product of Media Hype

For more than a decade groups that were later labeled "Nazi bands" vegetated in
the twilight of subcultural invisibility without being considered a societal problem.
This situation changed drastically at the beginning of the 1990s when Oi! music
was implicated in a sudden outburst of racist violence. The first association was
made during the investigation of a May 1992 fire raid in Hünxe in which two
Lebanese girls were killed. Here the perpetrators, all of them young skinheads,
stated that they were inspired to commit this crime by the song "Ich bin ein Bomber-
pilot, ich bringe euch Tod" ("I am a bomber pilot, I am bringing you death") by
the group Böhse Onkelz (Farin 1994:142).

This connection was made public by *Der Spiegel*, which made the first strong statements about the fascistic nature of this musical genre, just as it had done in the
case of punk a decade before. Other print media jumped on the bandwagon and
published numerous articles about a subcultural phenomenon that most of the journalists had never encountered and about music they had never had the opportunity to hear. Meanwhile, television broadcast almost daily reports about racist
attacks by right extremist youngsters and about the Nazi bands that were described
as their "secret seducers" (Baacke et al. 1994:7). Even the international pop music
press, *Billboard* in particular, could not resist sensationalism, and during Easter 1993
MTV dedicated a whole day to this topic. This overwhelming media coverage had
a number of effects.

First, the media constructed a public image of the skinhead subculture that had
little to do with its subcultural reality. The characteristics of the archetypal skinhead
style were exaggerated, and extremes were presented as the norm. Youngsters reported that they were sometimes paid by journalists to talk big or get photographed
in a Heil-Hitler pose (Matuscheck 1994:24).

Second, even though one of Böhse Onkelz's songs had already asked, "Do you
really believe everything I say?" and pointed out that the irony they played with was
the "shadow of our souls," the musical texts were taken at face value and read simply as political pamphlets. Commentators ignored the fact that the reception of pop
music, especially in combination with ecstatic dance, usually does not take place

on the cognitive level (Bruhn et al. 1985). They also missed the presence within the scene of different generations of skinheads with different attitudes, and the fact that different subgroups had different political orientations. Left-wing skinheads (such as Red Skins, Anarcho-Skins, Skinheads Against Racial Prejudice) were swept under the carpet, along with the main body of nonpolitical skins. The dominant image in the media was that of a Nazi skin dancing to fascist ideology and setting foreign citizens' houses on fire.

Third, the media intervention produced radical changes within the scene itself. On one hand, previously fragmented pockets of skinheads were reconstructed as a nationwide subculture with certain properties (Hohmann 1993:88). On the other hand, as if playing out a self-fulfilling prophecy, youngsters defamed as "Nazi skins" started to behave exactly as public opinion expected them to behave (Eberwein and Drexler 1987:46). The texts of the new bands, some of which were now formed for purely political reasons, became even more subversive. The fans, accused of being violent, became even more aggressive. The number of followers imitating every single detail of the skinhead image increased, and so did the number of arson attacks. Copycat attacks reproduced step by step the horror scenario that was being shown on television (Willems et al. 1993:87).

Fourth, Oi! music, once known only to insiders, was now disseminated on a broader scale. Members of the most subversive Nazi bands were herded from one talk show to another, and even beginners gained media attention. Furthermore, the more indignant the media reports became, the more intense was the interest in the ultra-hard "Nazi rock" (Farin 1994:145). For example, Böhse Onkelz sold half a million records almost immediately (Walter 1993b:29). They even got onto the charts, despite the fact that no radio station played their music.

Finally, there is no doubt that the basic goal of the media coverage was the suppression of neo-Nazi political tendencies.[11] In practice, however, it also provided a platform for right-wing extremists whom the media had previously refused to interview (Stark 1993b:6).

Rock Against Racism

Because of the Holocaust and the historical responsibility that Germany bears, Nazism is a very sensitive issue there,[12] and the media reports were followed by a fierce and emotionally loaded anti-Nazi-band campaign. The rock music scene as a whole was especially anxious to avoid coming under public attack and felt obliged to distance itself from nationalism, violence, and criminal acts. Concert organizers made sure that Nazi bands did not get the chance to perform, radio stations did not play Oi! music, and prominent rock musicians made their antiracist opinions public through talk shows, interviews, and advertisements in the daily press. Record companies that normally do not hesitate to sell the latest "rock revolution" kept their hands off this musical genre. Major distribution networks such as World of Music refused to sell records by bands seen as politically dubious, and the Gesellschaft für musikalische Aufführungs- und mechanische Vervielfältigungsrechte (GEMA), the organization that manages rights and royalties in Germany, adopted the following resolution:

> As for the Neo-Nazi actions, GEMA distances itself in the name of composers, poets and publishers it is representing from composers, poets and publishers of this kind of music and announces that it refuses to manage the royalties for any works whose content is aimed against the basic order of democratic freedom. Music that is used to glorify violence and call for racial hatred, crime, and hostility against foreigners does not belong to the world repertoire of musical works protected by GEMA. Recordings with the content mentioned, currently circulating on the market, were not produced by GEMA members. (*Musikspiegel* 1997:10)[13]

In the best Rock Against Racism tradition, in 1993 a mega-concert took place in Frankfurt, attended by some 150,000 people. This event was backed by public television stations, the pop music print media, and the Deutsche Phonoakademie, the umbrella organization of the German record industry.[14] Similar events were carried out in clubs and communication centers, with the German Rock Musicians Association appealing to its members to make an active contribution (*Rockmusiker* 1993:13–17). The following two examples show how these projects were typically designed:

- In Bavaria rock musicians' organizations, including the Rockzentrale Nürnberg and its newspaper, *Zentralnerv*, launched a project entitled "SOS Deutschland! Stop Rassismus! Stop Faschismus!" ("SOS Germany! Stop Racism! Stop Fascism!"). This consisted of a CD with antiracist songs in German, English, and Turkish and a tour by the groups involved. The income generated by this action was donated to a newly established antiracist news agency (*Zentralnerv* 1994:18).
- The "Rap for Courage" project was initiated by the Amt für Jugendarbeit in der Ev. Kirche von Westfalen (Bureau for Youth Work in the Evangelical Church of Westphalia) and financed by various sponsors, including the Ministerium für Jugend, Gesundheit und Soziales (Ministry for Youth, Health and Social Affairs). Though outlined as a broad youth culture project encompassing music, theater, video, painting, poetry, and photography, one of its driving forces was the Sons of Gastarbeita ("Sons of Guest Workers"), a rap group from Bochum consisting of young people from six different nationalities.

High-brow pop music critics who had mostly ignored the existence of "Nazi rock" in the past now drew attention to it. Of particular importance was a book by Max Annas and Ralph Christoph (1993) that brought together theoretical essays about Nazi rock and reflections on the role of music journalism in the events described. From their contributions to this project, it was evident that the journalists concerned had had a very hard time readjusting their position. This was because the right-wing extremism with which parts of the skinhead subculture were allied cancelled out what was considered to be a "historical pact" between youth subcultures and the "project of the left revolution" (Seeßlen 1994:175). The rise of neo-Nazi youth shook the foundations of a theoretical paradigm that had assumed that youth would be on the side of the left (Annas and Christoph 1993).

The main dilemma was as follows. On one hand this subculture possessed all the properties that were for decades praised as desirable for subversive subcultures: It was handmade, spontaneous, authentic, socially rooted, dissident, noncommercial, and powerful (Müller 1994:47). On the other hand "Nazi rock" appropriated subcultural codes that were previously considered generically leftist in order to promote right-wing extremism and violence. This was incompatible with the political correctness of alternative pop music journalism, and the leading magazine *Spex* went so far as to proclaim "the end of the subcultures" in an article entitled "The kids are not alright" (Diederichsen 1992).

Espionage and Censorship

For weeks in 1993 thousands of citizens gathered in demonstrations as political parties, schools,[15] and other public institutions moved the topic to the top of their agendas. Conferences were organized and research projects launched in order to analyze the situation and develop strategies for dealing with the neo-Nazi phenomenon. The previously neglected role of youth work was re-evaluated and more money made available. In 1992 the federal government contributed 200 million DM for youth and cultural work, and the Bundesministerium für Familie und Jugend (Federal Ministry for Family and Youth) in the eastern part of the country started a program against aggression and violence that cost 50 million DM (Lammert 1994:13). Local authorities fostered corresponding projects in youth culture, rock music, social work, and pedagogic initiatives (Bücken 1994:164).

In addition to the massive efforts being made to counter nationalism and violence through social and political work, education, and public discourse, repressive measures were applied. The crucial role here was played by the Bundesamt für Verfassungsschutz (Federal Office for the Protection of the Constitution),[16] which had been collecting data about the neo-Nazi skinhead scene for a long time but had not previously acted. In 1993, however, the office instigated a nationwide operation called Notenschlüssel ("the Clef") in response to the explosion of violence. Police searched the homes and offices of musicians and bands, looking for incriminating records, tapes, and fanzines. A criminal charge was lodged against Rock-O-

Rama from Köln, the chief producer and distributor of White Noise in Germany,[17] and in 1993 the police confiscated its stock of records and tapes, consisting of some 30,000 items.

Furthermore, members of the groups Störkraft, Radikahl, Tonstörung, Noie Werte, and Kraftschlag were put on trial for national incitement under paragraph 130 of the German criminal law (Strafbuchgesetz), whereby people who "violate the human dignity of other persons by (1) inciting hatred against other parts of the population; (2) encouraging violence or similar actions; or (3) insulting, maliciously disdaining, or defaming them will be punished with the withdrawal of freedom for three to five years." In most cases the prosecutions resulted in probation, although Jens Arpe from Kraftschlag was sentenced to two years in jail (<www.bloodandhonour.com/route88/html>; accessed Dec. 2001).

As another means of repression, on the recommendation of the Bundesprüfstelle für jugendgefährdende Schriften (Federal Examination Agency for Texts That Could Endanger Minors),[18] several records, tapes, and fanzines were put on the index. The *production* of these items was not forbidden henceforth, but selling them to people under the age of 18, advertising them, and distributing them became illegal (Bundesprüfstelle 1992). To understand the importance of this sanction, recall that the German constitution is based on the Universal Declaration of Human Rights and therefore explicitly excludes state censorship and guarantees freedom of art, science, and education. At the same time, the law limits freedom of speech in cases where (1) loyalty to the constitution is violated and (2) the dignity of another person is violated through words or pictures or youngsters could be morally or otherwise endangered (Gesetz über die Verbreitung jugendgefährdender Schriften— the Law on Distribution of Printed Matter That Could Endanger Minors).[19] Thus in addition to immoral texts in the traditional sense, items inciting crime and violence, stimulating racial hatred, or glorifying war had been, and continue to be, subject to indexing (Bundesprüfstelle 1992).

Texts of several Nazi bands met these boundary conditions and were registered on special lists.[20] This became increasingly common. During the 1980s only a few records, including "Der nette Mann" ("The nice man") by Böhse Onkelz, had been registered (Baacke et al. 1994:134). Between 1992 and 1995, however, 75 records, tapes, and CDs as well as 72 fanzines were indexed (Farin 1996), including a number of records and tapes from the eighties that had been freely available before. By the end of 1999, the Bundesprüfstelle für jugendgefährdende Schriften had put 140 records, tapes, and CDs on the index, most of them right-wing extremist Oi! music.

Attempts to forbid the activity of certain Oi! bands failed because there was no juridical justification for criminalizing playing in a rock band. Similarly, political justifications were seldom used to ban skinhead concerts. Instead, arguments for concert bans mainly centered upon the expected violent encounters between left extremist and right extremist youngsters.

The Effects of State Repression

The effects of the campaign against Nazi bands have been rather ambiguous. Initially, the campaign seemed to be successful, as bands that came under pressure from the authorities on one hand and public opinion on the other gave up their activities, and the production of Nazi rock temporarily decreased. Other bands kept going but distanced themselves publicly from right-wing extremism. Among these were Böhse Onkelz, who were published by Bellaphon and Virgin (Neitzert 1996) and celebrated by heavy metal magazines as "the German number 1 metal band."

Yet the most subversive and politically motivated bands retained their radical position and went underground. They simply adjusted to the new conditions, and by the mid-1990s the neo-Nazi skinhead scene had begun to reorganize itself in a way that proved that the basic aim of the anti-Nazi-band campaign—the repression of neo-Nazi tendencies in popular music—had not been achieved. The following points should be noted here:

(1) The number of Nazi bands increased again. According to the Federal Office for the Protection of the Constitution, after the Clef action there were some 30 bands left; in 1994, 40 bands were listed as active; in 1995, 50 bands; in 1996, 55 bands; in 1997, 70 bands; and in 1999, some 100 bands. Hundreds of CDs and tapes are on the market, and each year the Nazi rock repertoire grows by 50 to 100 new productions. In 1999, the turnover of this musical genre was about 8 million DM (Bundesamt 1999).

(2) The number of concerts increased. In 1994 only 20 skinhead concerts were recorded as having taken place. In 1995 there were 35 concerts; in 1996, 70 concerts; 1997, 106 concerts; and in 1998, 128 concerts (ibid.). The number attending these mostly secretly organized gigs varies. Since it is very difficult to acquire a license to hold a skinhead concert, in order to book an appropriate hall the events are often declared as "birthday parties" for some 30 to 200 "friends" (Trunk 1999).

(3) Since producers of neo-Nazi music fear continuous repression, the bands prefer to issue their CDs abroad, especially in Scandinavian countries and in the Czech Republic. Most of them are pressed by Gramofone Zavody in Lodenice and by CDC in Celakovice, near Prague. The deals are carried out by Adrian Preißinger, who is primarily a political activist and who has been prosecuted for right extremist political activities (Wagner 1999:33).

(4) Two opposing tendencies can be observed with regard to the content. The texts became less openly fascistic in order to avoid repression (Farin 1996), but a further radicalization has also been noted. Thus, for example, on the CD "Gute Zeiten, schlechte Zeiten" ("Good times, bad times") by the group Bonzenjäger ("Politician hunters"), death threats against leading politicians are articulated.

This CD was indexed. Another example is the video "Kriegsberichter" ("War reporter"), which includes a demonstration of how to murder a Jew: In one scene the British band No Remorse is shown in front of the burning home of some Rostock asylum seekers, screaming one of their popular songs, "Barbecue in Rostock." Furthermore, the video includes photographs, names, and addresses of anti-Nazi campaigners, mostly journalists and lawyers, along with the instruction "A bullet in the head" (Kleffner 1999). These videos were recorded by NS Records from Frederiksberg in Denmark (ZDF 1998). Their producer, Marko Jasa Jarvinen, has been imprisoned in Finland (<www.bloodandhonour.com/route88/html>; accessed Dec. 2001).

(5) The scene became commercialized to a previously unknown degree. For example, some army shops sell "German articles," including CDs, tapes, fanzines, badges, T-shirts, flags, and stickers, frequently ornamented with slogans, symbols, and neo-Nazi-style visuals (Spannbauer 1999).

(6) Thanks to the active involvement of some German neo-Nazi organizations,[21] the international Blood and Honour Movement,[22] and the Hammerskin Movement, the originally rather chaotic skinhead scene gained much firmer contours. By 1999 a quarter of all skinhead concerts were organized by the German chapter of Blood and Honour (Kleffner 1999).

(7) The neo-Nazi skinhead scene is making increasing use of the internet. In addition to purely musical pages, many home pages of right-wing extremists offer Nazi rock for downloading, as well as advertisements and links to bands, labels, and concert organizers. Since German providers have repeatedly banned home pages with right-wing extremist content, some political parties act as providers themselves (e.g., the Nationaldemokratische Partei Deutschlands, the German National Democratic Party, does this). Others make use of providers from abroad, mostly from the United States and Canada (the Thule Network). This route permits access to material (including music) that is forbidden in Germany (Bundesamt 1999).

(8) The musical spectrum of songs with neo-Nazi texts has been enlarged. The work of the singer-songwriter Frank Rennicke, a member of the illegal Wiking Jugend ("Wiking youth"), is particularly noteworthy. His CD "Ich bin Nicht modern, ich fühle Deutsch" ("I am not modern, I feel German") was indexed in 1997. There have also been some attempts to infiltrate the techno scene and parts of the esoteric scene. Further, some ultra-right texts were clad in the seemingly "innocent" sound of the German "Schlager" (popular song). An example is the CD "12 Doitsche Stimmungshits" ("12 moody German hits") by Zillertaler Türkenjäger ("Turk hunters from Zillertal"), which includes cover versions of well-known hits. With such musical packaging neo-Nazi political ideas became palatable for older listeners and appealed to a much broader public than the noisy Nazi rock was ever able to reach.

Squaring the Circle

When considering music and censorship, it could be argued that radical subcultures never live in a vacuum and thus that the fatal realism and fascistic messages of Oi! texts were not a phenomenon *sui generis* but a reflection of a specific political atmosphere. Echoing the "rhetorics of crisis" (Hebdige 1983) that dominated the public discourse of the early 1990s, "Nazi rock" in a certain sense "dramatized" the existing social pathology by boiling down complex political issues, such as the parliamentary debate on asylum, into simple slogans like "Germany for the Germans" and "Foreigners out."

In a similar generalization, the Nazi skinhead was constructed as the incarnation of evil. Society projected its dark side onto a group that was to become a scapegoat for the nation, thereby delegating to the youth a problem that it was unable to solve on the political level. From this point of view, the repression of the Nazi bands had the function of a symbolic purification, activating mechanisms of democratic self-control that—at least temporarily—re-established public agreement on anti-Nazism not only as a declared state goal, but also as one of the basic values of German society.

I agree with scholars like Dieter Baacke (1999) who argue that social problems cannot be solved by repressing their symptoms and who also disapprove of defaming a whole subculture as "Nazi." At the same time, it has to be acknowledged that parts of this musical scene consciously stimulated racial hatred, sometimes on behalf of right extremist political parties. Documents by the United Nations[23] and the European Union[24] describe racism and Nazism not only as major political problems endangering "the general welfare of a democratic society," but also as serious violations of the Charter of Human Rights. Consequently according to Recommendation XV (42) of the UN Commission for the Extermination of Racial Discrimination (Article 4 of the International Convention Against Racism), the suppression of ideas of racial superiority and racial hatred can be considered compatible with the right to free speech as stated in the Universal Declaration of Human Rights (UN Menschenrechtskommission 1997).

Bear in mind that "Nazi rock" was not only a matter of symbolic provocation, but was also associated with racially motivated crimes, including murder. Though none of the bands mentioned above was physically involved in violence, none of them tried to prevent it either. According to German law, failure to prevent criminal acts is punishable.

Overall the issue of the German Nazi bands produces more questions than answers. The emotionally loaded events described, including ideological overreactions, can be seen as condensing the spirit of the time—a struggle between global participation and provincial seclusion, between the enlightenment concept of individualism and new forms of corporatism, between nationalism and cosmopolitanism. They represent one of those borderline cases in which different philosophical, moral, political, and juridical issues collide and thus open up fundamental questions about the relationship between the individual and society, morality and law, culture and politics, nationalism and internationalism, tolerance and intolerance, the universal and the particular—as well as about the fluid transitions between radical musical expression and violence.

Notes

1. After the fall of the Berlin Wall, this movement also spread to the former socialist countries, and by 1993 Blood and Honour was already present in 20 countries.

2. A number of punk and post-punk artists flirted with fascism. Sid Vicious wore a red T-shirt with a swastika on it; Throbbing Gristle made an album entitled "Music from the Death Factory"; Joy Division—who took their name from the Treblinka concentration camp—published a picture of a Nazi drummer on the sleeve of the "Warsaw" album; the Residents issued a record entitled "Third Reich 'n' Roll"; Luxus brought out the song "Auschwitz"; the Cretins wrote a number called "Dachau Disco"; and the slogan "Today Your Love, Tomorrow the World," as used by the Ramones, was an allusion to the Nazi slogan "Heute gehört uns Deutschland und morgen die ganze Welt" ("Today Germany belongs to us and tomorrow the whole world").

3. Georg Seeßlen (1994:169) explained the output of these bands in terms of the "semantic catastrophe of postmodernism": thanks to the demystification of verbal and iconographic symbolism, the recontextualization of historical issues, and the playful appropriation of political topics, political symbols tipped over into empty signs, bereft of their ideological content.

4. Böhse Onkelz originated in Frankfurt—a left-wing city with a strong hippie dominance in culture and politics as propagated by the Green Party. The first punk singles circulated here through the Karl-Marx-Buchhandlung, a book shop managed by Daniel Cohn-Bendit, a leader of the student movement from the late 1960s and now a member of the European Parliament, and Joschka Fischer, minister for foreign affairs as this book goes to press (Walter 1993a:40).

5. Since Oi! was largely free of Afro-American musical influences, it was the first rock music genre that was co-optable by right-wing extremists (Annas and Christoph 1993:15). Up until then, their musical repertoire had predominantly consisted of traditional marches and "Heimatlieder" ("homeland songs"; see Deutsche National-Zeitung 1995:v).

6. Torsten Lemmer also belonged to the editorial board of the neo-Nazi newspaper Europa Vorn ("Europe Ahead") (Neitzert 1995). He issued Skinhead Rock (1994), a "theoretical" work on what he called "nonconformist music." In this book he explicitly argued that connections between the skinhead music scene and the right extremist political parties should be intensified.

7. The importance of these institutions for young people is evident from a study by the Deutsche Schell. In this report 60 percent of those questioned stated that they miss the

Youth and Pioneer organizations of the ex-GDR that they had previously rebelled against (Wicke 1992:2).

8. An exception was the magazine *Moderne Zeiten* ("Modern Times"), which was issued in an edition of 10,000 copies. One of its editors was Torsten Lemmer (Baacke et al. 1994:10).

9. The fact that in the eastern part of the country there were proportionally more right-wing skinheads than in the West was also due to the fact that the ideological vacuum left after the collapse of Marxism was relatively easy to fill with neo-Nazism, which found more competition in the pluralistic political scene of the West.

10. The following are free translations by the author.

11. The problem of neo-Nazism was not only a subcultural one. According to a study by Helmut Willems, in the early 1990s some 13 percent of German voters had a world view that was close to that of the extreme right wing. Moreover, the escalation of violence would not have been possible had the skinheads not been backed by at least a part of the adult population (Willems et al. 1993:91). That is why for Georg Seeßlen those implicated in the rise of the extreme right were not just the "proletarian kids," or skinheads, who started to "dance the Adolf Hitler" again. They also included politicians who were "blind on the right eye"; intellectuals who made restorative contributions to the ultra-right ideology; radical artists who turned barbaric masculinity into passionate pictures; noisy music; militaristic fashion; and the athletic cult of the body. Skinheads and Nazi bands merely took over these radical gestures, reduced their semantic content to a limited number of topics, and converted the (aesthetic) playing with violence into the actual physical use of aggression (Seeßlen 1994:174).

12. The sensitivity of this issue was shown by the case of a bass player from the German Opera of Berlin who signed his hotel bill "Adolf Hitler" during a tour of Israel in 1998. Although he is a prominent musician, he was fired from the orchestra, was expelled from the Deutsche Orchestervereinigung (German Orchestra Association), and lost his teaching position at the Berlin Music Academy Hans Eisler (*Frankfurter Rundschau* 1999).

13. The declaration by GEMA was merely a gesture, since no Nazi band was a member anyway. The reason for this was less the bands' political orientation than their low musical qualifications. Thus even if these groups had applied for membership, most of them would have failed to meet the artistic entrance criteria.

14. In order to stress the engagement of the music industry, in 1995 Sony Music issued an antiracism CD under the motto "Hand in Hand: All Different—All Equal," featuring prominent rap bands, among them Fettes Brot, Advanced Chemistry, Die Fantastischen Vier, and Weep Not Child.

15. Music education was put under particular pressure. Teachers' seminars were organized and corresponding teaching materials issued (*Zeitschrift für Musikpädagogik* 1996). Under the slogan "Music education—education to tolerance," a number of popular songs not previously deemed worthy were included in the school repertoire, including Michael Jackson's "Heal the World," which became a pedagogical hit.

16. Since Germany has experienced both Nazi and Communist totalitarian systems during its history, this office was established to secure human rights and the principles of a democratic society as they were put into legal terms by the German constitution.

17. Active since 1977, Rock-O-Rama was originally a punk label dealing with a wide range of music. The first records by Böhse Onkelz were issued by Rock-O-Rama, and even journalists from the sophisticated pop magazine *Spex* got records from this source. As the inter-

est in punk diminished, Herbert Egoldt, the owner of this label/shop, concentrated its activities on Nazi rock. This proved to be a very profitable decision (Farin 1996; Gotschalk 1993:110).

18. The Bundesprüfstelle is civic body composed of representatives of various secular, religious, and cultural institutions, organizations and associations, not a state one. However, its chair is appointed by the Bundesfamilienministerium, the Federal Ministry for the Family.

19. "Printed matter" here includes texts and audio, audio-visual, and multi-media materials.

20. Only German titles were indexed; English, French, and American songs were not considered, even though some of them were more subversive in terms of promoting fascistic ideas, such as the glorification of Adolf Hitler and Rudolf Heß, than those by the German bands.

21. The Nationaldemokratische Partei Deutschlands (NPD) is especially active. A member of its executive committee, Jens Pühse, owns a distribution firm for Nazi rock, Jens Pühse Tonträgervertrieb.

22. The fact that Blood and Honour understands its musical involvement as a political activity is evident from the editorial in the first number of its magazine *Route 88* (that is, "Route Heil Hitler" in the neo-Nazi code system): "This is a 'Blood and Honour' publication, but not just a music magazine. It is a political journal published to get you going as National Socialist activists, just like the White Power compact discs. We'll have interviews with White Power rock bands just as we'll have interviews with political activists. . . . We'll salute any NS ACTIVIST [emphasis in original], whether he listens to music or not. But we'll despise any NS person who listens to music and has no time for activism" (<www.bloodandhonour.com/routes88/html>; accessed Dec. 2001). The Blood and Honour home page claims that the website has been visited over two million times since 1996.

23. Statement of the Commission on Human Rights of the United Nations, 1997: "The Commission on Human Rights stresses its determination to exterminate completely and unconditionally racism in all its forms as well as racial discrimination. The Commission is firmly convinced that racism and racial discrimination are in total opposition to the principles of the United Nations Charter and the Universal Declaration of the Human Rights. Racism and racial discrimination belong to the most severe violations of the Human Rights which have to be fought against with all means available. . . . [The Commission] condemns categorically the role of some print, audio-visual, and electronic media which are inciting racist motivated violence . . . [,] supports the efforts of governments to abolish all forms of racism and racial discrimination . . . [and] . . . encourages all states to intensify their legal regulations in order to punish racist actions and racial discrimination" (UN Menschenrechtskommission 1997).

24. Statement of the European Commission on Racism, Hostility against Foreigners, and Anti-Semitism, 1995: "The continuous presence of racism, hostility against foreigners and anti-Semitism in all countries of the European Union is an enormous challenge to our society. . . . Racism is one of the basic threats to democracy. . . . Racism and hostility against foreigners are a danger not only for the stability of European society, but also for the normal functioning of the economy. . . . In order to secure human rights and basic freedoms as the central values of the European unification process, racism has to be condemned. The struggle against racism is a constitutive element of the European identity" (Europäische Union 1995).

Bibliography

Annas, M., and Christoph, R., eds. 1993. *Neue Soundtracks für den Volksempfänger*. Berlin: Verlag ID-Archiv.

Anti-Defamation League. 1995. *The Skinhead International: A Worldwide Survey of Neo-Nazi Skinheads*. New York: Anti-Defamation League.

Baacke, D.; Farin, K.; and Lauffer, J., eds. 1999. *Rock von Rechts 2: Milieus, Hintergründe und Materialien*. Schriften zur Medienpädagogik 28. Bielefeld: AJZ Druck und Verlag.

Baacke, D.; Thier, M.; Grüninger, C.; and Lindenmann, F., eds. 1994. *Rock von Rechts: Schriften zur Medienpädagogik 14*. Bielefeld: AJZ Druck und Verlag.

Bruhn, H.; Oerter, R.; and Rösing, H., eds. 1985. *Musikpsychologie: Ein Handbuch in Schlüsselbegriffen*. Reinbek: Rowohlt.

Bücken, E. 1994. "Rechtsorientierte Musik und Jugendarbeit," in D. Baacke, M. Thier, C. Grüninger, and F. Lindenmann, (eds.), *Rock von Rechts: Schriften zur Medienpädagogik 14*. Bielefeld: AJZ Druck und Verlag, pp. 162–169.

Bundesamt für Verfassungsschutz. 1999. *Rechtsextremismus in der Bundesrepublik Deutschland*. <www.verfassungsschutz.de>.

Bundesministerium für Bildung und Wissenschaft. 1994.: *Gratwanderungen: Jugendarbeit als Gewaltprävention?* Bonn: BMBW.

Bundesprüfstelle für jugendgefährdende Schriften. 1992. *Gesetzlicher Jugendmedienschutz*. Bonn: Informationsschrift.

Deutsche National-Zeitung. 1995. "Spitzenreiter der Woche," 5 May.

Deutscher Werkbund und Würtembergischer Kunstverein. 1986. *Schock und Schöpfung—Jugendästhetik im 20. Jahrhundert*. Darmstadt: Neuwied.

Diederichsen, D. 1992. "Abschied von der Jugendkultur," *Spex*, 11, pp. 13–18.

Drechsler, C., et al. 1993. "Punk im Turm," *Spex*, 1, pp. 34–39.

Eberwein, M., and Drexler, J. 1987. *Skinheads zum Wort kommen lassen*. Hannover: Selbstverlag.

Europäische Union. 1995. *Rassismus in Europa*. D.I.R. Archive, Marburg.

Farin, K. 1994. "Vom Rock 'n' Roll zur Skin-Musik," in D. Baacke, M. Their, C. Grüninger, and F. Lindenmann (eds.), *Rock von Rechts: Schriften zur Medienpädagogik 14*. Bielefeld: AJZ Druck und Verlag, pp. 141–146.

———. 1996. "Rechtsrock—Eine Bestandsaufnahme," PopScriptum, 5, pp. 4–14.

Farin, K., and Seidel-Pielen, E. 1993. *Skinheads*. München: Becksche Reihe.

Fischer, A., and Zinnecker, J. 1992. *Jugend '92: Lebenslagen, Orientierungen und Entwicklungsperspektiven im vereinigten Deutschland*. Opladen: Leske und Budrich.

Förster, P.; Friedrich, W.; Müller, H.; and Schubarth, W. 1993. *Jugend Ost: Zwischen Hoffnung und Gewalt*. Opladen: Leske und Budrich.

Frankfurter Rundschau. 1999. "Der Mann, der sich Hitler schreibt," 29 November. D.I.R. Archive, Marburg.

Funk-Hennigs, E. 1994. "Über die Rolle der Musik in der Alltagskultur der Skinheads," *Beiträge zur Popularmusikforschung*, 13, pp. 46–78.

Funk-Hennigs, E., and Jäger, J. 1995. *Rassismus, Musik und Gewalt: Ursachen, Entwicklungen, Folgerungen*. Münster: LIT Verlag.

Gotschalk, C. 1993. "Der Expertenstreit," in M. Annas and R. Christoph (eds.), *Neue Sound-tracks für den Volksempfänger*. Berlin: Verlag ID-Archiv, pp. 99–110.

Hebdige, D. 1983. "Subculture: Die Bedeutung von Stil," in D. Diederichsen, D. Hebdige, and O. Marx (eds.), *Schocker: Stile und Moden der Subkultur*. Reinbek: Rowohlt, pp. 38–72.

Heitmeyer, W., et al. 1992. *Die Bielefelder Rechtsextremismusstudie 1: Langzeituntersuchung zur politischen Situation männlicher Jugendlicher*. München: Juventa.

Hohmann, J. 1993. "Wilder Westen inklusive", in M. Annas, and R. Christoph (eds.), *Neue Soundtracks für den Volksempfänger*. Berlin: Verlag ID-Archiv, pp. 87–98.

Human Rights Watch. 1995. "Deutschland den Deutschen," in *Fremdenhaß und rassistische Gewalt in Deutschland*. D.I.R. Archive, Marburg.

Integration Contra Nationalismus. 1999. Website: <www.hvhs-hustedt.de/hvhs-hustedt/project.htm>.

Jäger, J. 2002. *Die rechts extreme Versuchung*. Münster: LIT.

Jahn, J. 1998. *Strafrechtliche Mittel gegen Rechtsextremismus*. Frankfurt: Lang.

Kleffner, H. 1999. "Über Musik zum 'Kampf': Die internationalen Kontakte der Neo-Nazis werden enger," *Frankfurter Rundschau*, 8 December.

Laing, D. 1985. *One Chord Wonders*. Milton Keynes, U.K.: Open University Press.

Lammert, N. 1994. "Jugendgewalt und Fremdenfeindlichkeit: Herausforderungen für Bildung und Kultur," in Bundesministerium für Bildung und Wissenschaft, *Gratwanderungen: Jugendarbeit als Gewaltprävention?* Bonn: BMBW, pp. 7–17.

Lemmer, T. 1994. *Skinhead Rock: Eine notwendige Klarstellung über nonkonforme Musik*. Düsseldorf: Verlag Mehr Wissen.

Lindner, R., ed. 1978. *Punk Rock oder: Der vermarktete Aufruhr*. Frankfurt: Verlag Freie Gesellschaft.

Matuscheck, I. 1994. "Jugendgewalt als Symptom gesellschaftlicher Krise," in Bundesministerium für Bildung und Wissenschaft, *Gratwanderungen: Jugendarbeit als Gewaltprävention?* Bonn: BMBW, pp. 18–26.

Melzer, W. 1992. *Jugend und Politik in Deutschland*. Opladen: Leske und Budrich.

Müller, R. 1994. "Oi!-Musik und fremdenfeindliche Gewalt," *Musik und Bildung*, 3, pp. 46–50; 4, pp. 44–48.

Musikspiegel. 1997. "GEMA distanziert sich von rechtsextremistischer, faschistischer und ausländerfeindlicher Musik," 18:10, p. 10.

Neitzert, L. 1995. "Dorfmusik in den modernen Zeiten," *Rechte Musik. Popscriptum*, 5, pp. 67–86.

———. 1996. "Die Speerspitze der Stammtische: Die rechtsextremistische Jugendmusikszene," in J. Terhag (ed.), *Populäre Musik und Pädagogik*. Oldershausen: Lugert Verlag.

Nevill, A. 1993. "The Good, the Bad and the Skins," in M. Annas and R. Christoph (eds.), *Neue Soundtracks für den Volksempfänger*. Berlin: Verlag ID-Archiv, pp. 47–64.

Reynolds, S., and Press, J. 1995. *The Sex Revolts: Gender, Rebellion and Rock 'n' Roll*. London: Serpents Tail.

Rockmusiker. 1993. "Musiker in Aktion: Heute die—morgen Du!" 1:1, pp. 13–17.

Seeßlen, G. 1994. *Tanz den Adolf Hitler: Faschismus in der populären Kultur*. Berlin: Tiamat.

Spannbauer, A. 1999. "Ku-Klux-Klan im Sommerschlußverkauf," *Taz*, 2 August.

Stark, J. 1993a. "Aufklärung oder Promotion? Konzertveranstalter Fritz Rau: Es gibt keine 'rechte Rockmusik,'" *Hamburger Rundschau*, 21 January.

———. 1993b. "Rock von rechts: Wem gehört die Rockmusik?" *Hamburger Rundschau*, 21 January.

Stark, J., and Kurzawa, M. 1981. *Der große Schwindel? Punk, New Wave.* Frankfurt: Verlag Freie Gesellschaft.

Sturzbacher, D. 1994. "Fremdenfeindlichkeit und Jugendgewalt im Wandel," in Bundesministerium für Bildung und Wissenschaft, *Gratwanderungen: Jugendarbeit als Gewaltprävention?* Bonn: BMBW, pp. 64–75.

Süß, W. 1993. "Was wußte die Stasi über die Neonazis in der DDR?" *Die Zeit*, 30 April.

Trunk, V. 1999. "Was Neo-Nazis unter Geburstagsfeier verstehen," *Frankfurter Rundschau*, 27 April.

United Nations. 1948. *Universal Declaration of Human Rights*, G.A. res. 217A (III), U.N. Doc A/810 at 71. Adopted on 10 December 1948 by the General Assembly of the United Nations. D.I.R. Archive, Marburg.

UN Menschenrechtskommission. 1997. "Rassismus, Rassendiskriminierung, Fremdenfeindlichkeit und verwandte Intoleranz." Auszug aus Resolution 1997/74 (E/CN.4/L.11/Add.8), D.I.R. Archive, Marburg.

Wagner, C. 1999. "Rock von rechts hat weltweit Konjuktur," *NMZ*, 3, p. 33.

Walter, K. 1993a. "Das Böhse Erbe der linken Onkelz," *Spex*, 1, pp. 40–44.

———. 1993b. "Dicker Stefan, gutes Kind," in M. Annas and R. Christoph (eds.), *Neue Soundtracks für den Volksempfänger.* Berlin: Verlag ID-Archiv, pp. 29–46.

Weigel, G. 1994. "Das Aktionsprogramm gegen Aggression und Gewalt," in Bundesministerium für Bildung und Wissenschaft, *Gratwanderungen: Jugendarbeit als Gewaltprävention?* Bonn: BMBW, pp. 76–86.

Wicke, P. 1992.: "Popmusik und Politik: Provokationen zum Thema—Hauptreferat zur Konferenz Popmusik und Politik." Manuscript. Oybin, Germany.

Willems, H.; Würtz, S.; and Eckert, R., eds. 1993. *Fremdenfeindliche Gewalt: Eine Analyse von Täterstrukturen und Eskalationsprozeßen.* Bonn: Bundesministerium für Frauen und Jugend.

ZDF (Zweites Deutsches Fernsehen). 1998. Kennzeichen D vom 5. IX. <http://newsaktuell. de>.

Zeitschrift für Musikpädagogik. 1996. "Musik und Gewalt: Musik und Unterricht," 36, pp. 1–57.

Zentralnerv. 1994. "SOS Deutschland!" January/February, p. 18.

Websites

Antifaschistische Nachrichten (1996–). Web archive: <www.infolinks.de>.

Archive of the Dokumentations und Informationszentrum für Rassismusforschung [D.I.R.], Marburg: <dir@mailer.uni-marburg.de>.

Blood and Honour. 1999. Website: <www.bloodandhonour.com/routes88/html>.

José Roberto Zan

12   Popular Music and Policing in Brazil

Urban popular music, with all its diverse genres and styles, was a major feature of Brazilian cultural life in the twentieth century. Composers and songwriters chronicled this period, and their work translated the social experience of rapid urbanization characteristic of the development of peripheral capitalism. Popular music was the target of political censorship at certain times because the lyrics' use of satire, parody, and metaphor had the potential to undermine the symbolism and doctrine of the Brazilian power elite.

Political censorship took a special interest in popular music in two periods. The first was during the New State (1937–1945), the dictatorial period under Getúlio Vargas; the other was during the 1964–1982 military dictatorship. In this chapter I look at the political and ideological contexts in which censorship was directed at this aspect of cultural life—and also at some more recent instances where censorship has intervened in popular music despite the current absence of specific legislation.

First, however, we will examine the formative period for urban popular music in the early twentieth century, and the social conflicts associated with the origin and consolidation of popular musical in Rio de Janeiro, the capital of Brazil at that time.

Origins of Brazilian Popular Music

Marcha, choro, and *samba* all emerged in Rio de Janeiro around the turn of the century as Brazilian society was being transformed by the abolition of slavery and the transition from imperial monarchy to republic.[1] A crisis was affecting coffee plantations in the Vale do Paraíba region, and since slavery had been abolished, large numbers of black workers migrated to Rio de Janeiro and swelled the ranks of laborers and the unemployed. Many settled in the Cidade Nova neighborhood, near Avenida President Vargas and the marshes. Later arrivals lived in overcrowded *cortiços* (rooming houses) in the Saúde district, and it was at this time that the first shantytowns sprang up in the hills and outlying areas of Rio (Tinhorão 1990:152).

Many of these former slaves were from Bahia and maintained their Afro-Bahian cultural traditions, such as the candomblé religion and other festive or religious activities, especially those associated with the Catholic feasts of Christmas and the Epiphany. These traditions evolved into samba and the Rio de Janeiro Carnival. The upper strata of Rio society took a very dim view of these activities, associating them with idleness, *malandragem*,[2] prostitution, and violence, and there was much police repression. Older *sambistas* say that the police identified the *malandros* by their fingertips, which were calloused from plucking the strings of the most popular instrument of the time, the guitar.

Many black families, usually extended families headed by Bahian women, roomed in large buildings in Cidade Nova. In the back rooms they held festive or religious ceremonies, the *candomblé, batucada,* and *capoeira* sessions that attracted police attention and repression. Dances and music (*choro*) took place in the rooms facing the street, since these activities were acceptable to Rio's high society and the gatherings were often frequented by politicians and intellectuals. These houses functioned as "cultural dividing screens," mitigating the conflicts occasioned by the uneasy blending of black people into white society (Sodré 1979:20). These were the devices the black population used to make room for their cultural practices within a white-dominated society.

After the turn of the century, the phonographic industry became a channel for the musical expression of these layers of society. Casa Edison was founded in Rio de Janeiro in 1900, initially selling phonographs, gramophones, and recordings. It went on to make Brazil's first mechanical recordings on disks; its first catalog appeared in 1902 and contained scores of *modinhas, lundus,* waltzes, polkas, and other genres recorded by popular Brazilian musicians (Franceschi 1984:37).

Many of the early Casa Edison recordings contain satire directed against politicians, governments, and public figures. The samba "Pelo Telefone," by Donga and Mauro Almeida, recorded in 1917, is a good example. The original version satirized Rio de Janeiro's chief of police and the campaign against roulette gambling waged by a local newspaper. The first few lines were: "The chief of police / By the telephone / Sent word / That on Carioca / There's a roulette / To gamble with." Fearing problems with the police, however, Donga introduced changes in the lyrics he submitted when he registered the copyright of the song. In the self-censored version, the lines read: "The leader of the dancers / By the telephone / Sent word that / Merry-making was to be left alone / So the fun can go on" (Moura 1983:76).

Until the mid-1930s, the Brazilian government had no specific legislation dealing with censorship of the mass media and music. The first incident involving censorship of popular music during this period was instigated by a radio station in reprisal against composers demanding higher copyright payments. In 1933 the Brazilian Confederation of Broadcasting set up a Censorship Commission with the prerogative of banning music that threatened official morality and established authorities. The first music to be censored by this organization was the samba "Lenço No Pescoço" ("Bandana Around My Neck") by Wilson Batista. This was recorded by Sílvio Caldas on 18 June 1933 for RCA Victor. The lyrics include the following lines:

> My hat cocked to one side
> Shuffling my feet along
> Bandana round my neck
> Razor in my pocket
> I go swinging by
> Staring them down and facing them out
> Proud to be such an idler.

This samba became a symbol for *malandragem,* or roguery, and the composer was accused by the censors of writing an elegy for idleness and violence (Cabral 1975:36).

Populism, Mass Culture, and Censorship

The president of Brazil from 1930 to 1945 was Getúlio Vargas. Originally from the state of Rio Grande do Sul, he left the army in 1902 and was elected state deputy in 1909 and state governor in 1928. In the March 1930 presidential elections, he was defeated by the candidate of the major coffee producers and exporters, Júlio Prestes of São Paulo. He won support, however, from factions of the regional oligarchies opposed to the coffee-planters' policies and from sections of the middle class and the junior army officers and went on to take power in a coup that deposed Washington Luiz and stopped president-elect Júlio Prestes from taking office.

Vargas came to power in 1930 against the backdrop of an economic, social, and political crisis deepened by the effects of the New York Stock Exchange collapse of the previous year. Brazil was at the end of a long and drawn-out transition from a country that mainly exported agricultural commodities to an urban-industrial economy. The process had resulted in the political exhaustion of the Old Republic and a crisis of hegemony. Vargas had support from the middle class and from ruling sectors such as the industrial bourgeoisie and some oligarchic factions not committed to an economic policy based on the export of primary sector products, but from the beginning he was forced to seek legitimacy in the eyes of the urban masses. With urbanization, new strata had emerged on the Brazilian political scene. Since the beginning of the century they had been gradually finding their voice and now constituted a new factor in both political and cultural life. It was in this setting that the new government made a definite populist turn combined with pronounced centralizing and paternalistic tendencies. Its survival depended in large measure on its ability to be "receptive to popular aspirations" (Weffort 1980:50–51).

The 1930s witnessed the spread of modern mass media such as newspapers, movies, records, and radio. The phonographic industry developed new methods of electrical recording that significantly improved sound quality. Sales rose in a promising market that was now attracting more investments, especially foreign capital. From 1933 through to the end of the Second World War, the Brazilian recording industry was almost totally owned by the three majors: Odeon (an EMI subsidiary), RCA Victor, and Columbia (Santos 1982).

Nevertheless, it was radio broadcasting that reported the highest growth figures. Although Brazil's first transmissions took place in 1923, consolidation and expansion came in the 1930s, when a Vargas decree allowed radio stations to charge for advertising and 52 new radio stations were launched around the country, eight of them in Rio de Janeiro.[3] The rapid growth of broadcasting closely resembled the pattern of the industry in the United States (Tavares 1997:57). Mass culture began to develop in Brazil, but with some unique characteristics shaped by the absence of two basic features that had helped to consolidate mass culture in the industrialized countries: a technical basis (i.e., a cultural industry) and the social basis of a real consumer society.

In Brazil, the expanding media of that period were not so well developed and systematically organized that they could be defined as a cultural industry. Their ability to co-opt the masses was still very much at an incipient stage (Ortiz 1988:48). At the same time, because of Brazil's weak industrialization and urbanization and its relatively backward market economy, this was not a fully developed consumer society (Lima 1982:55). As a result, the mass culture that began to emerge was quite different from that in the more advanced countries, in terms of both its origins and coverage and its function. The mass media acted much more as mediators between the state and the urban masses than as creators of a mass and integrating culture (Martín-Barbero 1987:178–179).

Vargas had a more developed understanding than other politicians of the usefulness of the mass media as political and ideological propaganda vehicles. He encouraged artistic and cultural events but censored those that ran contrary to the ideology of his explicitly authoritarian nationalist state.

Censorship Policy, Co-optation, and Resistance Under the New State

According to the 1934 constitution, Vargas was due to leave office in 1938. Instead, warning against the spread of ideologies that threatened the institutional order in Brazil and denouncing the "democracy of the party system" as a "threat to national unity," he ushered in a new constitution on corporatist lines, similar to the regimes then in power in Portugal and Italy. Vargas closed Congress, banned political parties, and appointed delegates of the central government to run the states. The New State, which he himself defined as a "strong regime, of peace, justice and work" (Skidmore 1969:50) was proclaimed on 10 November 1937.

The new regime was to last until 1945. To consolidate its rule, the government made particular interventions at the institutional and ideological levels as it sought to assimilate and discipline the working class. Vargas introduced a minimum wage, had government officials take over the unions, and funded them via compulsory union dues. This legislation was brought together in a new labor code in 1943. At the same time, Vargas carried out intense propaganda in the mass media with the aim of consolidating the government's image as one of "offering" benefits to the workers. In return, it called for workers to be disciplined and loyal in order to ensure the nation's progress. This government erected a major symbolic framework to support the New State and its ideology of *trabalhismo*—workerist populism or laborism (Weffort 1980:69).

The state took measures to integrate the working class with a new type of "scientifically organized labor." It sought ideological hegemony around the notion of the "New Man" who would fit into this economic and social order by being attuned to industrialization, interclass harmony, and national unity. In this context, censorship of cultural and artistic events took on more importance. The 1937 constitution instituted prepublication censorship for movies, newspapers, theater, music, and radio. In December 1939 the government's Decree Law no. 1.915 set up a communications agency, the Department of Press and Propaganda (DIP), with the following aims: "to carry out censorship of theater, cinema, recreational and sporting activities . . . broadcasting [including musical content], social and political literature, and the press . . . [to] promote, organize, sponsor or aid civic manifestations and popular festivities . . . [and] exhibitions showing the government's policies" (Legislação Federal Brasileira 1939:666).

The text of the law then explained that the DIP would not be charged only with censorship but also with encouraging cultural work compatible with the interests of the state. The DIP's attention was particularly focused on radio—the medium with the highest level of penetration among the urban masses—and, within that medium, on popular music as the main cultural content of broadcasting. The government saw the latter as a critical part of its strategy and clearly realized popular music's potential for mass influence. One New State ideologist, Alvaro Salgado, commented that "all the illiterate, rough and uncultivated people in the cities are attracted toward civilization, often through music" (Salgado 1941:84).

In January 1940, in accordance with its strategy for the co-optation of musicians and composers, the DIP promoted a Popular Music Night, a grand Carnival music competition. The winning samba was "Oh, Seu Oscar" by Wilson Batista and Ataulfo Alves. The lyrics were about a worker (a reformed *malandro*) who comes home from work only to find a message from his partner saying that she has decided to go back to her bohemian ways. Martins Castelo, one of the intellectuals who collaborated with the New State, said that this samba showed that the government's policy of "ennobling labor" was getting results. The figure of Oscar, he said, "only emerged later, with laws recognizing and supporting the rights of the workforce" (Castelo 1942:174). But it should be noted that this samba does not actually go so far as to defend the notion of work. On the contrary, despite being a hard-working man, the character continues to associate work with suffering, as seen in these lines:

> I did everything for her sake
> Even ended up down at the quays in the port
> Wracking my body night and day
> But it was all in vain
> She is a real bohemian
> And I gave it up!

In the same year, the DIP censored the lyrics of a samba by the same songwriters called "Bonde São Januário" (the title refers to a streetcar line) because it praised *malandragem*. The first lines of the original lyrics went like this:

> Those who work have got it all wrong
> I'll tell you that without fear of erring
> There goes another sucker on board
> The São Januário streetcar
> [but] You'll never catch me off to work.
>
> (Velloso 1997:113)

After the censors' veto and recommendations, Batista and Alves decided to change the lyrics to:

> Those who work have got it all right
> I'll tell you that without fear of erring
> The São Januário streetcar
> Is carrying one more worker on board
> And that's me on my way to work.

Recorded initially by Ciro Monteiro at RCA Victor in October 1940, the song was a big hit at Carnival time the following year and became a kind of symbol of the reform of the idle, good-for-nothing *malandro* into a diligent worker.

Despite censorship, the songwriters who identified with the theme of *malandragem* got their ideas across in ways similar to those described in the South African context in Chapter 9. Their language became more subtle, looking to irony and ambiguity to maintain a "critical and jocose spirit" (Matos 1982:110). Irony was almost always present in the relationship between officialdom and the lyrics inspired by *malandragem*. The latter had a certain dialogic character that, even under the New State, enabled it to undermine official language (Guimarães 1989:86).

In 1940 the DIP, as the official media department, banned 373 lyrics for "discordance with stipulations of the law" (Pedro 1980:80). The following year, according to a DIP report sent to the Presidency, 44 radio programs and 1,133 songs were banned (DIP 1941:3–4). There were probably many more cases during this period, but the surviving records are incomplete. Even so, the data available constitute an important sample of the impact of censorship on popular music during the dictatorial Vargas government. Censorship even affected Ary Barroso's "Aquarela do Brasil" (literally "Watercolor Painting of Brazil"), a classic of samba *exaltação* recognized by members of the political and intellectual élites as a symbol of Brazilian culture. The censors wanted to veto a reference to the "land of samba and tambourine," which they viewed as derogatory. The original lyrics were saved only by Barroso's powers of persuasion (Cabral n.d.:180).

With the end of the dictatorial regime in 1945, some songwriters revived the theme of rejecting the work ethic, thus pointing up the limited powers of the government and the relative ineffectiveness of *trabalhismo* as an ideology. One of the greatest successes at the Carnival that year was the samba "Trabalhar Eu Não" ("Working's Not for Me") by Almeidinha, which included the lines:

> I worked like a madman
> Until I got blisters on my hand
> My boss became wealthy
> And me a poor man without a cent.
> (Cabral 1975:40–41)

The end of the New State led to less censorship. Article 1 of Decree Law no. 8.356, 12 December 1945, proclaimed that "there is no requirement for previous censorship of ideas expressed on the radio; nevertheless, any abuses committed will incur responsibilities for the individuals concerned." The 1946 constitution restated this principle (Costela 1970:116–118). From 1945 to 1964 the political situation in Brazil was quite close to what might be described as a democratic order, and the amount of censorship decreased.

Censorship Under the Military Dictatorship

The early 1960s in Brazil saw the emergence of one of the most important manifestations of committed art in the country's history. The People's Center for Culture (CPC) was set up in 1961 under the auspices of the National Union of Students (UNE). The preliminary draft of the CPC's Manifesto, written in 1962, called on artists to become politically committed, since "in our country and in our time, there is no people's art that is not political art." Artists were to take up a "consistently revolutionary" position and should "become part of the people, its military detachments on the cultural front." CPC intellectuals saw "the people" as potentially the revolutionary subject, but hampered by a fragmentary and alienated culture. It was the task of intellectuals to approach the masses and provide the political consciousness needed to overcome alienation and produce truly "revolutionary people's art" using elements of the culture of the people itself (Martins 1979:67).

CPC militants were strongly influenced by the work of the intellectuals associated with the Higher Institute of Brazilian Studies (ISEB), which was set up in the mid-1950s by Brazilian philosophers, sociologists, economists, and political scientists determined to identify the factors that were impeding national development. In a sense, these intellectuals were developing a theory of the Brazilian revolution, which was understood by the more leftist sectors and by the young CPC members as a national and people's revolution.

CPC had several departments, the most important of which were active in theater, movies, music, and literacy campaigns. Gradually, the branches set up in several states began to promote cultural events for neighborhood associations, unions, student organizations, and similar groups with the aim of reaching out to the broad mass of the people. The music department was headed by Carlos Lyra, a popular songwriter associated with the *bossa nova*. His support for the CPC involved to some extent a break with the group that had launched this musical trend in late 1950s. The first phase of the *bossa nova* was profoundly lyrical, with themes centered on love, the beauty of Rio's women, and life in the middle-class neighborhoods of Rio de Janeiro's southern sector. On joining the CPC, Carlos Lyra told a Rio newspaper that *bossa nova* was "starved of content." The CPC influence brought about a new focus on social themes.

Seeking to broaden the reach of its cultural action, the CPC in July 1962 launched a single called "The People Sing," with four songs taking a good-humored look at the lives of Brazilians under an unjust social system subordinated to international capital. Some 11,000 disks were distributed within several states. Many popular musicians supported the CPC's work and began to write for its theater and film projects. Among them were Sérgio Ricardo, Geraldo Vandré, Edu Lobo, Gilberto Gil, Caetano Veloso, Nara Leão, Marcos Valle, and Vinícius de Moraes.

These composers and songwriters produced a vast repertoire associated with a new style identified at that time as "protest songs." A left bloc with a highly intellectual rationale and a middle-class public consisting mostly of university students were already identified with Brazilian popular music. Lyrics were connected to the dramatic social situation affecting workers, blacks, migrants from the Northeast, peasants, and other groups. The lyrical style of the *bossa nova* gave way to an epic-dramatic style. Metaphors referred to social movements, to the people taking to the streets and the imminence of social revolution. Musically, this repertoire ranged across several popular genres, such as *samba de morro, marchas de rancho,* and regional and folk music.

The military coup of 31 March 1964 unleashed violent political repression against the organized sectors of Brazilian society and the trade unions. The UNE and the CPC were closed down. Although the official decree issued on 9 April to justify the coup (Ato Institucional no. 1) made no specific mention of freedom of expression, unions and other associations were no longer allowed to hold cultural events. Committed artists and performers were now restricted to less public venues, with a narrower audience consisting mainly of intellectuals, students, and other artists.

At the end of 1964, a show called *Opinião* ("Opinion") was staged at the Super-Shopping Center in Copacabana, under the direction of Augusto Boal with songs by Zé Keti, João do Vale, Edu Lobo, Gianfrancesco Guarnieri, Carlos Lyra, Sérgio Ricardo, Vinícius de Moraes, Tom Jobim, and Ruy Guerra. Zé Keti's samba "Opinião"— which gave its name to the show—was about life in the impoverished hillside shantytowns around Rio de Janeiro. João do Vale's song "Carcará" referred to the backlands of northeastern Brazil, a region inhabited by extremely poor peasants. Agents of the Federal Department for Public Security thought that it suggested "open class struggle" (*Folha de São Paulo*, 2 November 1997).

Opinão was the first of a series of events that continued until 1968 and highlighted this kind of music and its creators. The initial audiences for popular protest songs were relatively small, but once they were transferred to television shows they had nationwide impact.

Brazil saw the widespread introduction of television in the 1960s, and numerous musical programs were launched after 1965. TV Record had a show called *O Fino da Bossa* ("The Best of Bossa Nova"), introduced by Elis Regina and Jair Rodrigues, which became almost exclusively a venue for the protest music then identified as "MPB"—Brazilian Popular Music. This was also the case for the Festivals of Popular Music organized by the television channels Excelsior, Record, and Globo. These major annual competitions featured the latest songs and highlighted new disks for the recording industry. Most people in the studio audiences rejected and jeered at any performers not identified with the new politically committed trend.

Until the end of 1968, the censorship had mostly affected the theater and the press; there were few bans on popular music. But after 1967 the political situation became more polarized and the government began to take measures laying the basis for stricter and more far-reaching censorship. On 13 March 1967 the government published Decree Law no. 314, subordinating the legislation governing radio, television, and news agencies to the New Law on National Security (Costela 1970:139). With the new constitution of 15 March 1967, censorship became a federal prerogative, and criteria were standardized nationwide.

By 1968 composers were facing difficulties from censors at song festivals. The censor advised Adílson Godoy, who composed "O General e o Muro" ("The General and the Wall"), to remove the words "General" and "bomb." Sérgio Ricardo's song "Dia da Graça" ("Day of Grace"), presented at the TV Record Festival, was thoroughly modified in order to make it more "optimistic." "Dom Quixote," by Os Mutantes, was also cut; the censor took Sancho and Quixote to refer to the president of Brazil and Che Guevara respectively, so that the lines "for Sancho to fall / And Quixote to rise" were supposed to be preaching revolution. However, the censors retreated on this one and allowed all three songs to be staged with their original lyrics (*Veja*, 27 November 1968).

The Third International Song Festival, organized by TV Globo in September 1968, was more politicized and controversial than ever and in many ways pointed to the political counterattack that followed a few months later. Chico Buarque won the major award with "Sabiá," written jointly with Antônio Carlos Jobim. Vandré was second with "Pra Não Dizer Que Não Falei de Flores" ("So They Won't Say I Didn't Talk About the Flowers"), which was virtually an ode to the Brazilian revolution. Gilberto Gil and Caetano Veloso introduced elements from international pop music via protest lyrics that were more in line with the student and counterculture movement in Europe. Most members of the festival audience were committed to a leftist-nationalist ideology and reacted against their new style. Gil's "Questão de Ordem" was disqualified. Veloso faced a jeering audience, made his performance of "Ë Prohibido Prohibir" into a "happening," and then dropped out of the competition in solidarity with Gil. Despite the jeers of the leftist audience, federal agents from the Department of Public Security were tracking every move of the two *tropicalistas*.[4] Their stage shows and their songs were seen as offensive to morality, Brazilian traditions, and even to the nation's symbols (*Folha de São Paulo*, 2 November 1997).

On 13 December 1968, the military government's decree Ato Institucional no. 5 came into force, and all recorded music had to be submitted to the censor. "Pra Não Dizer Que Não Falei de Flores" was banned for 11 years, and its author, Geraldo Vandré, had to leave the country clandestinely (*O Estado de São Paulo*, 5 August 1995). By the end of that month, Gilberto Gil and Caeteano Velloso had been arrested; they were released two months later to spend two years of forced exile in Britain.

The arbitrary nature of the regime's actions reached its peak on 29 March 1971 when President Médici signed a secret document giving the minister of justice the powers to apply Article 9 of the Ato Institucional no. 5 decree (AI-5), which allowed the president to "issue decrees complementary to the execution of this Institutional Decree and to . . . take the measures foreseen in lines *d* and *e* of paragraph 2 of Article 152 of the constitution which included a state of martial law authorizing the following measures of coercion . . . (d) suspension of the freedom of assembly and association, (e) censorship of correspondence, press, telecommunications and public entertainments." Special authorization by the president was no longer necessary for the exercise of censorship (Maklouf 1984:142–143).

The military dictatorship justified repressive action, including cultural censorship, by appealing to the Doctrine of National Security created by the Higher School of

War, a think-tank backed by the Brazilian military.[5] Whereas the Vargas government censored popular music mainly in order to combat the antiwork ethic of *malandragem,* as part of an overall campaign to consolidate its workerist-populist *trabalhismo* ideology, in the period of military government censorship was justified mainly on geopolitical grounds, under the Doctrine of National Security.

Over the 10 years the AI-5 was in effect, some 500 films and 450 plays were banned, as were 200 books, dozens of radio and television programs, and more than a thousand songs. In 1976 the following data were released in relation to censorship of popular music: Of 30,518 compositions analyzed, 292 had been vetoed; and singer-songwriters like Taiguara, Luís Gonzaga, Jr., and Milton Nascimento were targeted by the censors and often resorted to metaphors to avoid their interference (ibid.:144).

In the early 1970s, Chico Buarque used the pseudonyms Julinho da Adelaide and Leonel de Paiva in order to evade censorship. One of the songs produced by these alter egos was the samba "Acorda, Amor," on his album "Sinal Fechado," recorded by Phillips in 1974. The singer wakes his partner after a nightmare in which the police broke into his home. Then he realizes that the dream has become reality and the police are really there. Dismayed and bewildered, he yells: "Call the thief!" (Meneses 2000:70).

Retreat or New Rationale for Censorship?

In 1979 General President Ernesto Geisel began a gradual transition to political democracy. The repressive decree AI-5 was no longer in effect, and the government loosened censorship policy. Nevertheless, the legislation that had regulated censorship during the dictatorship was maintained until 1988. The following year an amnesty law was passed, and exiles began to return. Broad sections of society mobilized for direct presidential elections. In 1985 Tancredo Neves, the first civilian president after the military government, was elected not by the populace but by congressmen. Tancredo died before taking office, and Vice-President José Sarney took over. In 1987 the Constituent Assembly began its work, and the following year the new federal constitution was promulgated. Article 5 established that "the expression of intellectual, artistic, scientific and communication activity is free and does not depend on censorship or permission."

Yet censorship seems to have survived as a memory—and more. It threatens to re-emerge through initiatives taken by individuals or groups that nourish fond memories of the period of repression. It continues to have an effect as a traumatic experience that needs to be remembered in order not to be relived.

Because no legislation enables governmental bodies to censor now, initiatives of this kind have been restricted to individual actions or those promoted by civic organizations. In 1996, four cases involving censorship had a significant impact. The first concerned a lawyer's request that the attorney general seize copies of the British film *Trainspotting* on the basis that it encouraged heroin consumption. Soon afterward, copies of the Brazilian film *Corisco & Dadá* by Rosemberg Cariry were seized after relatives of the film's characters brought an accusation of "improper invasion of privacy." Finally, there were two cases involving popular music. One concerned accusations of racism in the lyrics of a song performed by clown-singer Tiririca; the other concerned an alleged endorsement of marijuana use during a Rio de Janeiro concert by the rock band Planet Hemp (*Folha de São Paulo*, 30 November 1996).

The Tiririca case began when a Rio-based nongovernmental organization, the Center for the Coordination of Marginalized Peoples, accused the singer of racism. In a song called "Veja Os Cabelos Dela" ("Look at Her Hair"), Tiririca sings of the "bad smell" and the "steel-wool-like" hair of a black woman. After a court hearing, 55,000 compact discs were withdrawn from stores, and Sony was forced to destroy 125,000 recordings. This brought an adverse reaction from many commentators, including sections of the press that had supported the court's initial decision and viewed racism as offensive and anticonstitutional. However, Minister for Justice Nelson Jobim did not reply to the Center's demand for his intervention in the case. In a press statement he said that "any action harking back to the past would be dangerous" (*Folha de São Paulo*, 1 August 1996).

During the litigation, four new actions were brought against Tiririca and the recording company, with average demands for awards of approximately one million dollars. Eighteen months later, the court absolved Tiririca. Nevertheless, he has been overwhelmed by his legal fees and is having difficulty rebuilding his career in show business (*Folha de São Paulo*, 28 October 1999).

On one hand, the case shows the successful development of organizations formed by black Brazilians over the last few decades, particularly from the 1970s onward, as they struggled for the affirmation of their ethnic identity and their rights as citizens. In 1942 the samba "Nega Do Cabelo Duro" ("Coarse-Haired Black Woman") by Rubens Soares and David Nasser had been a Carnival hit with the following lyrics: "Coarse-haired black woman / What comb is combing you." No organization at that time protested this portrayal of black women.

On the other hand, the case reflects a negative side of Brazilian society today. Law firms often drum up business through this kind of case. Huge damage payments are the objective rather than any real restitution of moral damages to individuals or groups.

The Planet Hemp case is a little more complicated. The band made a CD called "Usuario" ("User": an explicit reference to drug use) that was launched by Sony Music in 1995 with a photo of a leaf of *Cannabis sativa* (marijuana) on the CD case. In addition, some songs include a call for the legalization of marijuana. On viewing the video clip of the song "Legalize Marijuana Right Now," the Ministry of Justice ordered that it be broadcast only after 11 p.m. In several cities the band's shows were canceled by local judges, and police seized their CD and arrested dozens of people for possession of drugs. At a venue in Brasilia, the band was arrested and detained for several days on the basis of legislation dating back to 1996 that stipulated sentences of up to 15 years for possession, trafficking, or advocating drug use (*Veja*, 19 November 1997). In the end, the incidents provided useful publicity for Planet Hemp and the recording company, and their "Usuario" CD sold over 500,000 copies (ibid.).

These incidents raise a number of issues. First, it is important to highlight that, in contrast to the Getúlio Vargas period and the 1960s, Brazil now has a developed cultural industry. With the industrialization and urbanization of the last few decades have come consumer society and mass culture, in large measure now integrated into world cultural circuits. The various segments of the cultural industry function along highly globalized lines in relation to marketing and management. One consequence is a gradual process of autonomization of the cultural sphere in Brazilian society (that is, a tendency to develop on the basis of its own inner dynamics; see Ortiz 1988:193). Cultural products created by these business complexes are honed to mass-market specifications and are usually quite bland. The forms of sociability that emerge in correspondence with these productive systems are increasingly similar to those in other parts of the world. Social conflicts and crises are somehow more predictable.

On the other hand, Brazil's insertion into the circuit of global capital flow has led to a weakening of the state. In this context, symbolic constructions associated with national identity tend to lose their force. At the same time, a whole range of social subjects, particularly urban and rural workers, women, blacks, youths from the impoverished outskirts of the major cities, indigenous peoples, and so on, are now building or reworking their identities on the basis of everyday or local experiences in which they selectively incorporate globalized symbolic elements. New subjects are emerging at the same time that new social movements—the landless workers movement, the homeless, the black movement, the feminist movement, the hip-hop movement, etc.—are reshaping social conflicts. This dynamic is part of the cultural diversity that marks the contemporary world, even though it is articulated through increasingly provisional or volatile practices and representations of a local and global character (Hall 1992).

Identifying these processes may contribute to an understanding of the existence/absence of censorship of Brazilian cultural events. At present, there is no censorship based on coordinated action by the state, but there are initiatives from individuals and groups. Both the legislation and the repressive apparatus tend to be invoked by ordinary individuals or nongovernmental entities, and not necessarily by the government's own organs. In this context, censorship of the kind implemented in the 1930s and 1940s or the 1960s and 1970s becomes meaningless. Perhaps this was why the minister for justice avoided direct involvement in the accusation of racism brought against Tiririca. The minister did not really step back because it would be dangerous "to hark back to the past," but because action of this kind is no longer effective.

Notes

Acknowledgments: Thanks to Martha Tupinambá de Ulhôa, who suggested writing this article, and my friend Thomas Nerney, for invaluable assistance with translation and revision.

1. *Marcha:* a genre in two-four time with a heavily accentuated first beat. In Brazil, its popularity is associated with Carnival groups (*blocos*) and their slower-tempo *marcha de rancho* and the *marchina de salão*, with their standard sequence of instrumental introduction, verse, and chorus (Andrade 1989:307). *Choro* first appeared in Rio de Janeiro around 1870. It emerged from a local style of playing European dances such as polkas, mazurkas, and quadrilles, to which Brazilian instrumentalists added a new rhythmic element, African syncopation. This genre is played mainly by instrumental groups with guitars, cavaquinhos (small guitars), flutes, and percussion instruments.

2. *Malandragem:* activity associated with the *malandro,* a figure who originated within the "freeman" element of slave society. Since they were neither proprietors nor slaves, they made their living performing minor services and favors. With the ending of slavery and the expansion of the waged workforce, they began to live in the cities, especially in Rio de Janeiro. They were usually unemployed or underemployed and inhabited the boundary area between legality and illegality. They were generally very shrewd and sought an easy life by taking advantage of diverse situations. The figure of the *malandro* became something of a symbol of resistance to the world of work during the period of industrialization early in the twentieth century.

3. Many of the new stations were connected to the government. The most important, Rádio Nacional in Rio de Janeiro, was set up by the daily newspaper *A Noite* in 1936 and had grown rapidly by 1940, when it became federal property. Even when it became state-owned, Rádio Nacional, the country's leading station in the 1940s and 1950s, continued to operate on the usual commercial lines. It had a certain autonomy in relation to content and a somewhat ambivalent stance: While it was a spokesman for the state and the ruling classes, it also practiced a broadcasting style that made frequent use of symbolic elements from the lower classes; this was not compatible with the populist model of legitimation of the state (Goldfeder 1980:41).

4. Gilberto Gil and Caetano Veloso were seen, in the mid-1960s, as part of MPB. Their songs at the 1967 TV Record Festival differed from those of the other participants, who mostly presented protest songs in line with the ideas of their left-nationalist audiences. Gil's song "Domingo no Parque" and Caetano's "Alegria, Alegria" won awards at this festival, but their lyrics were not in the prevailing protest style and their arrangements made use of electronic instruments (guitars and keyboards) and other aesthetic elements from international pop music. For the nationalist left, this was "capitulation to cultural imperialism." Some

critics saw this as the emergence of a new movement in Brazilian popular music called *tropicália* or *tropicalismo* (Campos 1968:141).

5. The Doctrine of National Security was formulated by the intellectuals of Brazil's Higher School of War, an institution created in 1949 under the influence of the National War College of the United States. Its main aims were to ensure a military presence in a prominent position in the Brazilian state apparatus. This body emerged in the context of the Cold War and formulated its doctrine in order to legitimate the military's political action against "internal aggression"—the struggle of workers and people's political movements. It also sought to combat any reformist or revolutionary policies that posed a threat to the bourgeois institutional order, capitalism, or Brazil's position in the western bloc.

Bibliography

Andrade, M. de. 1989. *Dicionário Musical Brasileiro*. Belo Horizonte: Itatiaia.

Cabral, S. 1975. "Getúlio e a música popular brasileira," *Ensaios Opinão* (Rio de Janeiro), nos. 1–2.

———. 1990. *No Tempo de Almirante: Uma História do Rádio e da MPB*. Rio de Janeiro: Francisco Alves.

———. No date. *No tempo de Ari Barroso*. Rio de Janeiro: Lumiar Editora.

Campos, A. de. 1968. *Balanço da Bossa e Outras Bossas*. São Paulo: Editora Perspectiva.

Castelo, M. 1942. "O samba e o conceito de trabalho," *Revista Cultura Política* (Rio de Janeiro), 2:22, December.

Costela, A. F. 1970. *O controle da Informação no Brasil*. Petrópolis: Vozes.

Departamento de Imprensa e Propaganda (DIP). 1941. Report. Rio de Janeiro, Arquivo Nacional, Box 510.

Franceschi, H. M. 1984. *Registro Sonoro por Meios Mecânicos no Brasil*. Rio de Janeiro: Studio HMF.

Goldfeder, M. 1980. *Por trás das ondas da Rádio Nacional*. Rio de Janeiro: Paz e Terra.

Guimarães, S. 1989. "O Discurso Amoroso da (na) MPB." M.A. thesis, Instituto de Estudos da Linguagem, Universidade de Campinas.

Hall, S. 1992. "The Question of National Identity," in S. Hall, D. Held, and T. McGrew (eds.), *Modernity and Its Futures*. Cambridge: Polity Press, pp. 275–316.

Legislação Federal Brasileira. 1939. Vol. 3. São Paulo: Editora Lex.

Lima, L. C. 1982. *Teoria da cultura de massa*. Rio de Janeiro: Paz e Terra.

Maklouf, L. 1984. "A guerra da censura." *Retrato do Brasil: Da Monarquia ao Estado Militar*, vols. 1–2. São Paulo: Editora Três/Política Editora.

Martín-Barbero, J. 1987. *De los medios a las mediaciones: Comunicacíon, cultura y hegemonía*. Barcelona: Ediciones Gustavo Gili S/A.

Martins, C. E. 1979. "Anteprojeto do Manifesto do CPC," *Arte em Revista*, 1:1, January–March, pp. 67–79.

Matos, Cláudia Neiva de. 1982. *Acertei no milhar: Malandragem e samba no tempo de Getúlio*. Rio de Janeiro: Editora Paz e Terra.

Meneses, A. B. de. 2000. *Poesia e política em Chico Buarque*. São Paulo: Ateliê Editorial.

Moura, R. 1983. *Tia Ciata e a Pequena África do Rio de Janeiro*. Rio de Janeiro: Funarte.

Oliveira, E. R. de. 1976. *As Forças Armadas: Política e Ideologia no Brasil, 1964–1969*. Petrópolis: Vozes.

Ortiz, R. 1988. *A Moderna Tradição Brasileira: Cultura Brasileira e Indústria Cultural*. São Paulo: Brasiliense.

Pedro, A. 1980. "Samba da Legitimidade." Master's thesis. São Paulo: Universidade de São Paulo.

Salgado, Álvaro F. 1941. "Radiodifusão, fator social," *Revista Cultura Política* (Rio de Janeiro), 6, August.

Santos, A. 1982. *Discografia Brasileira: 78 rpm—1902/1964*. Vols. 1–3. Rio de Janeiro: Funarte.

Skidmore, T. 1969. *Brasil: De Getúlio a Castelo*. Rio de Janeiro: Saga.

Sodré, M. 1979. *Samba: O Dono do Corpo*. Rio de Janeiro: Editora Codecri.

Tavares, R. C. 1997. *Histórias que o Rádio não Contou*. São Paulo: Negócio Editora.

Tinhorão, J. R. 1990. *História Social da Música Popular Brasileira*. Lisbon: Editorial Caminho.

Velloso, M. P. 1997. *Mário Lago: Boemia e Política*. Rio de Janeiro: Editora Fundação Getúlio Vargas.

Weffort, F. 1980. *O Populismo na Política Brasileira*. Rio de Janeiro: Paz e Terra.

Paul D. Fischer

13 Challenging Music as Expression in the United States

> *Congress shall make no law respecting an establishment of religion, or prohibiting the free exercise thereof; or abridging the freedom of speech, or of the press; or the right of the people to peaceably assemble and to petition the government for a redress of grievances.*
> —First Amendment, United States Constitution

Culturally, the United States of America is a toddler—loud, willful, sometimes crude, self-centered, even conceited. Other cultures—European, African, Asian, Indian, Islamic—experienced thousands of years of continuous evolution; the United States has had slightly over 200. In spite of this, the indigenous musics of the United States, blues, jazz, rhythm and blues, rock 'n' roll, hip-hop, and more, have made significant contributions to national and world culture. Rooted in combinations of (mostly) European and African styles and forms, these musics are expressions of the multicultural nature of the U.S. population. However, they are not uniformly praised and prized at home. America's mainstream culture is predominantly white and Eurocentric. Holding out European forms of high culture (e.g., opera, ballet, symphonic music) as ideals to emulate and aspire to, these powerful arbiters of mainstream taste have overlooked, and even resisted, the intrinsic value of much of the United States' vernacular culture. This makes many forms of popular music in America minority expression and sometimes unpopular speech— exactly the type of expression the First Amendment seeks to protect.

W. E. B. Du Bois's *The Souls of Black Folk*, written at the outset of the twentieth century, plainly stated that "the problem of the Twentieth Century is the problem of the color-line" (Du Bois 1929:vii). In the wake of America's Civil War and Lincoln's Emancipation Proclamation, that line had to be renegotiated. Laws and constitutional amendments have been passed in efforts to right past wrongs, but in everyday effect many of the interrelationships and integrations essential to that process were initiated through connections to music. Beginning in the 1910s, America's recording industry strictly segregated music by marketing categories to ensure that music by black artists would reach exclusively black audiences and music by white artists would reach exclusively white audiences. The phenomenon of "crossover," blacks listening to white artists and vice versa, put the lie to such artificial divisions early on. Radio began airing rhythm and blues music to mixed-race audiences in the 1940s, and live performances brought fans of all races together in theaters. The popular crossover of rock 'n' roll to white teenage audiences in the early 1950s, made irreversible by the success of Elvis Presley, aroused white youths' interest in the black originators of these sounds.

Popular music's transgressions against the legally established color line made it unpopular with cultural elites. The frankness of lyrical content about intimate adult relationships that rock inherited from rhythm and blues transgressed against social mores derived from the nation's Puritan forefathers. Major record labels and publishers resisted signing contracts with both black artists and white artists who performed black styles. These artists, in turn, transgressed established power relationships in the music industry as they generated income for entrepreneurial "Others," the independent labels. The combination of the progressive, left-leaning social conscience of 1930s folk music with rock 'n' roll, engineered in the 1960s by Bob Dylan and others, transgressed even more directly against mainstream political philosophies. Organized resistance to the social, cultural, and political transgressions of popular music has taken social, legislative, and judicial forms at various times in the nation's history, and that struggle continues. To the extent that the personal is political, and the popular is political, song lyrics are speech worthy of constitutional protection.

Despite the ironclad language that Congress shall make no law abridging free speech, American courts have allowed several types of content-based restrictions on speech. Specifically, "obscene" and "inciteful speech" (fighting words) have been removed from First Amendment protection altogether, and material found "harmful to minors" may be restricted in ways that achieve the state interest of protecting youth from harm while making the least possible incursion on the rights of adults. Since the 1980s various aspects of popular music or its packaging have been challenged in American courts on all of these grounds. Thus far, the musical artists have consistently prevailed in these matters, usually on appeal beyond local jurisdictions. While no legislation has yet been introduced at the federal level, attempts have been made. Subcommittees of both the U.S. House of Representatives and the Senate have held hearings about popular music and its alleged impacts on listeners. In the 1990s legislation proposing content-based restrictions on popular music and other popular media was drafted and sometimes brought to the floor for consideration in several state legislatures. In this chapter I detail precedent-setting and current challenges to popular music as expression and highlight those standing guard to ensure its protection well into the new century.

Popular Music and the Renaissance of American Social Conservatism

During the election campaigns and years of the Ronald Reagan and George Bush presidencies (1980–1993), an overtly conservative political and social ethos came to be expressed by many of the country's political institutions and accepted by "mainstream" America. In a self-conscious reaction to the more progressive tone of the 1960s, the neo-conservatives of the Republican Party strove to reassert elements of the nation's Puritan heritage within late twentieth-century American culture. Elected officials and appointees alike promoted a sweeping social view of what was acceptably American—centered on the notion of "family values"—in order to satisfy a well-organized, politicized, overtly Christian segment of their party and ensure their continued hold on political power. Military operations were conducted in Grenada, Panama, and elsewhere, partly to erase the sting of defeat in Vietnam and partly to provide fodder for rhetoric about America as a Superpower and keeper of the arsenal of democracy. Despite a political philosophy based on less federal government, these Republican administrations took an increasingly paternalistic tone toward other nations and toward the U.S. population itself. With the economic and political collapse of the Soviet Union, the dismantling of the Berlin Wall, and a declaration of the end of the Cold War, conservative rhetoric quickly took credit for making the world a better place.

Without a universal, monolithic, external enemy, Communism, it became more difficult for the neo-conservatives in power to assert their moral authority in stark relief. It became politically and rhetorically advantageous to make examples of people outside the mainstream of American life as they defined it. Orthodox, Eurocentric notions of American culture were used to demonize internal enemies, and "culture war" was declared on those who would subvert or undermine the treasured "family values." Popular music became a frequent battlefield in what the historian James Davison Hunter (1991:49) calls "the struggle to define America." Patrick Buchanan wrote an essay entitled "Losing the War for America's Culture?" in the *Washington Times* (22 May 1989), and, as other political pundits followed suit, conservative politicians announced their intention to legislate culture. In the view of Richard Bolton, who edited the volume *Culture Wars: Documents from the Recent Controversies in the Arts*, "opponents of the NEA [National Endowment for the Arts] practiced a political strategy developed by anti-communists in the 1950s: accuse those with whom you disagree of sedition and immorality; but first marginalize the opposition and limit its access to public communication" (Bolton 1992:15). Buchanan's speech at the 1992 Republican National Convention brought this point of view to a prime-time television audience. The leap from high art to popular culture was an easy one.

The rhetorical device of declaring war suggests that there are only two positions that can be taken on the issue, and one of them must be "wrong." Arguing from a foundation of orthodox, social conservatism, the cultural warriors attempt to appropriate the moral high ground for themselves. Those who argue *for* popular music become, of necessity, their enemy. But as Peter Christenson and Donald Roberts (1998:6) put it:

> For every adult who is convinced pop music is responsible for the moral decay of our youth, there is an adolescent who believes music is the only positive force in contemporary society. For every critic who urges the censorship of rap and heavy metal lyrics, there is a free speech advocate who views these genres as the last bastion of meaningful social criticism.

While these two positions are irreconcilable, neither is, of necessity, demonically wrong. The deeper problem is that an entire middle ground of more nuanced positions is excluded because the polarized rhetoric frames the encounter not as a dialogue, but as a war. Reducing the discussion of complex cultural topics to binary oppositions, while excluding more speech and viewpoints from the realm of legitimacy, undermines the moral authority of the cultural warriors. Their tactics are elitist, paternalistic, and undemocratic. Most Americans, in Hunter's view, do not argue culture and politics from inflexible, religio-moral positions; rather, they are secularists: "A decided majority of secularists are drawn toward the progressivist impulse in American culture" (Hunter 1991:45). Yet despite the disengagement of broad segments of the American populace, the rhetorical skirmishes of the culture war played well in the media, effectively promoting the orthodox agenda to those most likely to vote in elections. In another reversal from the norms of the 1960s, the progressives had become the passive, silent majority. A new wave of highly visible challenges to popular music as expression that began in the mid-1980s must be understood in terms of this broader backdrop.

Late Twentieth-Century Opposition to Popular Music

In October 1984 the National Parent Teacher Association (NPTA) sent letters to major record companies asking them to voluntarily label any product whose lyrics might be objectionable to consumers. In July and August of 1985, a private lobbying group, the Parents Music Resource Center (PMRC), took similar actions, proposing a product labeling system directly modeled on the one operating in the motion picture industry:

> A rating of "X" was requested for "profanity, violence, suicide, or sexually explicit lyrics including fornication, sado-masochism, incest, homosexuality, bestiality and necrophilia." "DA" was requested for lyrics concerning drugs and alcohol, "O" for lyrics concerning the occult, and "V" for lyrics concerning violence. (Kaufman 1986:230)

The Recording Industry Association of America (RIAA) offered a compromise: a single sticker with the words "Parental Advisory: Explicit Lyrics." The day after this offer, the Subcommittee on Communication of the Senate Committee on Commerce, Science and Transportation announced that it would hold hearings on so-called porn-rock on 19 September 1985. Catalyzed by the concerns of the NPTA and the PMRC, government hearings on content-based labeling of popular music products raised the specter of possible legislation. Documents of the time indicate that both the NPTA and PMRC insisted that their efforts were driven by a desire for consumer information and child protection, not censorship. While they made no call for legislation, the hearings received high-profile media attention—in part because the PMRC membership included the wives of five senators (among them Mary Elizabeth "Tipper" Gore, wife of then subcommittee member Albert Gore, Jr.), six members of the House of Representatives, and several Bush administration officials (most notably Susan Baker, spouse of treasury secretary/chief of staff James A. Baker). Mrs. Gore insisted that the PMRC had not called for the hearings and that subcommittee chair John Danforth had—at the urging of his wife, also affiliated with the PMRC.

Emboldened by public reaction to the PMRC hearings on Capitol Hill and the growing ascendancy of cultural conservatism, new kinds of cases against popular musicians began appearing on court dockets. In separate actions, Ozzy Osbourne and the band Judas Priest were accused of contributing to suicides and a suicide attempt through their music.

The complaint against Judas Priest became a product liability case involving alleged "backmasked" messages in the recording. ("Backmasking" involves using professional recording technology to make full-speed backward recordings that can then be added to the overall "mix" of a piece of music.) The band's record company turned over the master tape for analysis by the prosecution, and there was extensive testimony about the practice and potential impact of "backmasking" and subliminal messages. Nevertheless, the band prevailed. In the Ozzy Osbourne case, plaintiffs took a different tack: trying to brand this musical expression "inciteful speech" in order to move it beyond First Amendment protection. The doctrine of "fighting words" had been set out in 1969 decision known as *Brandenburg v. Ohio*. In 1992 the U.S. Supreme Court allowed an appellate court opinion to stand in Osbourne's case, finding no causal connection between his music and a young man's suicide:

> In order for speech to be removed from first amendment protection in this manner, speech advocating action (historically, violent or criminal acts) could be proscribed when two conditions are satisfied: 1) The advocacy is *"directed"* to *"inciting"* or producing *"imminent"* lawless action, and 2) the advocacy is also *likely* to *incite* such action. . . . Under the *Brandenburg* test, it is not enough that recording artists, record labels, and broadcasters have intentionally disseminated music that is alleged to have

directly caused the unlawful action. Liability will only attach when the intention of dissemination was to cause the ensuing injury." (Block 1990:796–797)

The judge in Osbourne's case used this test and found that the song "Suicide Solution" was neither intended nor likely to produce the result of suicide. The plaintiffs in both these cases failed to demonstrate a causal link between listening to music and criminal action. Therefore, even these examples of heavy metal music are protected speech under the First Amendment.

There have been no subsequent cases raising similar challenges to popular music as speech. Other lines have been tried, however. In 1987, however, a case against Jello Biafra and his band Dead Kennedys was closed after a judge denied a prosecutor's motion for retrial. The band had been charged with distributing material harmful to minors—another category of speech not protected by the First Amendment. In this case the issue was not their music but a poster by the world-renowned fantasy artist H. R. Giger, enclosed in their third album, "Frankenchrist." Even though a warning label on the outside of the package warned about the potentially "shocking, repulsive, offensive" art within (Wishnia 1987:444), the band was forced to spend sixty thousand dollars to defend the suit (ibid.:446). Clearly, warning labels do not remove the threat of content-based prosecution. Where the NPTA and PMRC claimed to be calling only for enhanced consumer information to assist parents in their role as gatekeepers for their children's consumption of popular culture, this case took another step. Arguing from the existence of a state interest in the future and the importance of healthy youth to that future, an attempt was made to create governmental "protection" for youth, over and above parental efforts, from elements of America's popular culture. Although this attempt failed, it did not close off this avenue of legal reasoning. New cases, and even new laws, arising from this point of view can be expected.

In 1990 a musical work was declared obscene for the first time, thus raising the threat that popular music could be moved outside First Amendment protection in the third way allowed by Supreme Court opinions—potential harm to minors. Based on a request from law enforcement, on 9 March Broward County, Florida, judge Mel Grossman issued an order, an advisory opinion, that the record "As Nasty As They Wanna Be" by the rap group 2 Live Crew was obscene. The Broward County sheriff's office received and copied the order, and decided to "warn stores as a matter of courtesy" (*Skyywalker Records* v. *Navarro*, 739 F. Supp. 578 at 583 [S.D. Fla. 1990]). More than twenty record stores were visited by deputies in jackets marked "Broward County Sheriff," with their badges in plain view. Store managers were presented with a copy of the judge's order and, in a friendly, conversational tone, warned that further sales would result in arrest. These stores took the recording off the shelf, and as word spread others followed suit, making it unavailable for purchase throughout the county.

The next week Skyywalker Records, as plaintiff, filed suit in federal district court on its own behalf and that of the members of 2 Live Crew. Judge Jose A. Gonzalez, who heard the case, stated the issues succinctly: "Two distinct and narrow issues are presented: whether *As Nasty As They Wanna Be* is legally obscene; and second, whether the actions of the defendant Nicholas Navarro, as Sheriff of Broward County, Florida, imposed an unconstitutional prior restraint on the plaintiffs' right to free speech" (*Skyywalker*, 582). Judge Gonzalez' findings on both issues were positive: There was an unconstitutional prior restraint, and the recording was indeed obscene. This partial victory made it clear that even explicit musical material has the right to reach the marketplace and listeners until it has been found obscene in a court of law, not merely in an advisory opinion by a judge. 2 Live Crew appealed against the obscenity finding, which was overturned in May 1992. The U.S. Supreme Court chose not to hear a further appeal brought by Florida authorities.

There has yet to be another case involving music declared "obscene." It seems reasonable to conclude that if 2 Live Crew's utterances are not legally obscene, future prosecutions on these grounds have nearly insurmountable challenges to overcome. Thus far, popular music as expression has beaten back legal challenges that would have moved it into one of the areas of speech left unprotected by the Supreme Court. But although the pace of such prosecutions has slowed, there is nothing, save these precedents, to stop them from resuming.

Congress Continues

The next set of Capitol Hill hearings on pop music occurred in 1994. The genre now facing scrutiny was hip-hop and, more specifically, the subgenre known as "gangsta rap." As in 1985, a private lobbying group exerted pressure on members of Congress to hold hearings. This time it was the National Political Congress of Black Women (NPCBW), led by C. DeLores Tucker, who managed to have hearings called in both the House of Representatives and the Senate. The House hearings, presided over by Illinois Representative Cardiss Collins, were held on 11 February and 5 May 1994 on behalf of the Subcommittee on Commerce, Consumer Protection and Competitiveness, part of the Committee on Energy and Commerce. The Senate hearings were held on 23 February of that year, presided over by Illinois Senator Carol Moseley-Braun on behalf of the Subcommittee on Juvenile Justice of the Judiciary Committee. Both presiding officers were African-American women, and members of the Democratic Party.

One of the problems with these hearings was their low media profile. Unlike the PMRC hearings, which got extensive coverage, thanks to celebrity testimony and the involvement of legislators' wives, this probe went virtually unnoticed in the mainstream media. Another problem was that some of the most ardent protectors of popular music as expression were compelled to make their best evidence and strongest reasonings part of the public record, without a threat of legislation. Worst of all, the hearings provided a showcase for Mrs. Tucker's intolerant views on American culture. In her testimony, she charged that the music is

> injecting poison into the veins of America's future. It is our moral responsibility to halt the sale of not just gangster rap, but porno rap. Parents and elected officials need to be seriously concerned about gangster rap because it is obscene and sexist. . . . As I see it, the first three things to note about gangster rap is it is obscene, it is obscene, it is obscene. . . . The full authority of government should be used to restrict access of music and videos to minors. In particularly egregious instances, Congress should put forth measures to remove the offending product from the marketplace. . . . The record industry is out of control and if they don't clean up their own act, they must be regulated. (Subcommittee on Commerce 1994:12–14)

Calls for such regulation by the government would be likely to involve illegal prior restraints of the sort seen in the 2 Live Crew case. Further, findings of obscenity by individual citizens are not legally binding. For this argument to be persuasive, individual prosecutions must be brought. Mrs. Tucker did, however, manage to use the public-relations value of her appearances on Capitol Hill to raise her media profile and add clout to future private efforts against record companies made by herself and her organization. One of the few positive things that can be said about these hearings is that a broad range of witnesses were called, including record company executives, a spokeswoman for the RIAA, and even a performer or two.

Congressional interest in the impact of popular culture in general and popular music in particular did not end there. In the second week of November 1997, testimony was heard by the Senate Governmental Affairs Subcommittee on the Impact of Popular Music Lyrics on Youth. These hearings marked a new stage in the evolution of legislators' interest in popular music. They were catalyzed by members of the subcommittee itself, and the list of those invited to testify was severely limited. Only Hilary Rosen, president of the RIAA, spoke from an even vaguely pro-music position. These hearings centered on the testimony of a man whose 15-year-old son committed suicide, allegedly while listening to a Marilyn Manson CD. First, Senator Sam Brownback of Kansas introduced the hearings in his role as chair, stating in part:

> The majority of popular music does not contain violent or misogynistic lyrics. Our concern is not with popular music or even with a particular genre such as rock or rap. Our concern is with those songs that do glorify violence, racism, murder and mayhem and condone the abuse of women. That's the target. . . . It stands to reason that prolonged exposure to such hate-filled lyrics during the formative teen years could have an impact on one's attitude and assumptions and thus decisions and behavior. Understanding the nature and extent of the influence of music violence may well be the first step towards better addressing the problems and pathologies besetting our youth. (C-Span video 1997)

Brownback clearly wants Congress to consider content-based restrictions on musical speech. He proclaims the need to understand the impact on adolescents of exposure to this music, but did not see fit to call any social scientists who have studied the matter. Brownback was followed by his subcommittee colleague, Senator Joseph Lieberman of Connecticut, who spoke as a witness, thus ensuring that the viewpoint of those who called the hearings would appear prominently in its proceedings:

> Folks in the music industry which is mostly a very constructive, elevating industry have refused, I think, to adequately acknowledge our real concerns about this awful gangsta rap and shock rock music they produce. . . . The men and women who run the large corporations who turn out this music must stop hiding behind the First Amendment and confront the damage that some, and I emphasize some, of their products are doing. We're not talking censorship here, but citizenship. (Ibid.)

Lieberman, unlike Brownback, is willing to speak of the problem in terms of specific genres of music, though he cited no specific examples. He chides the music industry for "hiding behind the First Amendment," whereas the industry rarely, if ever, argues from that position—in part because when the industry agreed to sticker its product, it severely undermined its ability to argue at the level of rights and principles about popular music as expression. Lieberman's position is further undermined by a failure to produce credible studies that show a causal link between music exposure and action. Brownback's assertion that it "stands to reason" is an insufficient ground for encroachment on fundamental liberties provided by the founding documents of the United States. While some research has shown links between televised violence and violent action in those already at risk for such behaviors, no such study relating to popular music has ever been done. Both senators appeared to be ignorant of this—and also unaware of relevant case law and testimony from prior hearings that could have informed their statements. The major record companies are the targets here for blame and shame, neither of which is the proper purview of Congress. Private citizens or groups raising such issues directly with the corporations would be both more appropriate and more likely to achieve the desired results. It can only be assumed that the senators believe that bringing these matters to Capitol Hill will play well with constituents at home.

Brownback and Lieberman again held hearings on 16 June 1998 before the Senate Commerce, Science and Transportation Committee. Entitled "Labels and Lyrics: Do Parental Advisory Stickers Inform Consumers and Parents?" these hearings too featured a short list of witnesses and centered on the testimony of a middle school teacher from Jonesboro, Arkansas. Her testimony implied a causal link between listening to rap music and the nationally publicized shooting spree by two male students at her school. Again there was no effective countertestimony. The hearings seemed to treat the alleged connection between music and violence as though this was a new subject that had never been closely considered before. It is of the utmost importance that formal legislative consideration of matters relating to content-based regulation of any expressive art form include information from all previous hearings, relevant court cases, and social science research—not merely the gut feelings and hunches of inflamed legislators. This sort of rigorous consideration may, however, be an unrealized hope. Brownback and Lieberman promised at the close of these hearings that they were far from done, and that the topic would be revisited.

In the spring of 1999, in the wake of the shootings at Columbine High School in Littleton, Colorado, Congress acted again. Senator Lieberman and Senator John McCain of Arizona introduced the 21st Century Media Responsibility Act of 1999, which would require assessment of the amount and nature of violence in media products, giving the media industry six months to come up with a labeling standard (<www.narm.com/Content/NavigationMenu/Public_Affairs/Federal_Legislation/federal.htm>). Two days later, Senator Henry Hyde of Illinois proposed a law banning the sale to those 17 and younger of music, music videos, and computer games that are extremely violent. This legislation would also require music retailers to have on hand lyric sheets for all product they sell (<www.massmic.com/lyricsod1/html>, 10 June 1999). Hyde put this forward as an amendment to a juvenile crime bill. He was persuaded to withdraw it and said he would seek a resolution simply suggesting that retailers do so (ibid., 11 June 1999). The bill to ban the sale of violent material was voted down by a two-to-one margin (<www.massmic.com/dcmusicban.html>, 14 June 1999). Clearly, some lawmakers feel comfortable about their authority to regulate material deemed "harmful to minors." That door is still open.

On 4 August 1999, Senator Brownback, on behalf of himself and others, introduced Senate Resolution 172 regarding the establishment of a "special committee of the Senate to address the cultural crisis facing America." The proposed committee would be called the Special Committee on American Culture. Its stated purposes were:

1) to study the causes and reasons for social and cultural regression,
2) to make such findings of fact as are warranted and appropriate, including the impact that such negative trends and developments have on the broader society, particularly in regards to child well-being; and
3) to explore means of cultural renewal. (Text of Senate Resolution 172.)

This is clearly a broader reaction to perceived cultural ills than any of the hearings detailed above, but it includes calls for possible content-based regulation of aspects of American culture, both popular and otherwise, after facts have been found. Numerous terms in this resolution beg for more detailed definitions than the document provides. What exactly is the "cultural crisis facing America"? What are its dimensions and limits? What is "social and cultural regression"? By what standard is it measured? What qualifies as "cultural renewal"? From what source is it supposed to come?

On the basis of these ill-defined concepts, Brownback called for the establishment of a special committee of the U.S. Senate with power to spend contingent funds from the Senate's coffers, develop a staff, hold hearings, hire consultants, and subpoena witnesses and documents. It would last until the end of 2000, be empowered to spend up to $500,000, and make a final report to the Senate (ibid.). By late September the proposal had been downgraded to the creation of a "task force." By the month's end the proposal was dormant, if not dead, according to minority leader Tom Daschle. As this book goes to press, this is the most recent Senate action that could have an impact on popular music as expression. Clearly, some members of Congress believe it is both legal and appropriate for them to attempt to legislate culture.

State Legislatures

Many attempts have been made in state legislatures to exert control over music and other elements of popular culture that have come to the legislators' attention. A brief and incomplete history of such efforts follows. In 1989, bills were introduced in the state legislatures of Pennsylvania and Missouri requiring mandatory labeling of music product with certain kinds of content. Lobbyists communicated model legislation to many states in hopes of having it introduced if the early efforts succeeded.

> If the Pennsylvania measure becomes law, record manufacturers would be required to place a large fluorescent yellow warning label on LP's, tapes, and CD's that contain lyrics descriptive of or advocating "suicide, incest, bestiality, sado-masochism, rape, involuntary deviate sexual intercourse, murder, ethnic intimidation, and/or illegal use of drugs or alcohol." (*Los Angeles Times*, 11 February 1990)

The Reverend Donald Wildmon's Clear TV, Phyllis Schlafly's Eagle Forum, the American Family Association, and especially Focus on the Family and Media Update were among the groups that circulated model legislation but dismissed the concept of a unified national attack on rock. Thus far, no legislation on this model has passed.

The Washington State legislature did pass a content-based regulation, amending a 20-year old (unenforced) law against the sale and distribution of "erotic material" to include sound recordings. In a case brought on behalf of Washington State musicians, retailers, national record companies, and others, attorneys for the American Civil Liberties Union of Washington argued that the law was unconstitutional because it violated individuals' rights to free speech and due process, constituted a prior restraint, and was vague. On 29 October 1992, a King County Superior Court judge declared the law unconstitutional. Judge Mary Brucker's opinion stated: "[T]he basic flaw in the statute is the denial of persons affected to know that a sound recording has been determined to be erotic. . . . Knowing the possibility exists causes self-censorship, which deprives creativity" (*Tacoma Morning News Tribune*, 30 October 1992). Numerous attempts have been made to pass a reworded law, and in 1998 this ambition took the form of Substitute House Bill 1407, intended to regulate the sale and distribution of material harmful to minors. It stalled in committee.

That same year a bill was introduced in a committee of the Michigan State Legislature (SB 1100, 5/22) to allow local authorities to "rate" concert performances as "harmful to minors." This bill also died in committee before being considered by the full law-making assemblies. In 1999, however, a bill that would have required warnings on tickets and in all advertisements for certain concerts got to the floor. Determinations would be made on the basis of artists' recorded output in the previous five years, and whether any of that product had received a Parental Advisory sticker. Concerts by artists who had received the sticker would require warnings. The bill passed one house of the legislature but stalled in the second. It did not become law.

Also in 1998 a bill reached the floor of the Georgia state legislature that would have criminalized sale or rental to minors of stickered material (music, magazines, computer software, etc.). Curiously, this proposed law had no consequences for the creators of the material or the owners of the stores involved, but clerks would have faced a $5,000 fine for the first offense. The measure was voted down. A similar bill was introduced into house and senate committees of the Tennessee legislature, also in 1998. It stalled in committee, never made it to the floor, and has not been reintroduced.

A later version of content-based legislation regarding popular culture, the Tennessee 21st Century Media Responsibility Act of 2000 (H.B. 2158), began as a bill calling for industry labeling of music, movies, and computer games according to their violent content. The provisions for including movies and music were later dropped. It never reached the floor of the legislature. Built on the language of Senator Hyde's defeated federal bill, this would call upon the industry to create a system for labeling the nature, context, and intensity of violence in products and recommending a minimum age for exposure. If the industry does not provide such a rating system within 180 days after the passage of this bill into law, the state can prescribe such a system. This sort of legislation for content-based regulation of elements of popular culture is still circulating, searching for a first victory. Should one specimen pass, others are sure to be introduced. Once a prosecution occurs, the site of the struggle will likely return to the courts.

The Players, Pro and Con

There are few organizations whose stated purpose is protecting music as expression. Rock and Rap Confidential (RRC: <www.rockrap.com>) puts out a monthly newsletter edited by journalist/critic Dave Marsh and covering issues and happenings related to popular music. It recently absorbed Parents for Rock and Rap, which was founded by Mary Morello, mother of Rage Against the Machine's Tom Morello. RRC takes generally progressive positions, but is not explicitly activist. Its website provides links to several more activist organizations. Rock Out Censorship (<www.theroc.org>) was founded in 1989 to act as the "voice of music fans." Based in Ohio, this group has spearheaded antilabeling petition drives and had a presence on several concert tours. The Massachusetts Music Industry Coalition (MMIC: <www.massmic.com>) has the most extensive website of these groups. Led by the vocal and visible Nina Crowley, MMIC provides information on groups that have taken positions on all sides of music-related issues and links to their websites. The site also provides an archive of journalistic coverage of music-related issues, and Crowley is frequently seen in the media, speaking as a parent affronted by any and all calls for regulation.

Several organizations that do not make music-as-expression their primary focus are also active in matters pertaining to music. The Freedom Forum (<www.freedomforum.org>) provides links to many freedom of expression websites. The online news it provides often covers challenges to popular music as expression. The Freedom Forum's First Amendment Center, located at Vanderbilt University in Nashville, Tennessee, has held several panel discussions on issues related to music and popular culture and sponsored concert and conversation opportunities with recording artists such as Odetta, Tom Paxton, Jill Sobule, and John Kay of Steppenwolf. The Thomas Jefferson Center for the Protection of Free Expression (<www.tjcenter.org>) specifically mentions musicians among the artists whose works deserve protection, and Mike Mills of R.E.M. serves on its Arts Advisory Council.

Other mainstream civil liberties groups have provided assistance to anti-music-censorship efforts when called upon. The American Civil Liberties Union (ACLU: <www.aclu.org>) has provided local and national assistance when hearings arise or legislation is proposed. People for the American Way (<www.pfaw.org>) mentions music on its home page, which states its view of freedom of expression as a core issue and "pillar of democracy." The National Coalition Against Censorship (<www.ncac.org>) is an alliance of 48 nonprofits founded in 1974. Its focus seems to be largely literary, but it could be encouraged to defend music and musicians when real threats arise. The Institute for First Amendment Studies (<www.ifas.org>) and the American Communication Association (<www.americancomm.org>) say little about popular music. Two other websites valuable for the links they provide are those of the Free Expression Clearinghouse (<www.freeexpression.org>) and a Canadian site, Freedom Of Expression Links (<insight.mcmaster.ca/org/efc/pages/chronicle/censor.html>).

Censorship has been a recurring problem in American culture, and many organizations are poised to publicize censorship attempts and stop them. Music, however, is the primary focus of only a few such groups; how the rest will respond to calls for assistance has yet to be tested. Individuals who value music must be vigilant about attempts to censor both popular music and its associated culture in their local jurisdiction and prepared to make use of these resources should a problem arise.

Those opposed to freedom of expression in popular music consistently state that they are merely trying to provide consumers with better information about the music that their children might be listening to. They argue that they are attempting to shore up "family values" (as they define them), not to censor. Toward this end, many have moved away from supporting those who use the courts to prosecute musicians and retailers, and they have not pushed for legislative hearings for some time. Instead, they appear at corporate shareholders' meetings and hold public demonstrations to "shame" privately held companies into withdrawing support from artists they have contracted with, in hopes that the companies' largely white, economically elite board members will see things their way. If pressure within these companies means that artists are dropped from their record labels, distribution deals are discontinued, or product is not distributed, at one level that is not censorship because it will not have been done by the government. But it might serve to restrict recording artists' freedom of expression, leading to self-censorship in order to meet the demands of a seemingly conservative marketplace.

The Parents Music Resource Center is still around, though it has no online presence and has never offered much in the way of resources. Reverend Donald Wildmon's American Family Association, founded in 1977, believes that "the entertainment industry through its various products, has played a major role in the decline of those values on which our society was founded and which keep a society and its families strong and healthy." In an attempt to protect such values, the organization threatened to boycott Pepsi over its association with Madonna and her mid-eighties "Like a Prayer" tour. As a result, Pepsi pulled ads and walked away from a tour sponsorship deal. This fits the AFA's philosophy of action: "We believe in holding accountable companies which sponsor programs attacking traditional family values" (<www.afa.net>). The strategy of putting pressure on corporations to control the distribution of cultural products has gone mainstream via the PMRC, NPCBW, and others.

C. DeLores Tucker of the NPCBW has appeared publicly numerous times with William Bennett, one of the founders of Empower America, whose mission is to "promote progressive conservative public policies at both the state and national level based on the principles of economic growth, international leadership, and cultural empowerment" (<www.empower.org>). Bennett, author of the values-driven bestseller *The Book Of Virtues* (1993), believes in free markets, but also in the appropriateness of shaming corporations to make them conform to the set of values he promotes. For a time Bennett was director of Cultural Policy for the Heritage Foundation (<www.heritage.org>), which was founded in 1973 to "formulate and pro-

mote conservative public policies based on principles of free enterprise, limited government, individual freedom, traditional American values, and a strong national
defense." While music is not foremost on its agenda, it has supported content-
based attacks on popular culture in the past. Focus on the Family (<www.fotf.org>)
offers music reviews on its website and an archive of past reviews as well. While
not complete or exhaustive, the reviews provide coverage of many popular releases,
including assessments of their "Pro-Social Content" and "Objectionable Content"
and a closing "Summary/Advisory" that passes a moral judgment on the recording
artist, songwriters, and lyric content. Other groups who occasionally weigh in on the
negative impact of popular music are the Christian Family Network (<www.cfnweb.
com>), the Christian Coalition (<www.cc.org>), and the Family Research Council
(<www.frc.org>). All of these groups are party to, if not instigators of, the "culture
war" on American popular music, ready and willing to renew their battles when
they see an opportunity or sense weakness among popular music's supporters.

The spirit, uniqueness, and cultural value of blues, jazz, rhythm and blues, rock 'n'
roll, and hip-hop are widely acknowledged across the globe, but contested vigorously
at home. Societal groups harking back to the Puritan origins of Anglo-American
society still appear to be uncomfortable with these strong African-European and otherwise multicultural hybrids. Their Eurocentrism does indigenous American musics
a disservice. Even when these musics seem loud, raw, and unpleasant to Eurocentric ears, they often provide the truest expressions of this young, polyglot culture.
Ignoring these expressions in favor of an idealized, strictly European-derived American culture, often promoted as the world's "best," is an elitist fantasy.

The idea that America's musics bear principal responsibility for the ills of the culture at large is unsupported. If anything, the cries of rage, the protests against injustice, abuse of power, and structural inequalities heard in song, are symptoms, not
causes, of these problems. They are calls for recognition of these difficulties and for
their correction. For a society so fundamentally dedicated to freedom of expression,
these articulations are an integral part of a healthy, evolving, maturing culture. Popular music is an important element in the United States' cultural ferment—that
sometimes smelly, bubbling experimentation that can also lead to cultural advance.
The cultural worth of American popular music puts it firmly in the category of pre-
sumptively protected speech, and it deserves to be aggressively protected from governmental and nongovernmental challenges.

The legal notion of "harm to minors" appears to offer the most danger for popular music at this time. The challengers have argued and will continue to argue that
content—whether sexually explicit, violent, or just offensive or indecent from the
standpoint of the critics' value systems—should be regulated to protect youth. But
in a society devoted to "progress" and the capitalist imperative to exploit markets

and consumers for profit, an atmosphere of perpetual change (social, communicative, technological, cultural) is a given. The anthropologist Margaret Mead's 1970s study of American adolescents, *Culture and Commitment*, acknowledged this dynamic, calling American culture "prefigurative" (Mead 1978:62). In this type of culture the most valuable inputs, in terms of successful adaptation, are those most in touch with present trends and future dynamics. Mead viewed late twentieth-century American youth as "pioneers in time" (ibid.:63), always seeking out the best and most contemporaneous inputs to help them chart their paths.

To the extent that recording artists are in tune with the times and make use of perceptive and expressive abilities beyond the norm, they can be powerful sources of such guidance. This is an important, and often unstated, source of many cultural warriors' resentment of popular musicians. They may indeed be leading young people into a world different from that of their forebears, but that is the nature of contemporary American culture. It does not necessarily undermine all the most dearly held values of that world. Tarring all of popular music with the broad brush of charges that it causes violence or obscenity, and then calling for its regulation, is illogical. Content-based regulation of popular music, or even the exertion of private pressure to sanitize this segment of the popular culture marketplace, could rob American youth of some of its most valuable coping mechanisms in a prefigurative culture where the future is, by definition, unknown.

American youth and the future of this society could be seriously harmed if the free exchange of ideas in popular music is chilled. If popular artists rein in their perceptions and articulations about life in American society, and their criticisms of it, young pioneers in time could be moving into the future deaf and blind. Even proponents of regulation consistently acknowledge that only a very small percentage of popularly available material is objectionable to them and that the negative impacts of the popular music they fear are, at best, rare. Yet the calls for across-the-board regulation continue. These morally panicked calls to action could do greater harm to young people than the immediate ills they seek to redress. Pro-regulation forces are depending on moneyed corporate executives to succumb to elite peer pressure rather than face the costs and close scrutiny case-by-case prosecutions would bring. The obligation to demonstrate a causal connection between music listening, antisocial behaviors, and measurable harm rests on *them*. The burden they are shirking here must remain on them. Pro-music advocates must stop accepting hearings where they are not heard and legislation that penalizes minimum-wage retail clerks for failing to "protect" minors. So far the discussion has been framed by the would-be cultural warriors. The ferment and development of American culture hang in the balance. One successful state or federal bill or Supreme Court decision could put *all* the popular arts on a slippery slope. The Constitution's promise of "no law" should mean *no* law.

About the Contributors

Alenka Barber-Kersovan studied musicology, psychology, and aesthetics in Ljubljana, Vienna, and Hamburg. She is currently the executive secretary of the Arbeitskreises Studium Populärer Musik e.V. Her publications include *Popmusik und Lernen* (with H. Rösing, 1985) *and Krauts with Attitude* (with Simon Frith, 1998).

Vanessa Bastian is World Reports editor for the London-based trade magazine *Music Business International.* She is a contributor to the forthcoming *Encyclopedia of Popular Music of the World* and has done research for the European Music Office, the Musicians Union (UK), and other bodies.

Rob Bowman is a professor at York University in Toronto and the author of *Soulsville U.S.A.: The Story of Stax Records* (1997). In 1996 he won a Grammy for the monograph he wrote to accompany the 10-CD box set *The Complete Stax/Volt Soul Singles,* vol. 3: *1972–1975,* which he also co-produced.

Martin Cloonan is a senior lecturer in Adult Education at the University of Glasgow, Scotland, and the author of *Banned! Censorship of Popular Music in Britain 1967–1992* (1996). He has also written on popular music, education, and politics. When not pontificating on the state of popular music, he can be found watching Liverpool Football Club or wishing he was.

Michael Drewett is a lecturer in the Department of Sociology and Industrial Sociology of Rhodes University, South Africa. He has done extensive research on the censorship of popular music in South Africa and co-ordinated the successful Cutting Grooves exhibition on music censorship under apartheid, held at the Grahamstown National Arts Festival, South Africa, in July 1999.

Paul D. Fischer is associate professor in the Department of Recording Industry at Middle Tennessee State University. He holds a Ph.D. in American Culture Studies from Bowling Green State University and is president of the U.S. branch of the International Association for the Study of Popular Music.

Reebee Garofalo has been a professor at the University of Massachusetts–Boston since 1978, where he is affiliated with the College of Public and Community Service and the American Studies Program. In addition to *Rockin' Out: Popular Music in the USA* (2d ed., 2002), he has written numerous articles on racism, censorship, the political uses of music, and the globalization of the music industry.

Steve Greenfield is director of the undergraduate law degree program and co-director of the Centre for the Study of Law, Society and Popular Culture at the University of Westminster, London. Recent publications include *Film and the Law* (with Guy Osborn and Peter Robson, 2001) and *Regulating Football: Commodification, Consumption and the Law* (with Guy Osborn, 2001).

Mike Jones is course director for the MBA in Music Industries at the Institute of Popular Music at the University of Liverpool. He gained his music industry experience with the band Latin Quarter between 1984 and 1996. More details are available at <www.radioafrica.co.uk>.

Keith Kahn-Harris (né Harris) completed his thesis, "Transgression and Mundanity: The Extreme Metal Music Scene," at Goldsmiths College, London, in 2001. He has edited the book *New Voices in Jewish Thought*, vol. 2, and is a fellow at the Mandel School for Advanced Jewish Educational Leadership in Jerusalem. He continues to publish on music and youth culture and can be contacted at <kkahnharris@yahoo.co.uk>.

Jeroen de Kloet has completed a dissertation entitled *Red Sonic Trajectories: Popular Music and Youth in Urban China* and is currently affiliated with the International Institute of Infonomics (Heerlen, The Netherlands), where he is engaged in a research project on the uses of the internet in China and Indonesia.

Dave Laing is reader in the School of Communication and Creative Industries at the University of Westminster. He is an editor of the journal *Popular Music* and the author or co-author of a number of articles and books, including *One Chord Wonders* (1985) and the *Faber Companion to 20th Century Popular Music* (1995).

Guy Osborn is senior lecturer in law in the Centre for the Study of Law, Society and Popular Culture at the University of Westminster School of Law. His publications include *Contract and Control in the Entertainment Industry* (1998), *Regulating Football* (2001), and the edited collection *Law and Sport in Contemporary Society* (2000). He is a joint editor of the journal *Entertainment Law*.

David Parvo is a former Incident Updates editor and writer for Rock Out Censorship (<www.theroc.org>) and music reviewer for *Mo'Jams*. He is currently doing graduate work at the School of Architecture of the University of Texas at Austin while writing on a wide array of subjects.

José Roberto Zan teaches sociology of culture and arts at the Institute of Arts, University of Campinas (UNICAMP) in the state of São Paulo. His doctoral thesis and current research explore the origins and development of Brazilian popular music and its relations with the recording industry.